THE BURGESS FLOWER BOOK
FOR CHILDREN

ALSO AVAILABLE FROM LIVING BOOK PRESS

The Burgess Animal Book for Children (in color)
The Burgess Bird Book for Children (in color)

Home Geography - CC Long
Elementary Geography - Charlotte Mason
Viking Tales - Jennie Hall
Parables From Nature* - Margaret Gatty
Fifty Famous Stories Retold* - James Baldwin
The Blue Fairy Book* - Andrew Lang
      * in AO reading order

Richard Halliburton's Marvels of the Orient
Richard Halliburton's Marvels of the Occident

Charlotte Mason's Home Education Series

1. Home Education
2. Parents and Children
3. School Education
4. Ourselves
5. Formation of Character
6. A Philosophy of Education

And many, many more!

All Living Book Press titles are complete and unabridged, and presented with the original illustrations, sometimes from several sources, to bring these great books even more to life.

To see a complete list of all our releases or if you wish to leave us any feedback please visit www.livingbookpress.com

The Burgess Flower Book
For Children

THORNTON BURGESS

ILLUSTRATED BY
LOUIS AGASSIZ FUERTES

LIVING BOOK
PRESS

This edition published 2019
by Living Book Press
Copyright © Living Book Press, 2019

Original edition published in 1923.

ISBN: 978-1-925729-31-3 (softcover)
         978-1-922348-28-9 (hardcover)
         978-1-922348-59-3 (black and white softcover)

NATIONAL
LIBRARY
OF AUSTRALIA
A catalogue record for this
book is available from the
National Library of Australia

Contents

PREFACE

This book is offered as a companion volume to the Burgess Bird Book for Children and the Burgess Animal Book for Children. It is intended solely as an introduction for the youngest readers to the fascinating flower world. It makes no pretense to being a botany, or even a general hand book on flowers. Its purpose is to awaken and stimulate an interest in our wild flowers which may lead to a desire to know more about them and to seek such information in the many excellent books now available.

Because of the story method of treatment, and also because of the limited vocabulary of the little child, the use of scientific names and even the names of most of the parts of plants and flowers, save in the appendix for older people, has been avoided. This necessarily prevents that accuracy of description which the adult may desire. The vast number of flowers, which is America's rich heritage, makes it impossible to describe within the confines of a volume of this size more than a limited number. No small part of the task was the selection of the flowers to be included. Most of them were chosen because of their wide distribution. For the most part, only the commoner flowers, those most likely to be encountered in walks in field, meadow and woodland, have been chosen. A few of the rarer ones have been included because of their beauty, and the hope that the desire to find these may act as a stimulant to interest.

Peter Rabbit lives very close to the flowers. Peter is the beloved friend of childhood. Therefore Peter has been chosen as the guide for the little folk. If what Peter has discovered is not clearly told in the text I hope that the illustrations will enable the readers to make sure of identification. For the excellent photographs from which these illustrations were made I am indebted to Mr. L. W. Brownell, Mr. Henry Troth, the J. Horace McFarland Co. and The A. B. Morse Co., and to Miss C. M. Green for her careful work in coloring these photographs. I am also indebted to Mrs. Elizabeth G. Britton of the New York Botanical Garden for identification of the photographs, to Mr. Percy Wilson, Associate Curator of the New York Botanical Garden, for final review of the color engraving, and to Dr. G. Clyde Fisher of the American Museum of Natural History for critical reading of the manuscript and verification of scientific names. For the hearty cooperation and good will of these I herewith acknowledge my indebtedness and appreciation.

In the use of scientific names and in family names Gray's Manual has been followed throughout. Names in parenthesis are preferred and in common use by many botanists.

It is my earnest hope that at least some children will be led to that interest in our wild flowers which must develop into a love for them, and that through this love will be aroused a desire to protect them. Many species are in serious danger of becoming extinct because of the ruthless picking of the blossoms and tearing up of the roots by the thoughtless.

THE AUTHOR

TO THE AWAKENING IN CHILDREN OF
LOVE FOR OUR WILD FLOWERS AND
THE DESIRE TO PRESERVE THEM IN
THEIR NATIVE HABITATS FOR THE
BEAUTY AND JOY THEY GIVE TO THE
WORLD THIS BOOK IS DEDICATED.

X

1. Peter Rabbit Finds Signs of Spring

> "Winsome Bluebird's on the way:
> He is due here any day."

OLD MOTHER West Wind's children, the Merry Little Breezes, sang this softly as they danced over the Green Meadows and around the Old Briar patch. Peter Rabbit pricked up his long ears.

"How do you know? Who told you so?" he demanded.

"Nobody told us so; we just feel it, Peter," cried the Merry Little Breezes, and kept on singing as they danced.

"Huh!" exclaimed Peter. "Feeling isn't knowing. Perhaps Winsome is on his way and perhaps he isn't. I hope he is, for that would mean that Mistress Spring is on her way too, and she can't get here too soon to suit me. But I would feel a lot more sure of it if I could see some signs."

"Use your eyes, Peter! Use your eyes! There are flowers in bloom already, for we've seen them. What better sign that Mistress Spring is coming do you want?" chanted the Merry Little Breezes.

Peter jumped a foot off the ground. "Say, are you crazy?" he cried. "Look at this snow all over the Green Meadows! Do you expect me to believe any such story as that?"

"We don't care whether you believe it or not, it is so!" cried the Merry Little Breezes, dancing around Peter and throwing snow in his face.

> "Welcome Robin's on the wing;
> Very soon you'll hear him sing."

With this the Merry Little Breezes danced away across the Green Meadows towards the Green Forest, leaving Peter to stare after them as if quite sure that they really were as crazy as they seemed.

"Of course, it isn't true," muttered Peter. "The very idea of saying that they have seen flowers in bloom when the ground is still frozen and there is snow everywhere! I don't believe a word of it."

Nevertheless Peter couldn't get it out of his mind that the Merry Little Breezes had seen something that he hadn't. Thoughts of the glad springtime began to chase each other through his funny little head. Presently he began to have a queer feeling — which little by little he recognized as the very feeling the Merry Little Breezes had spoken of, — the feeling that Mistress Spring really and truly was on her way.

"Huh!" exclaimed Peter just as before, and shook himself. But he couldn't shake off that feeling. Then he thought again of what the Merry Little Breezes had said about signs and about using his eyes. "Huh!" said he again. "I guess if there is anything to see I would see it! There's nothing the matter with my eyes, and I haven't seen any signs of spring yet. Flowers in bloom! The very idea!"

Now, of course, Peter didn't really believe that the Merry Little Breezes had told an untruth. No, indeed! He thought that they were either just trying to tease him, or that they had been mistaken. But he couldn't get rid of the thought that perhaps they had seen something which he hadn't seen; and nothing upsets Peter more than the thought that others may know more than he does about what is going on in the Green Forest and on the Green Meadows.

"If there are any signs of spring which they have seen, I'd like to know where they are," muttered Peter, as he hopped all through the dear Old Briar-patch, looking sharply at all the bushes and little trees and brambles to see if any of the sleeping buds showed any signs of waking. But they didn't, and Peter felt satisfied that there were no signs of spring in the Old Briar-patch. Certainly there were none on the Green Meadows, for these were still covered with snow.

Then Peter made up his mind to visit the Green Forest just to make sure that he had missed nothing there. Nowhere could he see the least sign of the coming of Mistress Spring. Snow was everywhere. An idea popped into his head. "If they saw any flowers, it must be that they saw them through a window of Farmer Brown's house. I've seen them there myself," thought he. "But flowers up there are no sign of spring."

A few minutes later Peter came to that part of the Green Forest where in places it was swampy. You know a swampy space is where the ground is always very wet. This was the warmest place in all the Green Forest. The snow had disappeared in spots and in one of these a tiny stream of water was coming from a place where it bubbled out of the ground. It was a spring, and the tiny stream was the beginning of the Laughing Brook. Peter stopped on the edge of it. Just then along came the Merry Little Breezes and one of them tickled his nose with a queer smell. Peter sniffed.

"It smells to me as if Jimmy Skunk had left a little of that scent of his around here, but I haven't seen Jimmy's tracks anywhere," thought Peter. Again he sniffed. This time it seemed as if that smell came right out of the water in front of him. He stared at it a minute and for the first time noticed several queer brown-and-green things, like pointed hoods, standing in the water. Peter leaned forward to look at one a little closer, and right then he made a discovery. That smell, like Jimmy Skunk's perfume, came from that queer little hood! Peter hopped a step nearer that he might see better. On one side of that queer hood was an opening, a narrow opening. He was all curiosity now. He held his nose while he peeped in that narrow opening. You see, he didn't like that smell, and so close to that little hood it was very strong.

At first he saw nothing. But a moment later he discovered, down at the bottom of that little hood, a sort of thick stem all covered with something yellow. Peter's eyes seemed to pop right out as he looked harder than ever. Then he saw that the thick stem was covered with very, very tiny flowers, all yellow with the dust-like gold which most flowers have, and which is called pollen.

Peter jumped a foot straight up in the air. "Why, the Merry Little Breezes did tell the truth!" he exclaimed.

"Of course, we did!" cried the Merry Little Breezes, who had been watching him. "We always tell the truth. These are the first flowers of the year, the flowers of the Skunk Cabbage,[1] and the sure sign that Mistress Spring is on her way."

Peter remembered the big broad leaves he had so often seen growing here and in other swampy, places in the summer. He looked all about, but he didn't see even one. He wrinkled his brows in a puzzled way. "I thought the Skunk Cabbage was a big green plant," said he.

"So it is," laughed one of the Merry Little Breezes. "These are its flowers. They bloom before the leaves show at all. Queer, isn't it?"

"I should say so!" replied Peter. "I didn't know it had any flowers. I've seen these things early in the spring many times, but I didn't know what they were. I never thought anything about them."

"That comes of not using your eyes, Peter," cried a Merry Little Breeze. "There are many wonderful things all about you every day which you never see at all."

"What is there wonderful about these?" demanded Peter a little sharply, for he felt a little put out that any one should think he didn't see all there was to be seen.

"Isn't it wonderful that these little flowers can come up and be brave enough and strong enough to bloom when Jack Frost is still making everybody shiver?" asked the Merry Little Breeze.

Peter nodded. "That's so," he said slowly. "I didn't think of that. It is wonderful. I don't see how they do it." He looked at the tiny flowers with new interest. He saw how thick was the little brown-and-green hood inside of which they were blooming, and how warm and cozy it was in there with only a narrow opening for the light and air to enter. Then he began to understand how Old Mother Nature was protecting them.

"It is wonderful," he repeated. "I certainly have learned something today. I've always watched for the coming of Winsome Bluebird as the first sure sign of sweet Mistress Spring and

1   Look at the picture of the Skunk Cabbage on page 5.

SKUNK CABBAGE
Symplocarpus foetidus

YELLOW ADDER'S-TONGUE
Erythronium americanum

never once have thought that there might be other signs. Do you know, I rather like this smell now. It is — why, it is a sort of promise that winter will soon be over. Now I must hurry to tell Mrs. Peter the splendid news that the first flowers of the year are in bloom."

II. Two Surprises in the Green Forest

"DEE, DEE, dee, chickadee! Where are you going in such a hurry, Peter Rabbit?" cried a merry voice, as Peter was scampering down the Lone Little Path to reach the edge of the Green Forest on his way to the dear Old Briar-patch to tell Mrs. Peter the good news.

Peter stopped abruptly. "Hello, Tommy Tit," he cried. "I've just made the most wonderful discovery. I've found the first sure sign that Mistress Spring is on her way and will soon be here."

Tommy Tit the Chickadee flitted down to a twig just above Peter's head. "Is that so, Peter?" he cried, pretending to be very much surprised. "Is that so? What is it?"

"I've found flowers in bloom!" cried Peter. "Yes, sir, I've found flowers in bloom. I wouldn't have believed it if I hadn't seen them with my own eyes."

Tommy Tit's bright little eyes twinkled.

"What flowers are they, and where are they?" he asked.

"They are the flowers of the Skunk Cabbage, and they are in those funny little brown-and-green hoods down by the spring in the swamp!" cried Peter, and looked at Tommy as if he expected him to be greatly surprised.

"Dee, dee, dee! Do you call those flowers?" demanded Tommy rather scornfully.

"Certainly they are flowers," replied Peter rather sharply. "What is more, they are the very first flowers of the year. I think it is the most wonderful thing I've ever heard of that they are actually blooming now before the snow has gone."

Tommy Tit began to chuckle.

"What are you laughing at?" demanded Peter.

"To see you so excited over something I have known about for a long time," replied Tommy Tit. "I suppose those really are flowers, but I don't think much of them myself. They do come first of all, but they are not much ahead of some real flowers, flowers worth seeing. I saw some of the latter only a few moments ago, and they certainly did my eyes good."

Peter sat up very straight and stared very hard at Tommy Tit. "Do you mean to tell me that there are other flowers in bloom now?" he demanded. "I don't believe it, Tommy Tit."

Again Tommy Tit chuckled. "Peter," said he, "for a fellow who has lived in the Green Forest and on the Green Meadows as long as you have, you don't know much. No, sir, you don't know much. There are other flowers in bloom right this minute in the Green Forest, and I suspect that if I went to look for them I could find some right out on the Green Meadows, if there are any places where the snow has melted away. It doesn't make a bit of difference to me if you don't believe what I have told you. But if you will run up on the hillside back there and use your eyes as they were meant to be used, you will find some of the dearest, sweetest, bravest little flowers of all the year. I just love them. I watch for them every spring, and when I see them I know that winter is really over. Good-by, Peter." Before Peter could say another word Tommy Tit had flown away.

Peter was of two minds, as the saying is. He wanted to hurry home to tell Mrs. Peter of his wonderful discovery, and he wanted to go up on that hillside to see if Tommy Tit had told the truth. Somehow he just couldn't believe it. Then, too, his pride was hurt. He couldn't bear to think that he didn't know all there was to know. He started on towards home, but he only made a few hops before he stopped. Curiosity would not let him go on. Suddenly he turned and away he went, lipperty-lipperty-lip, for that hillside.

When Peter reached the foot of the hill he began to go up slowly. Snow lay in big patches all over it. "Of course," said Peter to himself, "those flowers will be where the snow has been melted longest." So he picked out the largest open spot and carefully hopped back and forth all over it. But all he found was a carpet of dead, brown leaves. Then he visited the next largest open spot with the same result. So he went from open spot to open spot until he had visited all of any size. Not a sign of a flower had he seen.

At last he sat down to rest. He was disappointed. Yes, sir, he was disappointed. "I don't believe Tommy Tit saw any flowers at all," muttered Peter. "No, sir, I don't believe he saw a single flower. He was jealous. He was jealous and he just made up that story. I'll rest a few minutes and then I'll hurry home to the dear Old Briar-patch."

Now right in front of Peter was one of the smallest open places on that hillside. It was so small that he hadn't thought it worth looking at. But as he sat there, his eyes just happened to rest on that little bare space in front of him. Suddenly Peter blinked and sat up very straight. Then he blinked two or three times more and gave a little gasp of surprise and unbelief. Right in the middle of that little bare space, standing bravely up above the dead, brown leaves, was something that looked very much like a flower! Yes, sir, it did so.

Peter jumped off the snow and hopped over to it. His face wore such a funny expression. Unbelief struggled with belief. But Peter knows that if he cannot believe his eyes he cannot believe anything. There under his very nose was the daintiest of little starlike flowers, a little lavender blossom bravely smiling up at him.

"Oh!" cried Peter under his breath. Then for a long time he simply sat there gazing at that little flower without saying a word.

It was a Hepatica.[2] It was about four inches high at the top of a woolly-looking stem, for that stem was covered with tiny fine hairs. Beside it, not yet ready to open, was a bud, and Peter saw at once that this also was covered with fine hairs and that it hung bent over. Though Peter didn't know it, this was to protect it from storms. Looking down, Peter saw other buds just starting up from the middle of a cluster of queer-shaped leathery-looking leaves. Some were green and some were purplish, and all lay almost flat.

Somewhat hesitatingly Peter stretched out his wobbly little nose and sniffed at that little blossom. "Why, it has a sweet

2   Look at the picture of the Hepatica on page 10.

HEPATICA
Hepatica triloba

SPRING BEAUTY
Claytonia virginica

smell!" he exclaimed.

"Have you just found that out?" asked a voice behind Peter. There was Tommy Tit, his small black eyes twinkling down at Peter.

"Yes," Peter owned up truthfully. "I remember seeing Hepaticas every spring, though I didn't know they came so early; but I hadn't noticed that they had any smell at all."

"Some don't," replied Tommy Tit. "Some, like this, are sweet-scented, and others have no scent at all. Even the sweet-scented ones lose that scent when they become old."

"I didn't know Hepaticas were this color, either," said Peter.

"Many of them are not," replied Tommy Tit. "Some are white and some are pinkish and others are almost blue."

"You seem to know all about them," said Peter a little enviously.

"Oh, no, I don't know all about them," replied Tommy. "But I've used my eyes and know some things. Do you know that they close at night?"

Peter's eyes opened very wide. "No," said he. "Do they?"

Tommy Tit nodded his black-capped little head vigorously. "Yes, sir," said he. "They even close on dark days. That is, they do until they get so old that they have begun to fade. Hello, it is beginning to snow! Just as if we hadn't had snow enough for one year! I think I'll get under cover."

So Tommy Tit flew away and left Peter sitting there, still staring at that little flower. Peter didn't mind a little snow. He knew it wouldn't amount to much, and somehow he didn't want to leave just yet. So he sat there looking at the brave little Hepatica. Presently he made a discovery that caused him to squeal right out. That little blossom was slowly closing. It didn't like the snow. Besides, it had grown quite dark. Slowly the little blossom closed and then Peter saw that its outer covering was overgrown with little fine hairs just as was the covering of the buds. "Why!" said Peter to himself, "the Hepaticas have regular little fur coats to keep them warm."

What Peter didn't find out until long afterward was that these same little hairs serve quite another purpose. They keep the ants and other crawling insects from climbing up and stealing the sweet juice which is called nectar, and which is hidden in the heart of each flower.

Another thing that Peter didn't learn until long afterward is that the colored parts which look like petals are not petals but are what are called sepals. The Hepatica has no true petals.

Finally Peter decided that nothing more was to be learned by sitting there, and once more he started for the dear Old Briar-patch, lipperty-lipperty-lip. He had so much to tell Mrs. Peter that it seemed to him he couldn't get home soon enough. "Flowers are wonderful. They truly are wonderful," thought Peter, as he scampered along. "I didn't know they were interesting at all. But they are, and I am going to find out all I can about as many of them as I can. Here it is early March and winter not yet really gone, and already I have found two kinds of flowers in bloom. I wonder what the next one will be."

It was a week before Peter got back to that hillside in the Green Forest. By that time all the snow had melted. That first brave little Hepatica had faded, but here and there all over that hillside were other little groups of Hepaticas. And Peter found that what Tommy Tit had told him was true; some were pink, and some were white, and some were a lavender which was almost blue, and some were sweet-scented, and some had no scent at all. But all were beautiful. "I love them," whispered Peter to himself. "I just love them. Now I know that sweet Mistress Spring is almost here."

Peter climbed up to the top of the hill. It was rocky up there. Peter likes to climb among the rocks sometimes. He didn't think of flowers up there, and so when he discovered a little cluster of tiny white, five-pointed, starlike flowers with yellow centers, growing, as it seemed, out of the very rock on which he sat, it is a question whether he was more surprised than delighted.

The stem was about four inches high and Peter looked at once to see if it also were covered with tiny hairs. It was. What is more, those tiny hairs were somewhat sticky. The stems sprang from the middle of a rosette of small, smooth, oval leaves with scalloped edges growing very close to the ground. It was then that he discovered that this little plant was not growing out of the rock, as at first glance it had seemed to be. There was a little crack in the rock filled with earth, and it was out of this that the plant was growing.

Peter looked all about. "I wish Tommy Tit was here," said he right out loud.

"Why?" demanded a very small voice. "I don't wish he was here."

Peter looked this way and that way, but could see no one.

"Where are you?" he demanded somewhat crossly. Just then he happened to glance at that cluster of tiny flowers. There, at work getting nectar from them, was a very small member of the Bee family. "Oh, excuse me!" exclaimed Peter.

The little Bee kept right on working. "What do you want of Tommy Tit?" she demanded.

"I want him to tell me what kind of a plant this is," replied Peter.

"It's the Saxifrage, the Early Saxifrage.[3] I thought everybody knew Saxifrage when they saw it," snapped the little Bee, keeping right on with her work.

"Isn't this a queer place for it to be growing?" asked Peter rather timidly.

"No, it isn't," retorted the little Bee. "It would be queer for it to be growing anywhere else. The Saxifrage loves the rocks. That is where you will always find it. They do say that people used to believe that it could split rocks and that is how it came by its name. Of course it can't do anything of the kind. That is all nonsense. But it does love to grow in little cracks like this one. That is where I always look for it. I'm very fond of the Saxifrage, because it comes when there are so few other flowers. Now I must go look for some more."

Away flew the busy little Bee and left Peter to think over the new knowledge he had gained.

---

3   Look at the picture of the Early Saxifrage on page 14.

EARLY SAXIFRAGE
Saxifraga virginiensis

LARGER MOUSE-EAR CHICKWEED
Cerastium vulgatum

iii. Peter Makes More Discoveries

Peter Rabbit slowly went down from the rocky top of the hill in the Green Forest. At the foot of the hill he turned towards the Green Meadows. He would make a few hops and stop. Then he would do it over again. He paid no attention to where he was going. The fact is, Peter was doing that most foolish of all foolish things for any of the little people of the Green Forest or the Green Meadows to do, forgetting to watch out. Like a great many people he can think of only one thing at a time, and just now he was thinking of flowers and not of possible danger.

So it happened that he almost walked into Reddy Fox. Just in time, the very nick of time, Peter saw Reddy. At the same instant Reddy saw Peter. You may be sure that all thought of flowers left Peter's funny little head then. There was nothing for him to do but to take to his heels. That is just what he did. Yes, sir, that is just what he did. He made those long heels of his fairly fly.

After Peter raced Reddy Fox. Reddy knows that Peter can run fast for only a short distance. He must reach a place of safety very soon. Reddy meant that this time Peter shouldn't reach a place of safety. Peter is a great dodger. He dodged around trees and jumped over logs and darted behind stumps. All the time he could see Reddy gaining on him, and in Reddy's eyes was a look of hungry eagerness which made Peter feel most uncomfortable.

Now Peter was down near the edge of the Green Forest where the trees were rather far apart. It was the kind of a place where Reddy Fox could run at his best. "Oh, dear!" panted Peter. "I must get to that old bramble-tangle on the edge of the Green Forest. If I don't, Reddy will surely catch me."

But that bramble-tangle was farther away than Peter had thought, and it began to look very much as if Reddy Fox would have a Rabbit for his dinner. Twice Peter dodged barely in time. He was in despair when he scampered around a big stump, and there between two roots was a hole just big enough for him to squeeze into. Peter didn't waste any time. He popped into that hole without waiting to find out anything about it. For all he knew there might be somebody in there. As his funny little apology for a tail disappeared, Reddy's teeth snapped so close to it that he actually pulled out a little bunch of white hairs.

Peter remained in that hole for a long time. He didn't even peek outside. He knew that Reddy Fox could be very patient at times and might be waiting around for him to come out. So Peter was content to be safe and wait. After he was quite over his fright, he began to think of flowers again, and the surprising things he had learned. Already he had found three kinds, yet rough Brother North Wind still howled at times through the Green Forest and Jack Frost still came around at night.

"I wonder," thought Peter, "if there are any other flowers. Tommy Tit said that he suspected he would be able to find some on the Green Meadows if he went to look for them. I wonder what ones he thinks he could find there this time of year. Oh, dear, I wish Reddy Fox had kept away from here! I want to go hunt for more flowers."

By and by Peter ventured to peep out to see if the way were clear. He could see nothing of Reddy Fox, but that didn't mean that Reddy wasn't somewhere about. He might be hiding. So Peter sat with only his nose out of that hole. Thinking of Reddy Fox, he forgot flowers until something pink just a little to one side caught his attention. It was a flower! There was no doubt about that. Peter ventured to poke his whole head out that he might see better.

"It is a pink Hepatica, I do believe!" exclaimed Peter to himself, and poked his head out still farther. Then he noticed the stem. It was very different from the stem of the Hepatica. It was longer, slender, and perfectly smooth. There were no little hairs on it. As he looked more closely he saw that while at first it had seemed to be all light green, it was slightly stained with red. It wasn't straight, but rather crooked, and halfway up were two leaves which right away made Peter think of grass, for they were long, narrow and pointed.

"Why-ee!" exclaimed Peter. "It isn't a Hepatica at all."

"Who said it was?" demanded a very small voice, which Peter at once recognized as that of the little Bee he had seen so busy at the blossoms of the Saxifrage. Then, without waiting for Peter to reply, the little Bee continued, "It is the Spring Beauty[4] which I've heard some folks call Claytonia. I like the first name best myself."

Peter nodded. "I say so, too," said he. "When I first saw it I thought it was a pink Hepatica. Are the Spring Beauties always pink?"

"No," mumbled the little Bee, as she sucked up the nectar from the heart of the flower. "Sometimes they are white with little pink veins. This is the first one I have found this spring, but there will be a lot of them around here soon, for this is the kind of a place they like. You notice that the ground is quite damp here, and the trees are so far apart that the sun can get in. It is a good thing that jolly, round, red Mr. Sun is shining, or we wouldn't have seen this little beauty."

"Why not?" demanded Peter.

"Because, like the Hepaticas, it closes when there is no sunshine. If you sit here long enough, you will find that it turns so as to always face towards the sun. It surely is a lover of sunshine. Just notice that it has five petals. There isn't any other flower quite like the Spring Beauty. By the way, Peter Rabbit, are there any dandelions yet on the Green Meadows?"

Peter shook his head. "I haven't seen any," said he.

"Pooh! That doesn't mean anything," said the little Bee. "I guess I could find some if I went to look for them. Dandelions and Common Chickweed can be found any month in the year if you look in the right place for them. Good-by, Peter Rabbit." The little Bee disappeared as suddenly as she had appeared.

Peter waited only long enough to make certain in his own mind that the way was clear. Then he started for the Green Meadows and the dear Old Briar-patch. A glint of yellow caught

---

4   Look at the picture of the Spring Beauty on page 10.

his attention on the very edge of the Green Meadows. Eagerly Peter turned that way. Could there be a Dandelion there? Yes, there was! There was no mistaking that round blossom of pure gold. Peter had known Dandelions ever since he could remember. Sometimes he got Dandelion leaves in his mouth and he knew just how bitter they are. But that spot of bright yellow where the grass had hardly yet begun to turn green was good to see, and as Peter looked down at the cheery little blossom he was filled with respect for this common plant.

A Merry Little Breeze came dancing along and saw what Peter was looking at. "Isn't it wonderful how so many flowers can grow together on one stem?" cried the Merry Little Breeze.

Peter stared about him, blinking rather foolishly. "I don't see but one flower," said he.

The Merry Little Breeze rumpled up Peter's hair and cried, "There must be something wrong with your eyes, Peter. You are looking at a whole bunch of them right now."

"I'm not!" retorted Peter. "I am looking at this Dandelion."[5]

"Look closer, Peter. Look just as close as you can. What you call a single blossom is made up of dozens and dozens of tiny flowers all growing together so as to look like one big flower," cried the Merry Little Breeze.

"What?" cried Peter. Then he looked very closely, as he had been told to do, and sure enough he discovered that the Merry Little Breeze had told him the truth. He was so astonished that for a few minutes he could do nothing but sit and stare at that Dandelion. At last he found his tongue. "And all the time," said he, "I have thought there was nothing wonderful about a Dandelion."

"Ignorance, Peter, ignorance," chuckled the Merry Little Breeze. "There is nothing in all the Great World more wonderful than some of the plants that people call common. You think it is wonderful because what you thought a single flower is made up of ever and ever so many tiny flowers. But there are other things just as wonderful about the Dandelion. At night all those little flowers are closed up in a little green house, for the Dandelion opens only after the sun comes up and closes before dark. By

5   Look at the picture of the Dandelion on page 69.

and by each one of those little flowers will become a seed on the end of a little feathery stem, and in the place of what you call a flower will be a feathery, little silver ball. Then I will come dancing along and blow, and away will go those little seeds, sailing far across the Green Meadows as if each were carried by a little balloon. It is great fun to blow them this way and that way. From each little seed will spring a new plant, and that is the way the Dandelions are spread. Have you noticed anything queer about that stem?"

"No," said Peter. "It is rather big, but that is all that I see queer about it."

"Well, it is hollow," replied the Merry Little Breeze. "If you should break it off you could blow through it. I suppose you know that the Dandelion got its name because some one imagined that those queer leaves with the notches on them are like a lion's teeth."

Just then Peter remembered the Chickweed. He wondered if that, too, were in bloom. Perhaps the Merry Little Breeze would know. So he asked. You know Peter never hesitates to ask questions.

"Certainly. Of course," replied the Merry Little Breeze. "You probably have seen it a dozen times since the snow left. I must say that for real pluck and bravery I know of no flower to equal the Common Chickweed. I've seen it in bloom in bare sunny spots in the middle of winter. There are some blossoms right over there now."

Peter looked, but at first all he saw was a mass of little plants a few inches high and having smooth little leaves growing in pairs along the stem and shaped something like the ear of a Mouse. Of flowers Peter saw none at all. Once more the Merry Little Breeze told him to look closely. Peter hopped over and put his nose right down to those little plants. Then for the first time he discovered the tiniest of white flowers, so tiny that always he had quite overlooked them. But they were real flowers. Peter counted the petals. There were five. Then he made a discovery. Each tiny white petal was notched so that it looked almost like two. Tiny as it was, it was really a beautiful little flower.

Peter noticed that the plants were branched and spread over

the ground. They looked too delicate for cold weather, yet the Merry Little Breeze had told him that even in the middle of winter blossoms of the Chickweed sometimes were to be found. The wonder of it filled Peter's mind as he once more turned towards the dear Old Briar-patch. He had made but a hop or two when he saw another little flower that caused him to stop again with eyes round with surprise.

"Gracious!" exclaimed Peter. "Here is one of those little flowers grown to be a giant."

It is not surprising that he thought so, for the flower at which he was looking, though small, was several times larger than the others, and in form was much like them. But presently Peter noticed that its stem was straighter and the leaves were a darker green and of different shape. Then he knew that this must be a different flower, but he was sure that it must be related to the other.

Peter was right. He had found the Larger Mouse-ear Chickweed,[6] a cousin of the Common Chickweed.

---

6.   See the picture of the Larger Mouse-ear Chickweed on page 14.

iv. Shy Blossoms and Fairy Bells

Peter Rabbit had climbed up the hill in the Green Forest to see once more the Saxifrage in bloom. Where, the first time he had visited that place, there had been but one cluster of blossoms there were now many peeping out from amongst the rocks. For awhile Peter sat and admired them. Then he started down the other side of the hill. He wasn't headed for any particular place and he had nothing in particular on his mind. As always, his wobbly little nose was continually in motion, trying to pick up news from the Merry Little Breezes.

"Ah!" said Peter, stopping very suddenly. Then he wriggled his wobbly little nose faster than ever; it had caught the sweetest of sweet perfumes. Peter sniffed long and hard. "Ah!" he exclaimed again. Then slowly he began to go forward in the direction from which that delightful scent came.

Little thrills of delight ran all over Peter. This was real fun. It was exciting. He knew that only a flower could give off that sweet fragrance, but he hadn't the least idea what flower was doing it. The wind was still cold, for it was early in April. But jolly, round, red Mr. Sun was doing his best to warm the brown earth.

Slowly Peter hopped along, looking eagerly ahead and to right and left in quest of a flower. But no flower did he see, nor any plant that looked as if it might have a flower. Still the sweet perfume grew stronger, and Peter sniffed and sniffed. Then just by chance he happened to look down at his feet. There, peeping out from the carpet of dead, brown leaves, was a beautiful little flower of the most delicate pink. It lay right on the ground. At least, that is the way it seemed.

Peter's first thought was that it had been dropped there. He always thought of flowers as having stems that stood more or less upright. He reached forward and brushed aside the dead leaves. Then he gave a little squeal of pleasure. You see he had uncovered a cluster of these beautiful, pink, fragrant little blossoms, and he saw at once that they were growing on a stem that, instead of standing upright, trailed along the ground. Peter had found that loveliest of spring flowers, the Trailing Arbutus.[7]

The stem of the plant was tough and woody. The leaves were thick, smooth on top, and somewhat hairy underneath. They were oval in shape, alternated along the stem, and were a dull, rather dark green with rusty spots on them. They looked old. Peter thought of that right away. The truth is they were old. They had grown the summer before and had remained green all winter. The new leaves wouldn't appear until the flowers had gone.

It seemed to Peter that he would never get tired of looking at those dainty, delicate little blossoms. They gave him a wonderful feeling. Somehow they made him sure that sweet Mistress Spring truly had arrived. They seemed to have in themselves the very spirit of Mistress Spring.

Peter hunted for more, and presently he found them. They grew in little patches here and there all over that sunny hillside. Some peeped shyly out from under the brown, dead leaves which had kept them warm all winter. Others were tucked away in patches of dead grass. Some of the loveliest grew beneath pine trees. Some were the most delicate pink, and others were a deep pink, while still others were pure white.

Lovely as were the Hepaticas, now blooming all through the Green Forest, and dainty as were the Spring Beauties down near the edge of the Green Meadows, these Arbutus blossoms seemed to Peter the loveliest and daintiest flowers he had seen. And with their beauty was that wonderful fragrance. It is no wonder that Peter kept exclaiming, "Ah!" and "Oh!" as he found the shy little blossoms modestly hiding in the grass or beneath the leaves.

Peter went back there again the next day. At once he discovered a boy and a girl there, and it didn't take him long to find out

7   Look at the picture of the Trailing Arbutus on page 23.

TRAILING ARBUTUS
Epigaea repens

MARSH MARIGOLD
Caltha palustris

that they, too, were in search of the Arbutus. They were picking them, and, because the stems were short, they often tore whole plants up by the roots. Peter was so indignant he didn't know what to do. Once he actually stamped with anger. This was a mistake, for the boy heard him and promptly came to look for him. Peter had to take to his heels while the boy shouted and chased him for a short distance.

Of course it was easy enough to get away from that boy, and the latter soon gave up. Then Peter stole back to watch the boy and the girl. They kept on hunting for the Arbutus and tearing them up by the roots. Peter grew angrier and angrier.

"Haven't they any sense at all!" cried Peter to himself. "Don't they know that if they tear those plants up by the roots there won't be any here next year? I never saw such stupidity!

Probably next year they will come here and wonder why they cannot find any flowers. Why don't they think a little? If they can't pick them without pulling them up by the roots, they should leave them alone."

Peter was right. Flowers are never so beautiful as when growing, and to take them by the roots is to rob the Green Forest and the hillsides of some of their greatest charms.

Peter finally left in disgust and wandered down to the Laughing Brook. As he hopped along the bank he came to a sunny spot where he found something which for the time being drove all thought of that boy and girl from his head. All about were little nodding yellow bells. At least, this is what they looked like. They looked as if they might be the bells of fairyland. Of course they were not. Of course they were not bells at all. They were flowers. Each hung from the top of a quite long, straight, slender, smooth stem that rose from between two large, oblong, grayish green leaves that were streaked and spotted with brown. They seemed to love the company of each other, for they crowded together along the bank and back and part way up the slope of a hill.

Peter had found the Dog's-tooth Violet, or Yellow Adder's-tongue,[8] sometimes called Trout Lily. The latter is really the better name, for it is a Lily and not a Violet. It is the first Lily

8   Look at the picture of the Yellow Adder's-tongue on page 5.

of the year. Though Peter didn't know it, he had found another flower that follows the light, turning on its stalk so as to always face jolly, round, bright Mr. Sun.

Peter looked for his friend, the little Bee, but he couldn't see her. In fact, those dainty little flowers appeared to have no visitors. Peter wondered if there were no nectar in them. It didn't seem possible that such lovely little flowers could be lacking in sweetness. That afternoon he returned for another visit and right away he discovered yellow Butterflies very busy among those nodding blossoms, and a number of small cousins of Bumblebee. Then Peter knew that the sweetness which is called nectar was in those flowers just as it was in the other flowers he had found.

Peter remained there watching the busy workers until the first hint of the Black Shadows warned of the approach of night. Then those dainty little Lilies began to close and the Butterflies and Bees departed. Remembering that he had found several colors among the Hepaticas, and that on this very day he had found both white and pink Arbutus, Peter made a careful search among the little Lilies to see if all were alike. They were. Each little bell was of a pale yellow, and Peter concluded that this was the only color of the Adder's-tongue. But in this he was wrong, for in some parts of the country it is white instead of yellow.

It was some weeks later that Peter returned to that place. Then he looked in vain for the fairylike flower bells. Not one was to be seen. What was more, he had hard work to find a trace of those big, spotted, grayish-green leaves. It was as if those beautiful little plants never had been. You see, shortly after the flowers withered and the seed was formed, those leaves began to wither also, and presently disappeared. The Adder's-tongue comes just to gladden the spring. Then, its duty done, it goes into a long sleep, to be awakened only when sweet Mistress Spring once more returns.

v. Tommy Tit Drops a Hint

"Dee, dee, Chickadee!
Look beneath the chestnut tree!
Pure as the drifted snow
Doth the dainty Bloodroot blow."

Peter Rabbit pricked up his long ears. "Bloodroot, Blood-root," repeated Peter to himself. "That must be the name of a flower. I wonder if I know it." He scratched a long ear with a long hind foot as he tried to remember if he had ever seen the Bloodroot. "I must have seen it," he muttered, "but somehow I can't remember what it looks like. It must be one of the very earliest flowers, for Tommy Tit says it is in bloom now."

"Dee, dee, Chickadee!
Look beneath the chestnut tree!"

rang the merry voice of Tommy Tit once more. Away went Peter, lipperty-lipperty-lip, towards the edge of the Green Forest in search of Tommy Tit. He soon found him industriously picking the tiny eggs of insects from the twigs of a tree.

"Hi, Tommy Tit!" called Peter. "Which chestnut tree is it?"

Tommy's tiny black eyes twinkled. "Which chestnut tree is which?" he asked mischievously.

"The one you were talking about. The one you said to look under to see the Bloodroot," retorted Peter.

"Oh," replied Tommy Tit, "that's it, is it? Well, it's right over in the Green Forest. Go look for it, Peter."

"But the Green Forest is full of chestnut trees," replied Peter impatiently.

"So it is. So it is," cried Tommy Tit. "Look under all of them, Peter. Look under all of them and then you'll be sure to find the right one. I have business up in the Old Orchard, so if you'll excuse me, I'll be on my way. If you haven't found the right tree by the time I get back, I'll show it to you." Before Peter could say a word Tommy Tit had flown away.

For a minute or two Peter was so vexed that he quite lost his temper. He stamped the ground angrily. But he was soon over his temper and curiosity started him on his way to look for that chestnut tree. "How can a fellow find the right tree among so many?" muttered Peter, as he hopped down the Lone Little Path. He was so busy thinking about this that he almost forgot to keep his eyes on the ground on both sides of the Lone Little Path.

So it was that he was almost past a certain big chestnut tree, which grew a little to one side of the Lone Little Path, when out of the corner of one eye he saw something white. He stopped for a good look, and then, with an excited jump, he headed straight for that tree. There, near the foot of it, was a beautiful pure white blossom. Peter remembered what Tommy Tit had said about the drifted snow, and he knew at once that he had found the Bloodroot.[9]

If Peter had known anything about measuring he would have said that it was nearly an inch and a half across. There were eight pure white petals, every other one just a wee bit longer than its neighbors. And the heart of it was a golden yellow. Later he discovered some of these same flowers with twelve petals. The stem was quite long, smooth and fairly stout.

Coming up from the ground close to the foot of the stem was a big leaf, which was not as tall as the blossom. This leaf was rounded and had very deep notches, so that it looked almost like a number of small leaves grown together. The under side was rough, for it was covered with fine ribs. But the upper side was quite smooth.

Looking to see if there were more of these blossoms, Peter discovered what seemed like a queer bundle wrapped in silvery green, just pushing up out of the earth. When he looked at it

9   Look at the picture of the Bloodroot on page 34.

closely he discovered that it was a Bloodroot bud wrapped in one of its own leaves, and thus it was protected from the wind and cold. As it grew higher that leaf would unfold and the blossom would push on and up until it was ready to open. He knew of no other flower that came out of the cold, damp earth so wrapped and protected.

Just then a Merry Little Breeze came dancing along, and when it had passed, several of the petals of the flower he had first seen lay on the ground, for despite its courage in blooming so early in the spring the Bloodroot is a most delicate flower. Like some of the other flowers Peter had found, it closes at night and on dull, dark days is never wide open.

As Peter turned to look for more of these little blossoms he accidentally stepped on a leaf and broke it off. A red juice came from it. Had Peter dug down and broken a piece of the root he would have found still more of that red juice. It is this that gives the plant its name of Bloodroot. Once upon a time the Indians used this juice for paint, and so in some places the plant is still called Indian Paint.

Peter soon discovered more of these dainty flowers growing under the trees, maples and oaks, as well as chestnuts. Then he understood that the Bloodroot is a lover of woodland, regardless of the kind of trees growing there.

Oddly enough, the Bloodroot is related to one of the most gorgeous of flowers, the California Poppy, for it is a member of the Poppy family. Its beautiful, brilliant cousin Peter had never seen. But had he lived out in the wonderful state from which the flower takes its name, it would have been perhaps more familiar to him than any other flower, for there in its season it covers the fields as with a cloth of gold. Or had he visited Farmer Brown's flower garden he might have found it there, for so beautiful is it that in the East, where it does not grow wild, it is cultivated in gardens. It seems strange that the modest little Bloodroot is related to such a gloriously brilliant flower as the California Poppy. [10]

Presently Peter made another discovery that almost made him forget the Bloodroot. Just a little way from where he had

10   Look at the picture of the California Poppy on page 29.

CALIFORNIA POPPY
Eschscholtzia californica

found the first Bloodroot he came upon a little group of flowers which, when he first saw them at a distance, he thought to
be Bloodroot. But when he had hopped over to them, he knew
right away that they were not even related.

At first glance these also seemed white, but when he looked
closely Peter found that some had the most delicate tint of
pink on the outside, while others had just the faintest touch of
blue. The flowers were not as large as those of the Bloodroot.
But it was in the stalks and leaves that Peter found the greatest difference. The stalks were very slender, and springing out
from each stem, about a third of the way from the flower to
the ground, were three to five leaves, each one deeply cut and
notched. They grew out from the same point on the stem so
that they made almost a circle around it. There was only one
flower on each stem.

"Wood Anemones!"[11] cried Peter in sheer delight. "I had
forgotten that it was time for these. They are the Windflowers.
How I love them!"

Just then, as if to show Peter why these lovely blossoms are
called Windflowers, a Merry Little Breeze came dancing along,
and all the flowers swayed and nodded and bent this way, that
way, and the other way. Peter remembered how the petals of the
Bloodroot had dropped at the rude touch of one of these Merry
Little Breezes. But the Anemones were quite unharmed. Even
had rough Brother North Wind blown upon them they would
simply have bent until he had passed, then lifted their lovely
heads again. This was because of those slender, wiry stems.

Just by chance Happy Jack Squirrel came along and dug for
a buried nut. In doing this he uncovered the root of one of the
Anemones, and Peter saw that the root, instead of going straight
down into the ground, turned sharply and ran along just under
the surface. It was quite thick and stout and from it grew many
little roots in all directions. Then Peter understood how the
Anemone is anchored in the ground and can stand the rude
winds without being torn up.

The finding of the Wood Anemones or Windflowers reminded
Peter that the spring before he had seen other flowers so like

11   Look at the picture of the Wood Anemone on page 31.

WOOD ANEMONE
Anemone quinquefolia

RUE ANEMONE
Anemonella thalictroides

them that he had guessed right away that they were cousins. He wondered if he could find these now, and promptly began to look. He didn't have to look far. In fact, he found them only a few hops away, for these cousins are most neighborly. Peter was glad of this, for it gave him a chance to compare the two.

The plants were much alike in the way they grew. These cousins also had slender stems, and the leaves were divided into leaflets. Such leaves are called compound. They, too, grew out from the same point on the stem so as to form almost a circle. But while there was just a single blossom of the Wood Anemone nodding above its circle of leaves, there were two or three blossoms above the leaves on each stem of the Rue Anemones,[12] for this is the name these dainty blossoms bear. The flowers were smaller. Most of them were pure white, though some were tinged with pink. They were for all the world like many-pointed little stars with yellow centers.

Remembering what Happy Jack Squirrel had accidentally shown him about the roots of the Wood Anemone, Peter dug down beside one of the Rue Anemone plants. Instead of a root like its larger cousin, he found the Rue Anemone had a cluster of little bulbs like very tiny sweet potatoes.

"Well," declared Peter. "If I couldn't tell those cousins apart by the flowers, I certainly could by the roots. But I guess there never will be any trouble in telling these two apart. All I have to do is to remember that the Wood Anemone has only one blossom, and the Rue Anemone has two or three. It is great fun hunting for spring flowers. It certainly is. I wonder what one I shall find next."

---

12   Look at the picture of the Rue Anemone on page 31.

vi. Gold and Other Treasures

Peter did not have long to wonder which of his flower friends he would find next. Indeed, it was only a short time later that, as he left the Green Forest to cross the Green Meadows on his way home to the dear Old Briar-patch, he came upon a whole army of little blossoms which are among the dearest of all that bloom in the early spring. Side by side they grew, so close together that many of them touched each other. They were like little soldiers on parade. Each flower was in the shape of a tiny tube opening into four oval petals.

"Bluets!"[13] cried Peter, as he sat down beside them. "I love them. I do so."

"So do I," said a sharp little voice, and there was Peter's friend of the Hepaticas, the little cousin of Bumblebee. "I suppose you love them to eat," added the little Bee.

"No," replied Peter, indignantly. "They are too pretty to eat. I love them because they look so pure and innocent. They are like tiny stars with gold centers, and it seems to me every one must love them. They add joy to the Great World just at this time of year when it is most needed."

"Pooh!" said the practical little Bee. "Pooh! Pooh! I love them for a better reason than that. I love them for more than looks. I love them for the sweetness that is in the heart of each. If it wasn't for this, I wouldn't take three strokes of my wings for a look at them."

"Which do you like the best, the white or the blue?" asked Peter, for he had just noticed that while some of these little stars were snowy white, many of them were bluish, some of them

---

13   Look at the picture of the Bluets on page 34.

BLOODROOT
Sanguinaria canadensis

BLUETS
Houstonia caerulea

quite blue, especially near the ends of the petals.

"They are all alike to me," replied the little Bee, busily buzz-ing from one to another and taking a tiny drop of nectar from each. "Color makes no difference so long as they have something to give me."

"You ought to be made to pay for it," declared Peter.

"I do pay for it," snapped the little Bee. "I carry that fine yellow powder which is called pollen from the heart of one to the heart of another, and this is necessary in order for them to make seeds by and by. I guess if it were not for some of us little winged people there wouldn't be so many of these Bluets you seem to love so much."

Peter didn't quite understand this, but as the little Bee seemed to be very sure of what she was talking about, he concluded that it must be so. Anyway, the little blossoms appeared to welcome the little Bee and not to begrudge the sweetness she took from them.

At first it seemed to Peter that these tiny flowers grew on a stem with no leaves, but when he looked closely he saw that tiny leaves grew out in pairs from opposite sides of this stem or stalk, and that the latter came up from a tuft of small leaves. There were dozens and dozens of these little flowers already in bloom, and dozens and dozens of tiny buds pushing up be-tween them to take their places when they should fade. Peter knew that within a week there would be such great patches of Bluets on the Green Meadows that at a distance they would look almost like snow. These flowers are also called Innocence and Quaker Ladies.

It was a week later that Peter again went flower hunting. This time he started for that part of the Green Forest where the Laughing Brook makes its way out into the Green Meadows towards the Smiling Pool. It is wet and swampy in there, and Peter had it in his mind that he might find a certain flower which loves to grow in such a place.

As he hurried, lipperty-lipperty-lip, through the Green Forest, he came to a part of it where the trees were not close together, and the earth was somewhat damp. There, just at one side of the Lone Little Path, two lavender blossoms a foot or more above the ground nodded a greeting to him. Each had five petals. These were almost whitish where they met around the heart of the flower. From this whitish base of each petal ran five fine lines out to the outer edge.

The leaves were cut very deeply into three to five parts, and each of these parts was divided many times. Some of the older leaves were spotted with white. The stalk was branched and was covered with tiny hairs.

It was an old friend Peter had found. It was the Wild Geranium, or Spotted Crane's-bill,[14] a flower brave enough to come early in the spring, but so delicate that it will not stand being picked. Though Peter did not know it, he had many times seen the long, quaint seed pod of this flower, which, when the seeds are ready, springs open and throws them out some distance.

Once more Peter started on, lipperty-lipperty-lip. When he reached the swampy place where the water stood between big grassy tussocks he began to pick his way carefully, for you know Peter doesn't like to get his feet wet. From tussock to tussock he jumped, this way and that way. Every moment or two he sat up and looked all about.

"Have you lost something, Peter? "cried Winsome Bluebird, from the top of a tall tree on the bank of the Laughing Brook.

Peter looked up and grinned. "No," said he. "No, Winsome, I haven't lost anything, but I'm looking for something. I'm looking for gold. If I don't find it pretty soon, I shall think that something is very wrong, very wrong indeed." With this Peter kicked up his heels, jumped over a puddle, and went on his way.

Winsome Bluebird scratched his head. "Gold!" he said to himself. "Gold! I always suspected that Peter Rabbit wasn't quite right in his head, and now I know it. The idea! The idea of looking along the Laughing Brook for gold! Whoever heard of such a thing!"

At first Winsome Bluebird thought he would hunt up some of his friends and tell them of Peter Rabbit's foolishness. Then he decided he would follow Peter and see what he was doing. He was just in time to see Peter dancing about and kicking up his long heels on the bank of the Laughing Brook, just on the

14   Look at the picture of the Spotted Crane's-bill on page 37.

SPOTTED CRANE'S-BILL
Geranium maculatum

COMMON CINQUEFOIL
Potentilla canadensis

edge of the Green Meadows. What could it mean? Winsome hurried over to see.

"I've found my gold, Winsome! I've found my gold!" cried Peter, as soon as Winsome drew near. He pointed down to the edge of the Laughing Brook.

Winsome looked eagerly. "I don't see any gold," said he, disappointedly. "I don't see anything but some yellow flowers, which I've heard some people call Cowslips and some call Marsh Marigolds."[15]

Peter laughed happily. "They are my gold!" cried he. "See how they shine! And they are full of golden meaning, for now I know that truly Mistress Spring is here to stay. I hoped I would find the very first ones to bloom, and I guess I have." Once more Peter kicked up his heels for pure joy.

The flowers Peter had found grew in a cluster above a mass of large, shining, rounded, green leaves that were heart-shaped at the base. They were growing on large, hollow stems, and the roots were on the very edge of the Laughing Brook. The flowers were much like large Buttercups, and they shone as if they were indeed of pure gold. The leaves were glossy, also.

Winsome Bluebird had been right in saying that they are called Cowslips and Marsh Marigolds. But they are neither true Cowslips nor true Marigolds, for they belong to the Crowfoot family, the same family to which the Buttercups belong. Another name for this plant is the Meadow Gowan. There is no mistaking these flowers, for no others at all like them grow with their feet in the water, as it were.

---

15   Look at the picture of the Marsh Marigold on page 23.

VII. Two Dainty Little Neighbors

SWEET MISTRESS Spring really had arrived. There was no longer the least doubt in Peter's mind. Gentle Sister South Wind, with the help of April showers, had swept away the very last of the snow. All through the Green Forest and all over the Green Meadows little people of every kind who had slept through the long winter were awakening. The little brown blankets that had wrapped and protected the leaf buds of the trees and bushes were bursting everywhere. Each day brought old feathered friends from the Sunny South where they had spent the cold weather.

Peter couldn't keep still. He just had to keep moving. It was such fun to greet the new arrivals, and to be the first to get the news of those who still were on the way, but had been left behind by the swifter-winged or those who were in a greater hurry to reach their old homes.

But with all his hurrying about to see his feathered friends, Peter didn't forget to keep his eyes open for new flowers. Every time he found one he had not seen before he tingled all over with pure joy. Not for the world would he miss one of these thrills of delight if he could help it. So as he scampered this way and that way through the Green Forest and over the Green Meadows, it was with a most delightful feeling that at any moment he might receive a happy surprise, and not a day passed without one or more of these surprises.

Very early one morning he was over in a part of the Green Forest where the ground was rich and damp. It was near the foot of the hill where he had first found the Saxifrage, and here and there big rocks were scattered about. It was as he came around one of these big rocks that Peter received one of these pleasant surprises. Right in front of him was a mass of soft, white, fuzzy-looking flowers that at once reminded him of the white foam he had seen on the edge of a pool in the Laughing Brook. Though Peter didn't know it, other people had been reminded of the same thing by these little flowers, and so had given to the plant the name of Foamflower.[16] And by this name it is very commonly known. It is also called the False Miterwort.

At first glance Peter was somehow reminded of those early friends of his, the Saxifrage flowers he had found higher up on the hill. And when you come to think of it this is not altogether strange, for the Foamflower belongs to the Saxifrage family. But when he came to look at them closely, they did not look so much like their relatives as he had thought. The tiny blossoms of the Saxifrage had been crowded together in little groups. These little flowers grew out from along the stem for some distance down from the tip and were not crowded. They were white and there were five tiny, somewhat pointed petals. From the heart of each little blossom there stood up ten of the little threadlike parts which are called stamens, each one tipped with a tiny package of the flower dust which we call pollen. It was these little stamens which at a distance made the flowers appear so soft and foam like.

The stalks were nearly a foot high, and when Peter looked closely he saw that they were covered with very tiny hairs. The leaves were of good size and on long stems. At the base they were cut in like a heart. The edges were very irregular and the veins showed very plainly. When he looked at these leaves closely Peter discovered that these, too, were slightly hairy on the upper side, and that along the veins on the under side were the finest of fine hairs.

How long Peter would have sat admiring these beautiful little friends had nothing happened no one will ever know. You see something did happen. Sammy Jay suddenly began to scream, "Thief, thief, thief!" at the top of his lungs from a tree just back of Peter. Peter looked up just in time to see Redtail the Hawk at the very instant that Redtail saw him. Peter made a flying jump right over the Foamflowers and dodged behind a big rock. He

16   Look at the picture of the Foamflower on page 41.

FOAMFLOWER
Tiarella cordifolia

was just in time, just in the very nick of time.

Redtail screamed with disappointment and flew away. He knew that it was a waste of time to wait for Peter to show himself again. Peter remained where he was, squatting under the overhanging side of that big rock, until he was sure that there was no longer any danger from Redtail. Then, quite as if nothing at all had happened, he started on his way.

He had gone but a short distance when he squealed right out with pleasure. Growing in rich, black earth which had been made by the decaying of countless leaves which had fallen among the rocks, were the quaintest little flowers Peter had yet seen. They hung from the under side of a slender, pale green, curving stalk. They were white, tipped with yellow, and looked like nothing so much as little white hearts hanging with the points down. In fact, they are often called Whitehearts. Had Peter ever looked in picture books, which of course he never had, he might have been reminded of the funny, baggy trousers which the little Dutch boys wear in Holland. You see two big petals were not shaped like petals at all, but grew together to make a sort of bag with two legs as it were, so that the flower was very much like a tiny pair of Dutch trousers hanging upside down. This is why these flowers are called Dutchman's-breeches.[17] They are also called Soldiers' Caps and Eardrops.

Each flower had two other very small and narrow petals at right angles to the longer ones, and these were arched over six yellow stamens. From some of the stems or stalks only three or four of the pretty and curious little blossoms were hanging, while from others there were as many as nine. Most of them were white, but a few of them were tinted pink. The leaves, which came up all about them, were compound, which, as you know, means that each leaf looked as if it was made up of many small leaves. Each of these parts which seemed like smaller leaves was also divided. They grew on long, slender stems and were very beautiful, dainty and delicate.

Peter just couldn't tear himself away. He wondered if these curious little flowers contained nectar, and if they did how any of the insect folk could get it. Presently he found out. Along

17   Look at the picture of the Dutchman's-breeches on page 43.

DUTCHMAN'S BREECHES
Dicentra Cucullaria

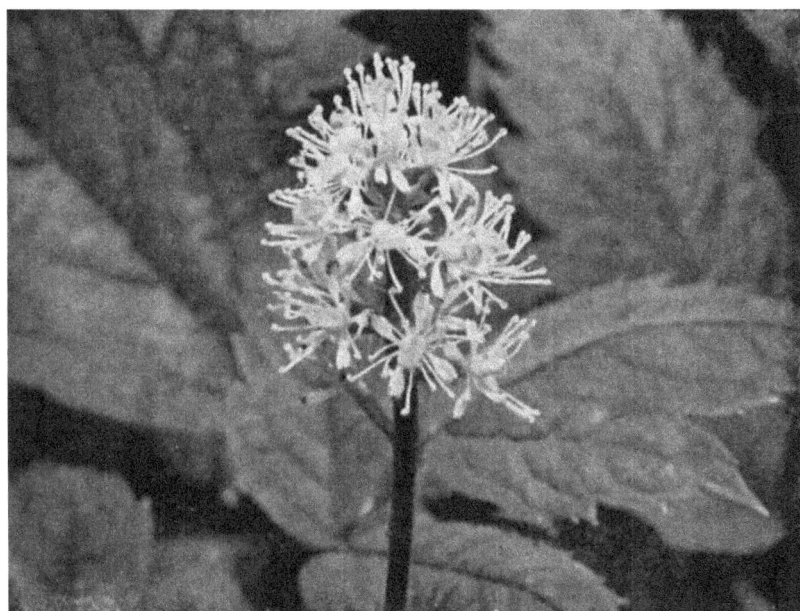

WHITE BANEBERRY
Aetata alba

came Lady Bumblebee. Now Lady Bumblebee has a very long tongue. She needed it now. From flower to flower she flew, clinging to each in turn. To make that long tongue reach the nectar in the heart of each little blossom Lady Bumblebee had to cling tightly to the flower, and in doing this she got herself well dusted with yellow pollen. Of course, when she visited the next flower she left some of that pollen there, which was exactly what Old Mother Nature had planned she should do, so that each little flower might in turn make seeds.

Peter was rudely startled by a shout. He turned hastily to see coming that way the boy and girl whom he had seen tearing up Arbutus earlier in the season. They at once began picking the beautiful little Whitehearts, and there wasn't a thing Peter could do about it. It made him boil inside! Such beautiful, dainty flowers were not intended to be picked. They would soon wither and fall from the stems. They belonged right where they were in the Green Forest, and nowhere else.

Even Peter knew that if no flowers were left there could be no seeds, and if there were no seeds there could be no new plants.

But the thoughtless children kept right on picking until not a blossom was left. Then away they went to search for more, while Peter sadly started for home in the dear Old Briar-patch. The finding of those Dutchman's-breeches had given him a great joy, but now that joy had been turned to sadness. There was something missing in the Green Forest, something that could not be replaced.

"I wish," said Peter, very fiercely, "that I were as big as Buster Bear. I'd scare those two-legged robbers so that they never, never would want to pick flowers again."

VIII. REDWING AND MRS. GROUSE HELP

O VER IN the rushes near the Smiling Pool was Redwing the Blackbird, telling all who would listen his joy in being back home once more. Way over in the dear Old Briar-patch Peter Rabbit could hear him. It reminded him that it was some time since he had been over by the Smiling Pool. Besides, he hadn't yet paid his respects to Redwing. He would do it now. First looking this way and that way to make sure that all was safe, Peter started lipperty-lipperty-lip, across the Green Meadows. Redwing saw him coming. "Hello, Peter!" he cried. "I certainly am glad to see you."

"You are no more glad to see me than I am to see you," replied Peter, as he reached the bank of the Smiling Pool quite out of breath. "I hope you and Mrs. Redwing passed a pleasant winter in the Sunny South."

"We certainly did," replied Redwing. "But it is good to be back here. Yes, sir, it is good to be back. This is home, you know, and there is no place like home."

"I know it," replied Peter. "That is why I never leave it. What is the news, Redwing?"

"I know of no better news than that the White Violets are in bloom," replied Redwing, promptly. "When I see them I know that it is time to think of nest building. Don't you love them, Peter?"

Peter nodded. But on his face was a look of disappointment. He hadn't seen any White Violets yet and he couldn't bear to have any one ahead of him. The truth is, he hadn't looked for White Violets. He had forgotten all about them. "Of course I love them," said he. "I can't imagine any one not loving them.

But how do you know they are in bloom, Redwing? Have you seen them?"

"Peter! Peter!" cried Redwing. "Where are your eyes? I can see dozens of them this very minute."

Redwing was perched on the top of a brown cattail. He was looking down at a place where the ground was low and wet just a few jumps from where Peter was sitting. Peter hurried over there. Sure enough, all about, modestly peeping up through the young grass, were the daintiest and dearest of all the Violet family, the Sweet White Violets.[18]

If Peter were disappointed at not being the first to find them, his disappointment gave way to joy.

Eagerly he leaned over to bring his wobbly little nose close to one of the little blossoms. At once he caught a fragrance as sweet and delicate as was the little blossom itself. Peter drew a long breath of pure happiness. How could one look at this beautiful little blossom, one of the smallest of all the Violets, and not be filled with happiness? The five white petals, the two upper ones curving back and the lower ones delicately marked with fine lines of purple, seemed to hold within them the very spirit of love and faith.

The little flower was not over two inches above the ground, though Peter remembered having found some in other years more than twice as high. The smooth stem seemed to spring directly from the ground, and around it, growing from the same spot, were several thin, smooth, light green leaves which were rather round, and heart-shaped at the base. The edges were very finely toothed.

Slowly Peter hopped about among the violets, stopping every hop or two to smell of them and always taking the greatest care not to step on one. Presently he noticed some of the beautiful little blossoms which grew taller than those he had been looking at. He would not have given them a second thought, had he not chanced to notice that the leaves were quite different. They were long and narrow instead of being nearly round. Then he knew that he had found a close cousin of the Sweet White Violet, the Lance-leaved Violet. The two are often found near together.

18   Look at the picture of the Sweet White Violet on page 47.

SWEET WHITE VIOLET
Viola blanda

FLOWERING DOGWOOD
Cornus florida

Having admired the Violets to his heart's content, Peter scampered over to the Green Forest where it was cool and shady. There he sat down to try to make up his mind where to go next. The ground was moist in there. Peter had about decided that he would go where it was drier when who should come along but Mrs. Grouse.

"Good morning, Peter," said she, for she and Peter are old friends.

"Good morning, Mrs. Grouse," replied Peter promptly. "I hope you are feeling as fine as you look."

The bright little eyes of Mrs. Grouse twinkled. "I don't know how I could feel finer," said she. "Isn't it good to have such fine spring weather? What is the news this morning?"

Peter scratched his head. For a moment he couldn't think of any news. Then he remembered the Violets. "The White Violets are in bloom!" he cried eagerly.

"That isn't news," replied Mrs. Grouse, scratching over some leaves to look for any stray bugs that might be hiding under them. "That isn't news, Peter. I saw them several days ago. By the way, it looks as if there will be plenty of Eyeberries by and by."

"Eyeberries!" exclaimed Peter. "What under the sun are Eyeberries?"

"Fie, fie, Peter! Don't tell me that you don't know what Eyeberries are. You must have seen them dozens of times," retorted Mrs. Grouse.

Peter shook his head. "I never heard of such a thing as an Eyeberry," he declared.

Mrs. Grouse chuckled. "You may not have heard that name," said she, "but you have seen the berries often enough. They are those white berries with a purple spot just like an eye. That is why I call them Eyeberries. There are no other berries like them."

Peter remembered at once having often seen those white berries on bright red stems early in the fall, and now that Mrs. Grouse had mentioned the purple spot on each, he understood why she called them Eyeberries. But it was April now and it would be weeks before he would see those berries. "What under the sun put those berries into your head just now, Mrs. Grouse, and how do you know there will be plenty of them?"

demanded Peter.

'Those flowers," replied Mrs. Grouse nodding towards a point just back of Peter. "Plenty of flowers means plenty of berries. Even you ought to know that."

Peter turned. Behind him were some tall plants. At least Peter called them tall, for when he sat up very straight he could not see over them. They were bushy. That is, the single stalk branched near the top. The dark green leaves were divided into leaflets, each leaflet sharp-pointed at the tip, and the edges were toothed. They were arranged in threes, and the veins showed very plainly.

But it was the flowers that Peter was interested in. At first glance they reminded him of the Foamflowers he had found a few days before. But when he looked more closely he saw that these were not quite so soft and feathery. They were little white flowers, having a varying number of petals which were very narrow at the base, and then broadened out. Each little flower had many of the little threadlike parts called stamens springing up from the center, and it was these which had reminded Peter of the Foamflowers. Each little flower was on a short stem which sprang out from a long stem, and this long stem grew out from the same point on the stalk that the leaf stems started from. The flowers were arranged around the end of the long stem in much the same way as were the Foamflowers.

Peter hopped over to smell of them. Then he made a wry face. They didn't smell good. No, sir, he didn't like the smell of them. Mrs. Grouse chuckled. "Those flowers are much like the berries they will turn into later — good to look at only," said she.

"Aren't the berries good to eat?" demanded Peter.

Mrs. Grouse shook her head in a very decided way. "They are poisonous," said she. "I advise you never to try one of them. I guess they are meant to be looked at and nothing more. Just the same, I like to see them in the fall just as I like to see these flowers now. Everything has its use, and I guess the use of these little plants is to add beauty to the Green Forest."

"I guess that must be it," said Peter. "I wonder what the name of these flowers is."

That Mrs. Grouse couldn't tell him. But you and I know that

he had found the White Baneberry,[19] which is also called the Cohosh and the Rattlesnake Herb. In some places these berries are called Doll's-eyes, and the plant goes by that name. A very near relative is the Red Baneberry, the berries of which are red instead of white.

---

19   Look at the picture of the White Baneberry on page 43.

ix. A Preacher and Nodding Beauties

Peter had it on the tip of his tongue to ask Mrs. Grouse if she had seen any other spring flowers which he had not found, when they were startled by a grunting and low growls, with an occasional little whine mixed in. Neither Peter nor Mrs. Grouse needed to be told who was making that noise. Very cautiously they stole along until they could peep down in a hollow. Just below them was Buster Bear. Yes, sir, it was great big Buster Bear.

Buster was very busy. He was digging. He was hard at work digging. But by the sounds he was making, it was clear that he was getting a lot of pleasure out of his work. The ground was soft down there, and Buster was tearing it up with his big claws, every now and then stopping to pick up something and eat it with the greatest satisfaction.

"What do you suppose he is finding down there?" whispered Peter, his eyes fairly popping out with curiosity.

"I haven't the slightest idea," replied Mrs. Grouse. "Whatever it is, he is digging it out of the ground. Perhaps he is getting roots of some kind. I have been told that Buster Bear eats various kinds of roots early in the spring when other food is hard to find. When he goes away we will go down there and see if we can find out what he has been digging."

So Peter and Mrs. Grouse watched Buster Bear until finally he stopped digging and shuffled away. When he was out of sight, Peter and Mrs. Grouse went down to where he had been at work. All about the soft, black earth had been torn up, but for some time they found nothing to show why it had been torn up. Then the sharp eyes of Mrs. Grouse discovered a little round root called a bulb, with little short roots growing out from it.

She guessed right away that it was bulbs like this that Buster had been digging for, and that this was one he had missed. She called Peter over.

Peter looked at the little bulb and then sniffed at it. It didn't smell particularly good, nor did it smell particularly bad. In fact, there wasn't much smell to it.

"If Buster Bear likes these funny little roots so much, they must be good eating," said Peter. I wonder what they taste like."

It's easy enough for you to find out," replied Mrs. Grouse. "I don't eat roots myself, or I would sample that one. Try it, Peter, and then you will know what it is like."

Peter didn't need any urging. Already curiosity had possession of him. He set his sharp teeth in that bulb and bit off a little piece. Then Peter Rabbit went crazy! At least Mrs. Grouse thought he had gone crazy. He jumped as if he had suddenly felt the sharp little lance of Lady Bumblebee. He danced about frantically. He rolled over and over. The tears ran down his cheeks. For a long time he couldn't say a word. You see his mouth was all puckered up. When he could speak he gasped, "I — I — I — I'd like to know what Buster Bear's mouth is ma-ma-made of!"

Of course Mrs. Grouse couldn't tell him. But she did show him a few minutes later what kind of a plant he had tasted the root of. She had found one which had been dug up, but from which the root had not been broken.

''Why, it is Jack-in-the-pulpit!''[20] exclaimed Peter in surprise.

And so it was. There was no mistaking Jack-in-the-pulpit for any other plant. A little way off they found two or three more plants. Coming straight out of the ground was a thick, green stalk from which grew a long-stemmed, three-parted leaf which looked like three leaves. At the point where the leaf sprang out from the stalk grew, at the end of a smooth stem, what looked very much like a striped, leafy vase with a top curving over in a pointed flap. It was green, striped with purple. But growing not far away was another which was light green striped with darker green.

Rising straight from the center, so as to peep out of that leafy vase, was Jack himself, in reality a smooth, green, little

20   Look at the picture of the Jack-in-the-pulpit on page 69.

club-shaped part of the plant. If Peter had known anything at all about pulpits and preachers, which of course he didn't, he would have understood at once why this odd little plant is called Jack-in-the-pulpit.

"I wonder," said he, talking to himself more than to Mrs. Grouse, "if that whole thing is the flower." Then there popped into his head a memory of the Skunk Cabbage he had found before sweet Mistress Spring really had arrived. He remembered those queer hoods, and how he had found the tiny flowers inside. Could it be that this leafy vase was for the same purpose as the stout hood of the Skunk Cabbage, to protect the real flowers?

Peter sat up in front of Jack-in-the-pulpit and tried to peep down inside. But that pointed flap which formed a sort of roof over Jack was in his way, and do what he would he couldn't see to the bottom.

"What under the sun are you trying to do, Peter?" demanded Mrs. Grouse.

"I'm trying to see if there are any flowers inside," replied Peter.

"Flowers!" exclaimed Mrs. Grouse. "Why, that whole thing is a flower, isn't it?"

"That's what I want to find out," retorted Peter. "I have an idea that it isn't. I have an idea that the real flowers are inside. I suppose I can tear this open and find out, but I hate to do it."

"There's one over there on the ground that Buster Bear dug up. Let's have a look at that one," said Mrs. Grouse.

So together they walked over to a plant that lay broken and trampled in the mud. The leafy vase had been torn on one side. Eagerly Peter peeped within. Sure enough, close around the base of the little green "Jack", at the very bottom of the vase, were tiny, greenish-yellow blossoms. Peter would hardly have known them for blossoms had he not seen those of the Skunk Cabbage.

"I thought as much," cried Peter happily. "Do you know, Mrs. Grouse, I believe Jack-in-the-pulpit must be a cousin of the Skunk Cabbage, because it protects its flowers in the same way."

Peter was right. The Jack-in-the-pulpit belongs to the same family as the Skunk Cabbage. It is the Arum family. That leafy vase is for the same purpose as the hood of the Skunk Cabbage, but because the weather is warmer when the Jack-in-the-pulpit appears, the flowers do not need as much protection as do the flowers of the Skunk Cabbage. Had Farmer Brown's boy happened along he might have told Peter that "Jack" is also a cousin of the beautiful Calla Lily. He could also have told Peter that Jack-in-the-pulpit is often called Indian Turnip, because long ago the Indians discovered that when the roots are properly cooked they no longer sting and burn in the mouth, but are excellent food.

"Speaking of flowers, have you seen the Columbine yet?" Mrs. Grouse asked, when Peter's curiosity had been quite satisfied.

Peter pricked up his ears. "I don't believe I know the Columbine," said he, though it was hard to admit that there was anything he didn't know.

"Oh, yes, you do," replied Mrs. Grouse. "Come with me."

She led the way through the Green Forest to the hill where Peter had first found the Saxifrage. Straight up the hill she went until they reached a place where it was rocky and in spots the earth barely covered the rock. It was open and sunny up there. Suddenly Peter fairly squealed with delight.

"Of course I know the Columbine!" he cried, as he hurried over to the nodding red-and-yellow blossoms of a plant with several branches, and which was a little more than a foot high. "Of course I know the Columbine![21] It had slipped my mind, that was all. Aren't these flowers lovely?"

"You said it, Peter Rabbit, and they are just as sweet as they are lovely," said a sharp, squeaky voice. "There is no flower I love more than I do the Columbine."

It was Hummer the Hummingbird who had spoken, and now his wonderful little wings, moving so swiftly that they made a humming sound, held him stationary in mid-air before one of the blossoms while he sucked the nectar from it. Then like a flash he had moved to another. So in turn he visited every one, and then darted away in search of more. He was gone before Peter could find his tongue.

Peter hopped a step nearer to look more closely at one of the blossoms. Without it was bright scarlet, while within it was bright yellow. It hung face down from a slender stem that bent

21   Look at the picture of the Columbine on page 55.

WILD COLUMBINE
Aquilegia canadensis

PINK AZALEA
Thododendron nudiflorum

over at the end. There were five petals, but these were unlike any petals Peter had seen, though in a way they reminded him of the queer little bag-like petals of the Dutchmen's-breeches. Instead of being flat each petal was in the shape of a tiny cone, tapering down very small and ending in a little rounded point. Hanging head down as the flower did, these little cones all pointed up. Peter counted them on several blossoms. In every case there were just five. Thrust out from the heart of each flower were many stamens, each with its tiny package of yellow pollen at the tip. With them were five other little threadlike parts without the little pollen holders at the tips. These are called pistils. Together the stamens and pistils were quite like a little tassel hanging from the center of the flower.

The leaves were light green above and beneath were almost whitish. They were divided into leaflets, each leaflet again divided into three or more parts with rounded notches on the edges. The stems were slender and somewhat wiry. With every passing Merry Little Breeze the flowers swayed and nodded.

For a long time Peter sat where he could look at and admire these brightest of the spring flowers. He watched Hummer the Hummingbird dart from one to another, not missing a single flower. Now he understood why Old Mother Nature had given Hummer that long bill, for without it he couldn't have reached the nectar held in the little rounded tip of each of those odd petals. What Peter didn't know was that Hummer carried the pollen from one flower to another, and thus paid for the sweets he gathered.

A memory of the boy and girl he had twice found gathering wild flowers came to Peter, and his face darkened. "I do hope they won't come up here," thought Peter. "If they should try to pick these flowers they would be almost sure to pull the plants up by the roots, and then never again would this old hillside be as beautiful as it is now. How it must hurt Old Mother Nature to see thoughtless people destroy the beauty she has worked so hard to create! I'm coming up here every day as long as the Columbine is in bloom."

x. Snow and Gold and Heaven's Blue

PETER'S SURPRISES were not over for that day. No, sir, they were not. He would have been quite satisfied not to have found another flower, for he felt that already the day was rich in the finds he had made. So it was with no thought of finding more that Peter at last left the hill where the Columbine grew and scampered along, lipperty-lipperty-lip, until he reached the edge of the Green Forest.

He had started out on the Green Meadows on his way to the dear Old Briar-patch when he happened to look over his shoulder back at the Green Forest. He cut a long jump short right in the very middle, and then turned and sat up to stare with unbelieving eyes at a point on the edge of the Green Forest some little distance below where he had left it.

"It can't be! It simply can't be!" Without knowing it Peter spoke aloud.

"What can't be?" demanded a Merry Little Breeze.

"Snow!" replied Peter.

"Of course it can't be!" chuckled the Merry Little Breeze. "What put such an idea into your head? It can't be, but by the look on your face I should say that you think that it is."

"Well, if that isn't snow over on one of those trees on the edge of the Green Forest, what is it?" demanded Peter.

The Merry Little Breeze laughed right out. "Go over and see, Peter. I'll race you over there," cried the Merry Little Breeze.

Away went Peter as fast as he could go, lipperty-lipperty-lip. And away danced the Merry Little Breeze just ahead of him. Peter went as fast as he could, but the Merry Little Breeze went faster. When they reached the tree which had seemed to be covered with snow, Peter had very little breath left, and what he saw when he looked up took away that little.

"Flowers!" he whispered under his breath. "Flowers!"

It was true. It was a small, irregular-shaped tree with broad, flat branches, and these were white with what looked like large, four-petaled flowers. How Peter did wish that he could climb like Happy Jack Squirrel, that he might get close to those flowers and see just what they looked like. Had he been able to do this, he would have found that many of them were not as white as they looked from a distance, but were tinted ever so lightly with pink. And he would have found that what he thought were petals, each with a little notch in its rounded end, were not true petals at all, but that they were the scales or coverings which had protected the real flowers in the bud. These real flowers were tiny, greenish-yellow and grew in a little cluster right at the center of the open petal-like scales.

But not being able to climb like Happy Jack Squirrel, all Peter could do was to look up and admire the Flowering Dogwood,[22] for this is the common name of the tree Peter had found. There is no mistaking it for any other. In the spring it makes the edge of the Green Forest beautiful with just such patches of white as had caught Peter's attention. In the fall the leaves become crimson and scarlet and gold around clusters of bright red berries. When other food is scarce in winter, certain of Peter's feathered friends are glad to get those berries.

Peter looked up at the Dogwood until his neck ached. Then he once more started for home. He did not go straight across the Green Meadows, but went around up on a little hillside where the ground was dry and somewhat sandy. As he hopped along he was still thinking of the beauty of the Dogwood. He wasn't even looking for more flowers, for it hadn't entered his funny little head that there might be any on that dry hillside. So his surprise was all the greater when happening to look down he found that he had almost stepped on a little yellow blossom that was smiling up at him.

It was so unexpected that Peter blinked rather foolishly. You see, it was a little friend with which he was well acquainted, but

22   Look at the picture of the Flowering Dogwood on page 47.

had forgotten all about. It was the Common Cinquefoil,[23] which is often called Five-finger. The latter name is given it because each leaf is made up of five parts which spread from the end of a hairy little stem like the fingers of a hand. Each part or leaflet is cut around the edges so that it appears to have little green teeth. Had Peter stopped to think about it, those little leaves would have reminded him of the leaves of the Strawberry, though the leaves of the latter have only three parts. These leaves grew in little clusters from a stalk that crept along the ground like a vine.

But it was the little bright yellow blossom that interested Peter most. It was very like a tiny, single, yellow Rose. As a matter of fact it belonged to the Rose family. There were five petals, broad and rounded, each with a little notch in the outer edge. There were many little stamens, and in the very center were crowded together many little green pistils.

Peter remembered that the year before this hillside had been yellow with these blossoms, and he knew that it would be so again. What Peter didn't know was that later in the season, in the very beginning of summer, there would be a cousin of the Common Cinquefoil, which, instead of creeping along the ground, would boldly grow from a few inches to four feet high, with many branches and with flowers two to three times the size of these he was now looking at. This is the Shrubby Cinquefoil or Prairie Weed, and while it likes damp places best it is also found in dry, sandy places. It is easily recognized by its bushy growth and by the leaves, which are more truly like fingers, for the leaflets are long, narrow, and widely spread.

"At this rate I'll never get home," muttered Peter, as he turned from the little Cinquefoil and once more started on. It began to look as if Peter was right for he had made but a few hops when he fairly squealed aloud with delight. "Violets!" he cried. "Bird's-foot Violets![24] Oh, how I love them!"

With a couple of swift bounds Peter reached a little group of flowers that seemed to have taken their color from the sky, and from the Purple Hills at the hour just after jolly, round, bright

---

23   Look at the picture of the Common Cinquefoil on page 37.

24   Look at the picture of the Bird's-foot Violet on page 60.

BIRD'S-FOOT VIOLET
Viola pedata

COMMON BLUE OR MEADOW VIOLET
Viola papilionacea

Mr. Sun has gone to bed. The two upper petals, which bent back, were of this soft, rich purple, while the three lower petals were the blue of the sky at midday. Orange-colored stamens growing close together gave each flower a heart of gold.

Peter knew that these are the largest of the Violets, and because of the sandy soil in which they delight are sometimes called Sand Violets. "All the Violets have a strong family likeness, no matter what color they may be," thought Peter. "One could never mistake a Violet for any other flower. And one never can mistake this one for any other member of the family," he added, as he glanced down at the leaves.

He was quite right. The leaf is divided into from five to nearly a dozen long, narrow parts with the longer middle ones notched on the ends. Some of these parts or leaflets are grouped together in such a way that if spread out flat they remind one of the foot of a bird, and this is how the plant comes by its name. Unlike other Violets the Bird's-foot often blooms a second time in the fall. Occasionally one is pure white instead of purple and blue. Often the two upper petals, instead of being dark purple, are practically the same color as the lower petals. In fact this is the commonest form. In some parts of the country the Bird's-foot Violets with the two upper petals rich purple are called Velvet Johnnies or Velvet Johnny-jump-ups.

The finding of these Violets reminded Peter that he had quite forgotten to look for the one of all the family he knew best and loved the most, the Common Blue Violet or Meadow Violet.[25] He knew that it must be in bloom, for it comes before its cousin, the Bird's-foot Violet. Peter sat up and looked across the Green Meadows towards the Smiling Pool. He knew just the place down there where the Meadow Violet would be at its best.

"How stupid of me," muttered Peter, "not to have thought of the Meadow Violets when I saw the White Violets down there early this morning. Well, I have just got to see them."

He looked up at the blue, blue sky to be sure that Redtail the Hawk was nowhere to be seen. He looked this way and that way over the Green Meadows to make sure that Reddy Fox was not prowling about. Then he started, lipperty-lipperty-lip, for

25   Look at the picture of the Meadow Violet on page 60.

the Smiling Pool. Past the sweet-scented little White Violets he hurried with merely a glance at them. Just a little way beyond, where the grass already had a good start, and where the ground was damp but not really wet, Peter found the little friends he had been sure were there. On long smooth stems they lifted their beautiful blue faces to the sky whose color they matched. Some were light blue, some were dark blue, and a few were even striped. Each had a heart of gold.

A Merry Little Breeze danced over them and they swayed gently on their long slender stems. Having in mind the leaves of the Violets he had just left, Peter eagerly looked at the leaves above which these beloved little friends raised their bright faces. These leaves were so different from those he had just seen that it didn't seem possible that they could belong to the same family. They were large, heart-shaped, broad at the base, pointed at the tip, and with very fine scallops along the edges. On the young leaves the lower parts curved upward. Each leaf stem had a groove its whole length on one side, while the stems of the flowers were smooth.

"Oh, you beautiful things!" cried Peter. "You beautiful, beautiful things! I just love you. I do indeed."

In this Peter differed not at all from the rest of the world, for who is there who can look at the Meadow Violet nestling amid the young grass of the meadow and not love it?

> The violet blue! The violet blue!
>   It sets my heart at rest.
> So fragile in the grass it lies,
> It seems a flower of the skies,
>   And hope springs in my breast.
> The violet blue! The violet blue!
>   It sets my heart at rest.

XI. A Day to be Remembered

"Cheer up! Cheer up! Cheer up! Cheer!
Strawberry time will soon be here."

WELCOME ROBIN was perched in the top of a little tree just above Peter Rabbit's favorite resting place in the dear Old Briar-patch. Over and over he kept repeating that message, and there was joy in every note. Peter looked up at him.

"What of it?" he demanded, when he had grown tired of hearing Welcome Robin say the same thing over and over again.

"What of it?" repeated Welcome Robin, after him. "Why, it means that some of us are going to have a feast by and by."

Perhaps so, and perhaps not," retorted Peter. Strawberry time doesn't always mean a lot of Strawberries. Perhaps there will be only a few this year. I've known such things to happen."

"So have I," replied Welcome Robin, promptly.

"But it won't happen this year. No, sir, it won't happen this year. There will be more Strawberries than I've ever seen before."

"Huh!" grunted Peter. "Much you know about it! Much you know about it, Welcome Robin! There will be no Strawberries for some time yet, so how can you know whether there will be many or few?"

"Because the plants are in blossom right now, Mr. Smarty," retorted Welcome Robin. "Never have I seen so many Strawberry[26] blossoms at one time as there are up in the Old Pasture right now. Any one who knows anything at all knows that plenty of blossoms means plenty of berries."

By this time Peter was already hopping along one of his pri-

[26]   Look at the picture of the Wild Strawberry on page 80.

vate little paths on his way out of the dear Old Briar-patch. "Hi, Peter! Where are you going?" called Welcome Robin.

"I'm going up to the Old Pasture," replied Peter over his shoulder, and disappeared among the brambles of the dear Old Briar-patch.

When Peter reached the Old Pasture he was not long in discovering that Welcome Robin had told the truth. In every little open grassy place clusters of white flowers with yellow centers smiled up at him. They were every place where there was the least chance for them to grow.

They grew in little clusters, each flower on a little stem which branched out from the main stem. This in turn sprang up from a little tuft of dark green, three-parted leaves. Each part or leaflet was cut into teeth around the edges. Both the stems of the leaves and the stems of the flowers were hairy.

The blossoms were very wide open so that they were almost round. There were five white petals. In the center was a little green cone just the shape the berry would be by and by. Out of this little cone grew many little pistils, and around it clustered the yellow stamens. Busy Bee was hard at work among the blossoms, carrying pollen from one to another, and taking her pay in the nectar which would go to make honey.

The meeting with Welcome Robin reminded Peter of a certain little blossom which takes a part of its common name from Welcome himself. It was the Wake-robin or Purple Trillium[27], sometimes called the Birthroot. Just why it should be called Wake-robin Peter couldn't understand at all, because Welcome Robin always is on hand and very much awake long before this queer little blossom appears.

No sooner did Peter think of the Wake-robin than he started off to look for it. He knew it was in bloom. He headed straight for a certain rather swampy part of the Old Pasture. He felt quite sure he would find it there. Sure enough, he discovered it at once. Had he not seen it, his nose would have told him it was there, for it has an odor which is not at all pleasant excepting to certain insects which have a fondness for bad odors and search for it to get its pollen.

27   Look at the picture of the Purple Trillium on page 65.

PURPLE TRILLIUM OR ILL-SCENTED WAKE-ROBIN
Trillium erectum

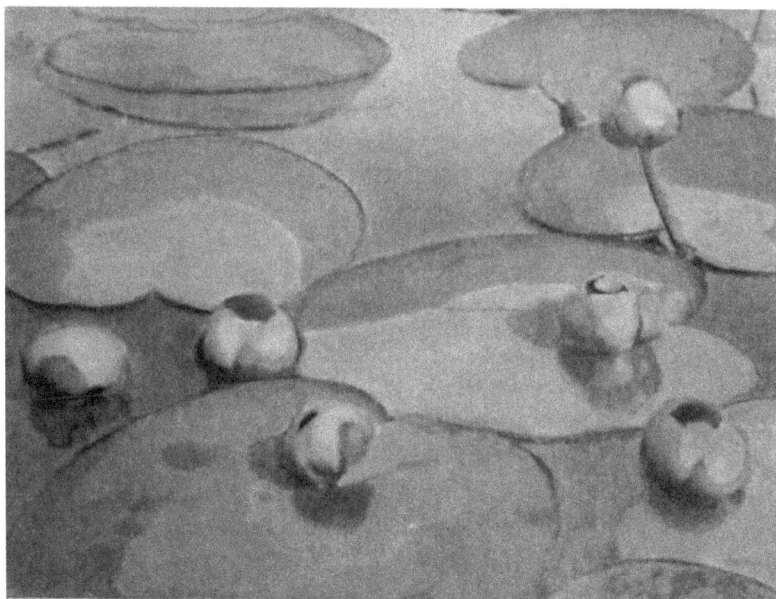

LARGE YELLOW POND LILY OR SPATTER-DOCK
Nymphaea advena

There is no mistaking a Trillium for any other plant because it is arranged in threes. From the top of a smooth, stout stalk three broad, oval leaves ending in sharp points droop. Just above, springing from the point where the three leaves meet is a three-petaled flower, which to some folks is not at all attractive to look at because of its dark, purplish-red color. The petals are oval, and there are six stamens and one pistil. The tip of the pistil is divided into three short, curving parts.

Peter didn't stay there long. After the sweet scent of the Strawberries he couldn't stand the odor of the Ill-scented Wake-robin. He was glad to turn away to look for some sweeter flower. Happening to glance above him on the hillside, he caught a glimpse of something pink. Instantly he was off to see what it could be. The moment he reached it he knew. There before him was a little bush covered with the loveliest of pink blossoms. At first it looked as if there were no leaves, for the latter had only just started, while many of the blossoms were fully open.

They grew in clusters. Each blossom was in the shape of a long tube, spreading into five petals which opened out quite flat. Out of that tube five long, curved, red stamens and a single long pistil were thrust. Some of the flowers were quite a deep pink, and others a very light pink.

"The Pinkster!" cried Peter, happily. "It is the Pinkster!"

Peter was right. That is one of its common names. It is also called the Pink, Purple or Wild Azalea,[28] and the latter name is perhaps the best, for it is an Azalea. In some places it is called the Wild Honeysuckle. This is a mistake, for it is not a true Honeysuckle.

Looking about, Peter found other bushes, some of them quite six feet high and others not more than two feet high, on which the pink buds were swelling or had already burst into bloom. Once again Peter thought of the boy and girl whom he had twice seen picking flowers, and with all his heart he hoped they would not find the Pinksters. He knew that they could not be picked without serious harm to the bushes on which they grew. In this he was wholly right. The Wild Azalea makes rarely beautiful the spot wherein it grows, but it has no place elsewhere.

28   Look at the picture of the Wild Azalea on page 55.

Leaving the Old Pasture, Peter went down to the Smiling Pool in search of Grandfather Frog. Peter likes to have a little gossip with Grandfather Frog once in so often. You know Grandfather Frog is accounted very old and very wise. But when Peter reached the Smiling Pool he quite forgot Grandfather Frog for the time being. You see almost at once his attention was caught by half a dozen bright yellow spots near the shore at the lower end of the Smiling Pool. Peter hurried around there at once. Sure enough, those yellow spots were just what he suspected they were, flowers. They were like yellow balls, somewhat flattened at the top. They were quite large, some of them being almost three inches across, and at first glance most of them seemed to be floating on the water in the midst of big, oval, thick, green leaves, heart-shaped at the base, which also seemed to be floating on the water. But presently Peter noticed that one of the flowers was quite a bit above the water on a stout stem.

They were Lilies, the Large Yellow Pond Lily,[29] Cow Lily or Spatter-dock. One of the blossoms was near enough for Peter to reach out and smell it. He didn't like it. It wasn't pleasant, in which respect it was quite the opposite of its beautiful cousin, the White or Sweet-scented Pond Lily.

Peter didn't stop to look into the blossoms closely. It was enough for him to know that they were there. No one can fail to recognize them because there are no other flowers growing in the water at all like them. Had Peter looked more closely, he might have found that what looked like yellow petals were really not true petals at all, but that the true petals were inside and were narrow, fleshy, and looked a great deal like stamens. But it was enough for him to know the flower, so he promptly turned his back and hurried to look for Grandfather Frog.

---

29   Look at the picture of the Large Yellow Pond Lily on page 65.

XII. The Joy of Bees and Hummer's Delight

Peter was sitting at the edge of the dear Old Briar-patch, undecided where to go. "Buz-z-z-z. It's a fine morning for Clover, Peter Rabbit," said a voice almost in his ear.

Peter ducked his head. That sound had been too close for comfort. Lady Bumblebee, looking very handsome in her black-and-yellow cloak, chuckled. "I wouldn't sting you, Peter," said she. ' You ought to know me well enough by this time to know that I never sting any one who doesn't bother me. But gracious, I can't stop to gossip here! Clover time is busy time for us Bees. Buz-z-z-z."

By the time Peter had recovered from his surprise enough to find his tongue it was too late to ask questions. Already Lady Bumblebee was almost out of sight. "She said Clover time is here," muttered Peter. "I haven't seen a Clover blossom this season. But if she says that the Clover blossoms have come, they have. You can always trust Lady Bumblebee to know when there is a Clover blossom anywhere around."

Away went Peter after Lady Bumblebee. He could just see her, a little speck above the grass. He didn't try to keep her in sight. It was enough for him to know the direction in which she had gone. He knew that she would go in a straight line to those Clover blossoms, and that all he need do was to follow that line. It was some distance out on the Green Meadows that Peter finally caught up with Lady Bumblebee. But for the moment he gave her no thought. You see, right before him was a little group of Red Clover[30] blossoms.

"Ha!" cried Peter, happily, and stretched out his wobbly little

---

30   Look at the picture of the Red Clover on page 69.

COMMON DANDELION
Taraxacum officinale

JACK-IN-THE-PULPIT
Arisaema triphyllum

COMMON RED CLOVER
Trifolium pratense

ROBIN'S PLANTAIN
Erigeron pulchellui

nose to the nearest blossom to smell of it. He sniffed and sniffed. It seemed as if he never could get enough of that sweet odor. You see it was a long time since he had had a chance to smell it. Peter has known the Clovers ever since he was big enough to know anything. Clover leaves are one of Peter's favorite foods. Before this he had never given any thought to the flowers. They had been just flowers and nothing more to him.

But now, as he looked at the beautiful flower heads, he suddenly remembered how he had learned that the Dandelion blossom is not a single flower, but really a mass of tiny flowers growing together, and a suspicion that the same thing might be true of these pinkish and crimson Clover heads led him to look at them more closely. Sure enough, he saw at once that each head was composed of tiny flowers crowded together, each tiny flower, or floret as it is called, being like a little tube, white at the base.

Lady Bumblebee was very busy, working as only a Bee can work. In each of those tiny flowers was the nectar or sweet juice that she likes best, and she didn't mean to miss any of it. When she alighted on one of those Clover heads she went all over it, running her long tongue down into each tiny tube. Only one with a long tongue like hers could possibly reach that nectar.

But to Peter the leaves were more interesting than the flowers. You see Peter had not yet had his breakfast. So while Lady Bumblebee sucked up the nectar from the flowers, Peter started to fill his stomach with the leaves. These, of course, were three parted, each part or leaflet very narrow at the base, oval, and each bearing a V-shaped whitish mark. The plants were branched and the stems were hairy.

Peter ate his fill. It took some time to fill that big stomach of his, and meanwhile Lady Bumblebee had carried home her load of sweets and returned for more. When at last Peter's appetite was satisfied, he bade Lady Bumblebee good-bye and headed over towards the Green Forest. As he drew near it he caught a glimpse of blue quite unlike the Clover he had just left. "I wonder if there is such a thing as blue Clover?" thought Peter, and turned aside to find out.

But when he was near enough to see clearly he discovered some flowers that were wholly different. In shape they reminded him of the Daisies that later would whiten parts of the Green Meadows. They were very like small Daisies, only bluish-purple instead of white. As a matter of fact this flower is often called the Blue Spring Daisy. Two other common names for it are Robin's Plantain[31] and Robert's Plantain.

Remembering the Dandelion and the Clover, Peter knew at once that he had found another plant whose blossom is composed of many tiny flowers growing together. Such flowers are called composite, which means that they are made up of many little flowers arranged together so as to look like one. The flower heads grew two or three together at the top of a quite tall, very hairy stem which was thick and hollow, and had a few small scattered leaves widely separated. It rose from the center of a cluster of leaves like a flat rosette close to the ground.

While the flower heads were much like some of the Asters which would come later, the plant itself was not at all like Aster plants. The Asters never have their leaves arranged in a little flat tuft close to the ground.

"Two flowers and I have only just started out!" cried Peter. "I wonder what the next one will be."

He soon found out. As he entered a thicket on the edge of the Green Forest he caught his breath. Above his head in a small tree were clusters of flowers of brilliant red. Peter sat up and tipped his head back that he might see them better. "I didn't know," muttered he, "that any of these trees bore red flowers. I must find out about this."

Just then he discovered Hummer the Hummingbird darting from flower to flower. "Oh, Hummer!" he cried. "What kind of flowers are those?"

"Honeysuckle. Trumpet or Coral Honeysuckle,"[32] replied Hummer. "The idea of not knowing a Honeysuckle when you see it!"

"But I thought Honeysuckle flowers grew on bushes, and these are growing on trees," retorted Peter.

"Use your eyes. Use your eyes. These are not growing on

---

31   Look at the picture of the Robin's Plantain on page 69.

32   Look at the picture of the Coral Honeysuckle on page 72.

ARETHUSA OR INDIAN PINK
Arethusa bulhosa

LARGER BLUE FLAG
Iris versicolor

CORAL HONEYSUCKLE
Lonicera sempervirens

BULBOUS BUTTERCUP
Ranunculus bulbosus

trees at all. They are growing on a vine," retorted Hummer, in his high, squeaky voice.

Sure enough, they were growing on a vine. Peter saw this as soon as his attention was called to it. It was a vine that wound itself about the branches all over the tree. The leaves were a dark shining green on the upper side and were rounded oval in shape. They grew out from the stem in pairs opposite each other. As his eyes followed the vine, he made an odd discovery. The pair of leaves nearest the blossoms grew together all around the stem so that they made almost a cup with the stem coming out of the middle.

But Peter paid little attention to the leaves. Why should he with those bright, red blossoms to look at? They grew in little groups or clusters, and each blossom was like a little red trumpet an inch and a half long or less. Within they were yellowish. Five stamens and a single pistil barely showed beyond the spreading mouth.

Peter looked in vain for Busy Bee and her cousin, Lady Bumblebee. There seemed to be no one around those beautiful little fairy-like trumpets excepting Hummer the Hummingbird. Finally Peter expressed his surprise that none of the Bees had found those flowers, which by their bright color were so very showy.

"Oh, they have found them all right," said Hummer, in his thin, squeaky little voice, "but they are not interested."

"Why not?" demanded Peter. "Haven't such lovely flowers any sweetness in them?"

"Of course they have," replied Hummer. "Do you suppose I would waste my time around them if they hadn't? But the Bees know that they can't get that nectar and they are too wise to waste any time trying. Their tongues are not long enough. It is for just such flowers as these that Old Mother Nature gave me my long bill and long tongue."

"Oh," said Peter, and then for the time being forgot all about flowers as he watched Hummer dart from flower to flower with wings moving so fast that Peter couldn't see them at all.

XIII. Beauties of the Swamp

APRIL WITH its showers had passed, and May had come with its longer sunny days. All the little people of the Green Forest and the Green Meadows were busy with the building of new homes, or with the care of babies. I said all the little people, but this isn't quite true. A few there are who seldom spend much time in such cares. Peter Rabbit is one of these. Peter leaves most of the care of his growing family to Mrs. Peter. So it was that Peter still had time to try to satisfy his never-ending curiosity.

Not yet had he lost interest in flowers. Indeed, his interest had grown. It was still a delight to find a flower he had not seen before this season. And wherever he went, he kept his eyes open for newcomers. Many of the flowers which had so delighted him when he discovered the first blossoms were now so numerous that he hardly gave them a thought. It was not that he loved them less, but that he was so eager to find new ones that he couldn't spend time with those he had already learned about.

One morning he happened to think that he had not yet seen his old friend, Longbill the Woodcock. "Of course he is here," thought Peter. "I'll find him over in that swampy place where the Laughing Brook comes out of the Green Forest on its way to the Smiling Pool. He is always there this time of year. I'll just run over and pass the time of day with him."

So away went Peter, straight over to where the Laughing Brook enters the Green Meadows. Redwing the Blackbird had a nest in there, and Peter stopped to inquire how many eggs there were in the nest. Of course Redwing wouldn't tell him, for it really was no business of Peter's. He was just about to go on in something of a huff when on the very edge of the swamp he caught sight of a big, blue flower that caused him to squeal right out with joy and forget all about Redwing and those eggs.

This flower was very stately as it stood erect above long, narrow, pointed leaves like giant blades of grass. It was at the top of a stout, straight, green stalk, and even when Peter sat up was above his head. Peter gave little attention to leaves and stalk, for he had no eyes for anything but the beauty of that wonderful flower. Truly, it was beautiful. It was quite the largest flower he had yet found. It was violet-blue with lines of white, green, and yellow.

Peter counted the petals, at least what he thought were the petals. There were nine, and they were arranged in groups of three. The three largest were broad and rounded and bent gracefully downward. They were beautifully marked with white and yellow on a wonderful background of violet-blue. Really they were not petals, though Peter was quite excusable in thinking they were. They were sepals, which are those parts which are usually green and form the outer covering for the true petals when the flower is in the bud.

The true petals, of which there were three, were smaller, narrower, and stood nearly erect. They were violet in color and marked with delicate purple veins. The other three petal-like parts were narrower, smaller, notched at the tips, and each curved outward directly over the base of one of the sepals. Although they did not look it at all, these were really divisions of this flower's curious pistil, which, as you remember, has to do with the seed-bearing part. Hidden directly under each was a slender, yellowish stamen.

So Peter had found a flower as interesting as it was beautiful. It was a flower beloved by Bees, for in the heart of it was much of the sweet nectar of which they are so fond. Then, too, blue is their favorite color. The parts of this flower were so curiously formed by Old Mother Nature for the express purpose of making it impossible for the Bees to get the nectar without becoming dusted with the golden pollen, and this meant that they could not visit another flower of the same kind without leaving some of that pollen there.

It was an old friend, and one Peter was delighted to find.

It was the Larger Blue Flag,[33] which is also called Blue Iris and
Fleur-de-lis, a flower you cannot mistake for any other, for
there is none like it.

"You are staring at that Blue Flag as if you had never seen
one before," said a voice.

Peter turned quickly to find the very one he had started over
to the swamp to look for, Longbill the Woodcock. "Hello, Longbill!" cried Peter joyously. "I was hoping I would find you over
here. I came over purposely to see you. How is Mrs. Longbill?"

"Mrs. Longbill is fine, thank you. She is on our nest and
doesn't want to be disturbed, or I would take you to see her,"
replied Longbill politely.

"What is there about that Blue Flag that interests you so
much?" he inquired as an after thought.

"All flowers interest me," replied Peter. "Until this season
I never had thought about them much, but now I am learning
more every day of the beauty and wonder of them. Isn't that
Blue Flag lovely?"

"I suppose it is," agreed Longbill, without showing any particular interest. "I am not much interested in flowers myself.
But if you are, I can show you one that to my way of thinking
is really worth while, and one I don't believe you have seen."

Peter pricked up his ears. "Where is it?" he cried eagerly.

"Follow me," replied Longbill, and led the way into the swamp.

The ground became more and more wet and in places very
muddy. Peter would never have thought of going in there to look
for flowers. He began to doubt if Longbill really had found a
flower there. But Longbill kept on. You know he is very much at
home in a swamp. Presently he disappeared behind a big tussock
of grass. Peter hurried to catch up. When he came around that
tussock the first thing he saw was a beautiful little pink blossom
that fairly took his breath away. Yes, sir, it did so.

"Oh, how beautiful!" he cried, and for the moment forgot
all about Longbill. He squatted down and stared at that flower.
This one really was new to him. Never before had he found it. It
was six or seven inches above the ground at the top of a smooth,
very slender stalk, and there were no leaves.

33   Look at the picture of the Larger Blue Flag on page 72.

The flower was a bright, purplish-pink. Here again was another flower in which the sepals or outer coverings were colored like the petals. In fact, they were very much like the petals, and all were partly united. They arched over a curious drooping part called the lip, which was broad and rounded and had three little white, hairy ridges. It bore little blotches or spots of purple. Peter's wobbly little nose already had discovered that it had a scent much like that of Sweet-scented Violets.

"What is it?" he asked at last.

"I don't know," replied Longbill, "but I guess you'll admit that you never have seen anything prettier."

Peter nodded. "Yes," said he, "I'll admit that. I wonder why I have never seen it before."

"Probably because you have never been where it grows," replied Longbill. "I see it every spring. But it isn't very common. People who see it have to look for it."

"I wonder why it hasn't any leaves," said Peter.

"There will be only one leaf, and that will come later and be much like a blade of grass," replied Longbill.

Peter remained for some time admiring the wonderful little flower and wondering what it could be. It was the Arethusa[34], often called Indian Pink, and sometimes called Dragon's-mouth, and it belonged to the Orchid family, the family which has the strangest and most interesting of all flowers.

---

34   Look at the picture of the Arethusa on page 72.

xiv. Umbrella Plants and Flower Butterflies

WHEN AT last Peter bade farewell to Longbill the Wood-cock he headed towards the Green Forest which began just beyond the edge of the swamp. Here the ground was still damp and rich. Peter was thinking of the beautiful Arethusa as he hopped along rather aimlessly. Presently his attention was caught by what appeared like curious, little, green, folded umbrellas pushing their way up through the earth. Peter's curiosity was aroused at once and he stopped to look at them. Of course he saw immediately that they were leaves which had not yet opened.

"Now I wonder what these are," said Peter to himself, and looked around for some fully opened. He didn't have to look far. All about were plenty of them. They were beautiful great leaves nearly a foot across, each cut into five to nine long, narrow parts starting from a common center. If the folded leaves looked like closed umbrellas, the open leaves were quite as much like opened umbrellas. They were dark green above and much lighter green beneath. Though Peter didn't know it children often call them Umbrella Plants.

Of course Peter at once began to look for flowers. He found one presently. It was a little more than a foot from the ground, nodding from a very short stem which grew out from a point on a stalk where two leaves similar to those he had been looking at, but smaller, sprang out.

The flower was pure white, almost round, saucer-shaped, about two inches across, and was waxy looking. In this one there were six petals, and these were covered with a network of very fine veins. There were twice as many stamens, each with a big yellow anther, arranged in a circle around a large pistil. Looking among other plants Peter found more of these pretty flowers, some of them having as many as nine petals. He had to look to find them, for most of them were quite hidden beneath the broad umbrella-like leaves.

Of course Peter smelled of them, and he promptly turned up his wobbly little nose. They were good to look at, but not to smell of. He knew what they were. Long ago he had learned not to eat the leaves of this plant, for they were poisonous. It was the Mandrake, or May Apple.[35] Because in midsummer it bears a yellow fruit it is also called Wild Lemon and Hog Apple. The latter name is given it in the South, where hogs delight to eat the fruit.

"Three flowers this morning," said Peter to himself. "I wonder what the next one will be." He found out in a very few moments. Leaving the Mandrake he went on up among the pine trees, and there almost at once he caught sight of a whole colony of quaint, little, pink flowers only a few inches above the ground. Delightedly he hurried over to them.

There was something about them that at once reminded him of the Arethusa he had left so short a time before down in the swamp. It was the fact that these little flowers also had colored sepals which looked like petals. There were five sepals, but only two of them were colored, and these two were rose-pink and like a pair of wide-spreading wings. They were much larger than the three other sepals.

The three true petals were formed into a slender tube, and the lower one, which was parted and extended beyond the others, was beautifully fringed. Within this tube were six stamens and a single pistil. In most cases there were two to four flowers on short, slender stems growing from among the oval-shaped leaves clustered at the top of a stalk.

The flowers reminded Peter of gay little butterflies. In fact they are often called Gay-wings, but their proper name is Fringed Milkwort, for they belong to the Milkwort family. Fringed

---

35   Look at the picture of the May Apple on page 80.

WILD STRAWBERRY
Fragaria virginiana

MAY APPLE
Podophyllum peltatum

Polygala[36] is another name for them, and they are also called Flowering Wintergreen. The reason for this Peter found out. Accidentally he uncovered the root of one and out of curiosity smelled of it. It smelled like Wintergreen.

A thing that Peter didn't know, and that very many people do not know, is that these strange little plants have two kinds of flowers entirely different. One of them is borne underground, strange as that may seem. Probably you would not recognize it as a flower if you should see it. But it really is one. It is Old Mother Nature's provision to insure seeds in case something happens to the gay little flowers above ground. The leaves of the Fringed Milkwort remain on the plant through the winter, becoming reddish in color.

When Peter left the bright little Gay-wings he decided that he had seen enough for one day and would go home to the dear Old Briar-patch. Perhaps his conscience pricked him a little for having left Mrs. Peter there alone to care for their lively youngsters.

On his way across the Green Meadows he suddenly remembered that it was a long time since he had had breakfast. He knew of a certain patch of Clover which he had not visited for some time, so he promptly turned in that direction. When he reached it, he discovered that since his last visit something had happened in that patch of Clover. All over it were what at a distance appeared to be white flowers. But close to some proved to be pure white, some a creamy white and many decidedly pinkish.

Of course, like the Red Clover, what appeared to be a single flower was made up of tiny flowers growing in the form of a head, but smaller and not so pointed as the head of the Red Clover. How sweet they smelled! It seemed to Peter he could not get enough of their fragrance.

And how busy Busy Bee and her friends were among them. Well they knew that there is no nectar like the nectar of the White Clover[37] for making honey, and they didn't intend to miss a drop of it.

---

36   Look at the picture of the Fringed Polygala on page 120.

37   Look at the picture of the White Clover on page 82.

WHITE CLOVER
Trifolium repens

LARGE-FLOWERED WAKE-ROBIN
Trillium grandiflorum

There was little for Peter to learn about this Clover, for had it not been one of his favorite foods ever since he was big enough to nibble? Unlike the Red Clover it is a creeping plant, spreading over the ground and frequently taking root at the joints. There are no leaves on the flower stems and the plant never grows high. Its leaves are divided in three parts like all Clovers, and usually there is a V-shaped whitish band on each leaflet.

Of course, Peter knew nothing about the good fortune that is supposed to follow the finding of a Clover leaf divided into four parts, but he could have told any one who asked him that this is the kind of Clover which most often has the four-parted leaves. He had found many of them in his time.

There is a relative of the White Clover known as the Tree Clover because sometimes it gets to be almost ten feet high. This one is also called White Sweet Clover, Honey-lotus and the White Melilot. It has a widely branching stalk and the flower heads are long and slender.

Peter ate his fill and then once more started for the dear Old Briar-patch. Happening to glance up he discovered Redtail the Hawk high in the blue, blue sky. Redtail saw Peter at the same instant. It was fortunate for Peter that he had not far to go. And how he did go! It was hard work running on a full stomach, but the mere thought of Redtail's great claws gave added speed to Peter's long hind legs. He reached the dear Old Briar-patch just in time, for hardly had that funny little white tail of his disappeared as he dived into one of his private little paths under the brambles when Redtail checked himself in the midst of a headlong rush downward, and with a scream of disappointment flew away.

"Why don't you stay at home?" demanded timid little Mrs. Peter sharply. "One of these days that fellow will catch you on one of these foolish trips of yours."

"They are not foolish trips," retorted Peter. "I learn something on every one of them, and nothing is foolish which adds to one's knowledge. I wish, my dear, you could have seen the flowers I saw this morning."

"Pooh!" said little Mrs. Peter, turning up her wobbly little nose. "I have something more important to think about than flowers." And with that she went to look after her babies.

xv. Buttercups and Lily Cousins

CAROL THE Meadow Lark had stopped at the dear Old Briar-patch for an early morning call on Peter. Of course he knew, as by this time everybody knew, of Peter's interest in flowers. "Have you seen the Buttercups yet, Peter?" he asked.

"No," cried Peter, pricking up his ears. "Do you mean to say the Buttercups have come?"

"One has, anyway, for I saw it only yesterday," replied Carol.

"Where? Tell me where, Carol, that I may see it too," Peter begged.

"I am surprised at you, Peter. I am much surprised at you that you should ask such a thing," replied Carol, with a twinkle in his eyes that Peter couldn't see.

"Why?" demanded Peter, looking very much surprised and puzzled.

"Haven't you learned yet that half the pleasure in finding things lies in hunting for them and finding them without help?" inquired Carol.

"That's true," replied Peter, thoughtfully. "I hadn't thought of it before, but it is true. I don't want you to tell me where you saw that Buttercup. No, sir, I don't want you to. If there is a Buttercup in bloom I am going to find it myself. If you should try to tell me now, I would stop my ears. I would so."

Carol chuckled, then flew away. Peter watched him drop down in the grass far out in the Green Meadows and guessed that somewhere near there Carol had a nest. "Let me see," said Peter, talking to himself. "If Carol has seen a Buttercup it must be somewhere on the Green Meadows, for that is where Carol lives. Now I think of it, I have usually seen the first Buttercup on the Green Meadows, so that must be the place to look. I'll start out right away."

First making sure that the way was clear and no enemy in sight, Peter started out. He didn't know which way to go. That Buttercup might be almost anywhere. One place was as good as another. So Peter hopped about aimlessly, this way and that way, sitting up every few jumps to look about him on all sides. He hunted and hunted until at last he was becoming discouraged. He was just about to give up and go over to the Green Forest when he thought he saw a tiny yellow spot off at one side.

"Probably it's a tall Dandelion," muttered Peter, as he started over towards it.

But it wasn't a tall Dandelion. Peter knew that as soon as he got near enough to see the shine on that yellow blossom. It was the same shine that had made the Cowslip he had found earlier in the season glisten in the sun. "It is a Buttercup!" cried Peter, happily, and hurried forward.

Peter was right; it was a Buttercup. It was like a little cup of shining gold with its five glossy yellow petals and yellow stamens. The plant wasn't as tall as would be the Buttercup Peter would find later in the season, the Common Meadow or Tall Buttercup, for this was one that comes just before that. The stalk and leaves were much the same. The latter were many times divided, and each leaflet was again divided into narrow parts. The stems were quite hairy, much more so than the stems of the Meadow Buttercup.

Had Peter dug down to the root, he would have found it swollen into something very like a bulb, which is not the case with the root of the Meadow Buttercup. From this it gets its name of Bulbous Buttercup,[38] and it is because this root is so big that it has stored in it the energy to make quick growth in the spring, and so be the first of the Buttercups to bloom.

It was with a sense of great contentment that Peter at last turned towards the Green Forest. He had hunted for and found that first Buttercup without help from any-one, and he would be quite satisfied if he didn't find another flower that day.

But Peter was to find other flowers that day. He found one

---

38   Look at the picture of the Bulbous Buttercup on page 72.

almost as soon as he had entered the Green Forest. It was near the place where he had found the Wake-robin, or Purple Trillium, a place where the ground was rich and damp. He had passed several of these plants without more than a glance, for he had taken them to be the Wake-robin he had already found. The leaves were much the same, three of them at the top of a smooth, stout stalk. He was hurrying on when he happened to glance directly at one of these plants, and then he stopped short. He stopped short and simply stared. Just above those three broadly oval and sharply pointed leaves was a pure white flower. He could hardly believe it, for you see had he thought about it at all he would have expected to see a purple flower there.

This flower was in shape like that of the Purple Trillium, but it was much larger and pure white, very lovely to look at. The three, long, pointed, white petals turned outward in a graceful curve. They were rather less pointed and somewhat broader than the petals of the Purple Trillium.

Of course Peter knew that he had found another member of the Trillium family.

"I wonder if this one smells as badly as the other," said he, and stretched forth his wobbly little nose to sniff. It didn't smell bad. In fact, there was no smell at all, whereat Peter was glad. It was the Large-flowered Wake-robin,[39] also called the White Trillium, and this is scentless.

Peter continued on his way, still thinking of the Trilliums. He decided to first visit the Laughing Brook. Almost the first thing he saw when he reached it was another group of Trilliums growing a little back from the bank. Just out of idle curiosity he hopped over to them to see which kind these were. Imagine his delight when he discovered that they were neither of the two he had already found. The plants appeared much the same, but the blossoms were more beautiful than either of the others. There were three petals, as is the case with all of the Trilliums. They were waxy-white like those he had just left, but the edges were wavy, and each petal was beautifully striped at the base with pink.

"Oh!" cried Peter. "This is the loveliest yet!"

---

39   Look at picture of Large-flowered Wake-robin on page 82.

And so it was, for Peter had found the Painted Trillium,[40] which is the most beautiful of all the family. Should he come that way later in the season, he would find in the place of each flower a bright red, egg-shaped berry, while the fruit of the Large-flowered Wake-robin is nearly black.

One more Trillium Peter found and later learned that it was the most common of all. This was the Nodding Trillium, or Nodding Wake-robin, so called because the white or pinkish blossom hangs downward from its short stem so that often it is quite hidden by the leaves. The Nodding Trillium is one of the earliest of the family to bloom. All the Trilliums belong to the Lily family.

Wanting to see the beautiful Blue Flag again, Peter followed the Laughing Brook down to the Green Meadows. Another blossom had opened on the Blue Flag, and for some time Peter sat admiring these wonderful colors. Finally he started along out on to the Green Meadows. Here where the ground was moist he unexpectedly came upon some small, blue flowers like tiny blue stars with yellow centers.

"Well, I never!" exclaimed Peter. "I didn't know before that grass has such pretty little flowers."

"What are you talking about?" buzzed Busy Bee, who happened along just in time to overhear him. "That isn't grass. You ought to know that without being told." Then before Peter could make a reply Busy Bee was on her way.

Peter looked a little more closely. Then he saw that what he had taken for grass leaves were really stems and leaves of a plant not even related to grass. But they looked very grasslike, for they were long, narrow and shaped much like blades of grass. They looked so much like some kinds of grass that Peter felt he was really excusable for making the mistake.

The little blue stars were at the top of stalks about a foot high, and these stalks were flat and two-edged, which made them rather grasslike. There was one little blossom at the top of each stalk, and one or more buds not yet open. It was lucky that Peter had happened along on a bright, sunny morning for otherwise he would not have seen them at all. You see, they open

40   Look at picture of Painted Trillium on page 88.

PAINTED TRILLIUM OR PAINTED WAKE-ROBIN
Trillium undulatum

EASTERN BLUE-EYED GRASS
Sisyrinchium atlaniicum

only in the bright sunshine of the morning. In the afternoon they would close tightly, never to open again, for they open but once and remain open only a few hours.

Peter had found the Blue-eyed Grass,[41] which in some places is called Eyebright, although that name is also given to another flower. Blue Star is another name sometimes used.

"Well," said Peter, looking at the leaves again, "this may not be grass, but it certainly looks like it."

"Perhaps it does to people who do not use their eyes, but any one who looks closely enough will never mistake a cousin of the Blue Flag for a member of the grass family," buzzed Busy Bee, who had just returned.

"What!" cried Peter, and his surprise was funny to see. "Do you mean to tell me that these little blue flowers are related to that wonderful Blue Flag back there? I don't believe it."

"What you believe or don't believe doesn't matter the least little bit. Facts are facts, and these little flowers belong to the Iris family and so does the Blue Flag," retorted Busy Bee.

Busy Bee was right. The Blue-eyed Grass is a member of the same family as the wonderful big Blue Flag.

---

41   Look at the picture of the Blue-eyed Grass on page 88.

XVI. A Trap for Living Insects

Tommy Tit the Chickadee had stopped in the dear Old Briar-patch for a brief call on Peter Rabbit. Tommy knew all about Peter's interest in flowers. "I suppose," said he, "that you know that the insect eaters are in bloom." His eyes twinkled with mischief.

"Insect eaters in bloom? What are you talking about, Tommy Tit?" Peter wrinkled his brows in a funny, puzzled way.

"I'm talking about the plant that catches and eats insects," replied Tommy Tit.

"There isn't such a thing," declared Peter.

"How can a plant catch insects? What nonsense!"

Tommy's eyes twinkled more than ever. "There is no nonsense about it," he declared. "There is a plant that catches insects for food, and if you had half used your eyes in the past, you would know the plant I mean."

Now Peter had never known Tommy Tit to tell him a thing that wasn't so. Still Peter couldn't quite believe this. He thought Tommy must be joking and said so.

"No," replied Tommy Tit, "I'm not joking. You think you have found out a lot about plants, Peter, but what you have found out is nothing to what you have yet to learn. There are several kinds of plants that catch insects and use them for food, just as we birds do. But I don't ask you to take my word for it. Just run over to the edge of the swamp and see for yourself. I hope the next time I make you a call you will not be so impolite as to doubt my word. Good-by, Peter."

"Wait a minute, Tommy Tit! Wait a minute!" Peter cried. But Tommy was already on his way to the Old Orchard and didn't turn back.

Of course Peter fairly ached with curiosity. He waited only long enough to make sure that the way was clear. Then he started for the swamp as fast as his legs could take him, lipperty-lipperty-lip. "I don't believe it because I can't believe it," said he to himself. "But if it is so, I am going to find out, though how I am going to do it I don't know. Tommy Tit might have told me what kind of a plant to look for. As it is I haven't the least idea. Anyway, if I don't find it I won't be disappointed, because I don't believe there is such a plant."

Just on the edge of the swamp the ground was boggy, and great masses of a certain kind of moss grew. Peter hesitated. He didn't want to get his feet wet. Then out in the middle of that boggy place he saw something which for the moment put all thought of what he had come for out of his head. He no longer thought about wet feet, but hurried over to it. It was a flower. There was no doubt about it. But it was a flower wholly unlike any Peter had yet found.

It nodded from the top of a long, smooth, light green stalk, and was quite as high above the ground as the top of Peter's head when he sat up. It was a large flower, quite two inches across. There were five sepals which were purplish-red on the outside and light green on the inside. There were five petals, and these were also a purplish-red. They were odd in shape, for they narrowed in the middle and then rounded out broadly, and these rounded ends folded over a big round part which was really a part of the pistil, though Peter had never seen anything like it before. It was like a little umbrella spread over the case which later would hold the seeds.

But odd as was this flower the leaves of the plant were even more odd. They grew out in a circle around the base of the flower stalk, and each leaf was like a little purple and green pitcher with a little hood at the top. Perhaps it would be nearer the truth to say that each leaf was like the curved horn of a cow with the narrow part at the bottom, and with a thin, broad wing on the side which curved in.

Just out of curiosity Peter peeped into one of these hollow leaves. It was half filled with water. He peeped into another and found this partly filled with water. It was the same way with every one of the leaves of that plant, for Peter looked into every one to find out.

But it wasn't the water that surprised him most. No, sir, it wasn't that at all. It was the fact that in every one of those leaves were many drowned Flies and insects. Peter hardly gave the matter a thought when he saw them in the first leaf into which he looked. But as he looked into leaf after leaf and found that the same thing had happened in each, he began to wonder. At first he thought these little Flies and insects had been accidentally drowned. Then he began to wonder how they had happened to go into those leaves.

And then quite suddenly he remembered what Tommy Tit had said. Could this be the plant that made a business of catching insects for food? Peter backed off a step or two and stared at that plant as if he were just a little bit afraid of it. Of course he wasn't really afraid, but the idea that he might be looking at a plant that lived in part on insects, just as so many of his feathered friends did, gave him a queer feeling.

As he sat there staring he saw a little Fly alight on the edge of one of those leafy cups or pitchers. Peter leaned forward to watch. It was plain there was something just inside that pitcher that was very tempting to the little Fly. Peter could tell that by the way the Fly acted. It crept inside, then suddenly slipped and fell!

Of course it fell in the water. But it fell at one side and not in the middle. Thus it was able to start to climb up without getting very wet. But it couldn't climb up very far. It had climbed but a little way when again it slipped and fell. This led Peter to look into that cup more closely, and he found that there were tiny hairs on the sides pointing down. These were what prevented the little Fly from climbing up. Then the little Fly tried to fly straight up, but hairs at the top prevented its escape, and down it fell again. Each time it got a little wetter, and each time it had less strength. Finally it could do nothing but struggle helplessly on the surface of the water, and after a little these struggles ceased. The little Fly had been drowned.

Then Peter understood. These pitcher-like leaves half-filled with water were traps. The unlucky Fly or insect tempted to enter by a sweet juice just below the edge was almost certain to fall, and once in had very little chance of getting out. It was quite clear that the queer shape of these leaves was well-adapted for catching insects, and of course that meant that the plant must get part of its food from them instead of getting all of it from the ground through the roots as most plants do. It was hard to believe, but Peter could not doubt his own eyes. He sat there for a long time and saw the same thing happen over and over again.

This strange plant is called the Pitcher Plant,[42] the Huntsman's-cup and the Indian Dipper. But the first name is the most common one. It belongs to a family of its own.

Late that afternoon Jenny Wren happened over to the dear Old Briar-patch and at once Peter started to tell her about what he had seen that morning. "Tut, tut, tut, tut, Peter. I know all about it," said she. "Way down south where I go in winter are several other members of the family, one of which has leaves that, instead of being curved, grow straight up and are like a trumpet with the small end springing from the ground. Over the top is a flap something like the flap Jack-in-the-pulpit has over his head. I have peeped into one of those leaves and seen it nearly filled with dead insects."

"Ugh!" exclaimed Peter. "I can't make it seem right that a plant should get part of its living in the same way that Old Mr. Toad and most of the birds do."

"Right or wrong, the Pitcher Plants do it, and there are a number of other plants that do it, too. And why shouldn't they? Insects are very good eating, very good eating," replied Jenny Wren.

---

42   Look at the picture of the Pitcher Plant on page 94.

PITCHER PLANT OR HUNTSMAN'S-CUP
Sarracenia purpurea

SMALL YELLOW LADY'S-SLIPPER
Cypripedium parviflorum

XVII. How The Lady's-Slippers Were Saved

PETER HAD gone over to the Green Forest. He was hopping along the Lone Little Path where it winds in and out among the pine trees. He was startled by hearing a shout just ahead of him.

"I've found one! I've found one!" cried a voice. Peter stopped abruptly. He didn't like that voice. He knew it the instant he heard it. It was the voice of the boy he had seen picking Arbutus, and who had chased him that time.

"I wonder what he is doing over here," muttered Peter. He stole forward very carefully. At last he reached an old stump from behind which he could peep out and see what was going on. A boy, the same boy he had seen before, and a girl, the same one who had been picking Arbutus, were running about hunting for something.

"I've found one!" cried the little girl, and held up a beautiful pink flower.

Even at that distance Peter knew what it was.

It was the beautiful Moccasin Flower or Pink Lady's-slipper.[43] Sudden anger filled Peter so that he almost choked. "They are at it again," he muttered. "Yes, sir, they are at it again. They are picking all those beautiful flowers, and that means that there will be no seed. Why can't they be satisfied with just one or two? If they picked only one or two, there would be no great harm done, though what they want to pick them for at all I can't understand. But they are picking every one they see. There is nothing more beautiful in all the Green Forest than these flowers, but some day if all the blossoms are picked, there will be no

---

43   Look at the picture of the Pink Lady's-slipper on page 97.

plants left. That would be dreadful. I wish I could stop them."

But of course Peter couldn't stop them, and there was nothing for him to do but to sit there and vainly wish that he were as big as Buster Bear.

Suddenly the little girl screamed and started to run as fast as she could. "A snake! A snake! A horrid, great, black snake!" she screamed.

"Pooh!" said the boy. "I'm not afraid of snakes. Where is he?"

The little girl didn't stop running until she was at what she thought was a safe distance. Then she turned and pointed to a big tree. "He is right over at the foot of that tree," said she. "I was just going to pick a flower when I saw him. He is the biggest snake I have ever seen. You better keep away from there."

But the boy said "Pooh!" again, and picking up a stick slowly walked over towards the tree his sister had pointed out. Now the boy pretended to be very brave and unafraid. That was because his sister was watching. In his heart he was foolishly afraid of snakes. He hoped that by the time he got over to that tree that snake would have disappeared.

But Mr. Blacksnake, for that is who it was, was still there. He was big. Yes, sir, he was big, though not nearly as big as he looked to the boy. When the boy was a few feet away Mr. Blacksnake decided that was no place for him and started away from there in a hurry. Now when Mr. Blacksnake is in a hurry he moves fast, very fast indeed. It looked to the boy as if Mr. Blacksnake were rushing right at him. The boy didn't wait. He turned and ran faster than his sister had run. When she saw him do this she turned and once more ran. When he caught up with her he took her hand and together they raced out of sight.

Peter, who had seen it all, chuckled. "This," said he to himself, "is the first time I've ever seen any good in Mr. Blacksnake. He certainly scared that boy and girl, though I have an idea he was just as badly scared himself. I guess they'll keep away from here now. I hope Mr. Blacksnake will stay around until those flowers are through blooming."

Then Peter hopped out from behind the old stump and began to look for flowers. He found a number of plants from which the flowers had been picked, but for some time the only one

PINK LADY'S-SLIPPER
Cypripedium acaule

he found with the flower still in bloom was the one the little girl had started to pick when she saw Mr. Blacksnake. Peter sat down beside it to admire it. Rising from the brown pine needles on the ground were two large, thick, pointed, oval leaves which were slightly hairy and had many ribs. Close to the ground the leaves were clasped around each other. From between them rose a quite long, slender stem, at the top of which hung one of the most beautiful of all the flowers of May, and at the same time one of the most interesting. There were both petals and sepals, which were narrow, pointed and looked much alike. They were greenish-purple in color.

But it was not these that made the beauty and wonder of the flower. It was the curious shape and beautiful color of one of the petals. This was in the shape of a dainty bag with a slit nearly its whole length on the upper side, and having the edges folded inward. It was a most beautiful, delicate pink, and covered with little veins or lines of darker pink or purple.

Lady Bumblebee came along and alighted on the beautiful pink bag. Then she forced her way in through the opening on the upper side, which immediately closed after her. It looked very much as if she were in a trap, and Peter wondered how she would get out. For a time she was quiet. You see she was sucking up the sweet nectar within.

Then Peter heard her begin to buzz rather angrily, and he watched to see her try to get out by the way she had entered. But she did nothing of the kind. To Peter's great surprise he saw her head finally appear at an opening in the neck of that pink bag close to where it was attached to the stem. She seemed to be having hard work to force her way out, but finally she was free. All down her back was pollen. She had got it there in her struggle to get out.

"Phew!" said she. "One certainly does have to work to get the nectar from these flowers. At least one has to work to get away with it. But it is worth the trouble. Yes, sir, it is worth the trouble." Then off she flew to look for another, and Peter knew that when she tried to squeeze her way out of the next flower she would leave some of the pollen which had stuck to her back, and at the same time get a new supply.

Though Peter didn't know it, the Lady's-slipper is a member of the Orchid family, and therefore is in a way related to the beautiful Arethusa which he had so much admired. It is a family which contains some of the most beautiful and most wonderful flowers in all the Great World.

A little later this same month Peter found a cousin of the Pink Moccasin Flower. This was the Large Yellow Lady's-slipper, or Yellow Moccasin Flower. It was growing in the Green Forest where the ground was quite wet. The plant itself was quite different from its cousin growing under the pines. Instead of having only two leaves it had several growing out from a stalk nearly two feet in height.

At the top hung a flower much the same shape as that of its pink cousin, but the curious bag-shaped lip was pale yellow, streaked with fine purple lines. The sepals were pointed and quite broad, but the two other petals were narrow, long and twisted, and were brown in color.

Of course Peter was delighted with his find, but he was still more delighted when a few moments later, and growing quite near, he found another Yellow Lady's-slipper, this one only about half the size of the other. It was not only lovely, but fragrant, as Peter's wobbly little nose soon found out. Like its larger cousin it had two twisted petals above the bag-like yellow petal. It is commonly called the Small Yellow Lady's-slipper.[44] How glad Peter was that none of these blossoms had been picked!

---

44   See picture of the Small Yellow Lady's-slipper on page 94.

XVIII. The Delightful Reward of Curiosity

PETER RABBIT sat just outside of the dear Old Briar-patch. He wanted to go somewhere, but he didn't know where. He simply couldn't make up his mind. Blacky the Crow decided the matter for him. Blacky began cawing as if he were greatly excited. "Caw, caw, caw, caw!" screamed Blacky. "Caw, caw, caw, caw!"

Peter pricked up his ears. "Blacky is up in the Old Pasture," thought he. "I wonder what the black rascal has found now. If he were over in the Green Forest, I should think he had discovered Hooty the Owl, and was tormenting him. But Hooty wouldn't be over in the Old Pasture. Blacky must have found some one or something else to excite him."

"Caw, caw, caw, caw!" Blacky was hardly stopping long enough to get breath. And now there were answering "caws" over in the Green Forest, and Peter saw some of Blacky's relatives heading for the Old Pasture to join Blacky.

Curiosity began to get the better of Peter's common sense. The longer he listened to that cawing, the more he wanted to know what it was all about.

"I believe I'll run over there," said Peter to himself. "I may as well go over there as anywhere else. To be sure Reddy Fox has his home over there, but there are plenty of bramble-tangles for me to hide in. My, what a racket those Crows are making! I simply must find out what it is all about."

So away went Peter, lipperty-lipperty-lip, for the Old Pasture. About the time he reached the edge of it Blacky and his friends stopped their noise. A few minutes later Peter saw them flying back to the Green Forest. He was disappointed. He had come over there for nothing. He was tempted to go back home, or else to go over to the Green Forest. But he didn't do either.

"Now that I am here I may as well see if there is anything new in the Old Pasture," said he to himself. "I'll call on Old Jed Thumper, the gray old Rabbit who lives over here. He'll probably try to chase me out, but I don't care if he does."

So Peter started on into the Old Pasture. For a wonder he wasn't thinking of flowers. In fact, he had quite forgotten to look for them at all. So his surprise and delight were all the greater when he came upon a little bush covered with clusters of feathery white flowers.

"Ha!" exclaimed Peter, and stopped to look closely at his find. It was a small bush a little over two feet high. The leaves were oval and pointed, and each leaf had three ribs. The edges were cut into fine little teeth, and the surface of the leaves was hairy.

But as usual it was the flowers which interested Peter most. They were very tiny and were crowded together around the ends of long slender stems. Each tiny blossom had five petals and five stamens. So small were these little blossoms, and so dainty, that each little mass looked soft and feathery. Of course he at once tested them with his wobbly little nose. There was a faint fragrance.

Peter scratched a long ear with a long hind foot. "I wonder what I've found now," said he.

But there was no one to tell him. He happened to think of the root and wondered what it was like. To find out he dug around it and discovered at once that it was of a deep reddish color.

"I guess I'll have to name this thing myself," said he. "I'll call it Red-root. Yes, sir, that's what I'll call it."

Now it just happens that what Peter had decided to call it is the very name that other people have given it. However, it is much better known as New Jersey Tea.[45] Way back in the days when this country of ours was first settled tea was a great luxury, and many people could not get it at all. Then they used to take the young, downy leaves of this plant, dry them and use them for making tea. So the plant became known as the New Jersey Tea plant. From the roots a dye was made, and so you see this little plant was very useful.

45   Look at the picture of the New Jersey Tea on page 102.

NEW JERSEY TEA
Ceanothus americanus

SWEET-SCENTED WHITE WATER LILY
Castalia odorata

Peter felt that already his trip to the Old Pasture was quite well worth while, and he was in a very happy frame of mind as he continued on his way to look for Old Jed Thumper. But Old Jed Thumper was soon forgotten. On the edge of a bramble-tangle Peter found the first Rose of summer. It was the Low or Pasture Rose, the most abundant of all wild Roses, and a flower that Peter had loved from the days when he had started out in the Great World to find a place for himself.

The bush Peter had found now was not much above his head, though he knew places where the bushes grew as high as the head of a tall man. The leaves were compound. That is, they were divided into leaflets, each one of which was like a complete leaf. In most cases there were five of these leaflets, though Peter found one or two with seven. These leaflets were oval, rather shiny, and the edges were cut into irregular little teeth.

The branches were covered with little sharp thorns. At least, that is what most people call them, though they are not true thorns, but prickles. They grow out from the bark, but true thorns grow out from the wood itself and are really branches which have been changed into thorns.

But it was the flower itself that interested Peter most. How he loved it! Later there would be countless numbers of them all through the Old Pasture, but this was the first one, and Peter feasted his eyes on it, and his wobbly little nose rejoiced in the fragrance of it. There were five soft, pink petals, for the Rose goes in fives. You know there were five leaflets to each leaf as a rule. Back of the beautiful pink petals were five sepals. In the center was a cluster of pistils, and around these a circle of many bright yellow stamens.

While Peter sat there Busy Bee came along. To Peter's great surprise she hardly gave the Rose a look. He had thought that she would be as delighted as he was, but she appeared not at all interested.

"What is the matter with that Rose that you do not draw out its sweetness to make honey?" asked Peter.

"There is no sweetness in it to make honey of," retorted Busy Bee. "It would be a waste of time for me to look for any there." And with this Busy Bee went on in search of other flowers.

But if Busy Bee was not interested in the Pasture Rose, some of her relatives were. They came to it to collect the pollen with which it was most generous. Peter knew that in the fall where the beautiful blossom now was there would be a bright scarlet berry, and then certain of his feathered friends would be quite as interested as he now was.

It was with real regret that Peter finally started on his way. He knew that there would soon be many of these beautiful blossoms, but there is never quite the joy that comes with the finding of the first one. A little later he would find the Swamp Rose[46] on the edge of the swamp. This would have stout, hooked prickles, while those of the Pasture Rose were straight. Then would come the Meadow Rose, sometimes called the Smooth Rose, which would have few if any prickles. The blossoms of all are much alike.

The Rose family is a large one, and contains many members that at first sight would seem not to be related at all. Most of our fruit trees belong to the Rose family, and you remember that the Wild Strawberry and the Cinquefoil are also little cousins of the Rose.

By this time Peter had forgotten all about Old Jed Thumper, and instead of keeping on to look for him he hurried back to the dear Old Briar-patch to tell little Mrs. Peter that Rose time had begun.

---

46   Look at the picture of the Swamp Rose on page 105.

SWAMP ROSE
Rosa Carolina

WILD LUPINE OR WILD PEA
Lupinus perennis

xix. White and Yellow Cousins

BUBBLING BOB the Bobolink poured out the joy which filled his heart as he mounted in the air and then dropped down out of sight in the grass of the Green Meadows. No one could hear that rollicking song and not know that Bubbling Bob was as happy as a bird could be. Peter, watching him from the edge of the dear Old Briar-patch, knew the cause of that happiness. He knew that somewhere safely hidden in the grass Bubbling Bob had a nest, and that he was singing to the little brown-cloaked mate who was sitting on the eggs in that nest.

Every spring Bubbling Bob and his mate nested not far from the dear Old Briar-patch, and every spring so far Peter had wasted much time looking for that nest. He and Bubbling Bob were the best of friends, but a nest is a secret not to be shared with any one, and so Bubbling Bob had watched Peter hunt and hunt, and instead of telling him where that nest was had led him far from it. This spring Peter had been too much interested in hunting for flowers to be even curious about nests. But now as he listened to Bubbling Bob, the old curiosity became too much for him. He had nothing special to do, so to while away the time he decided he would once more try to find out Bubbling Bob's secret.

He had seen just where Bubbling Bob had dropped down in the grass, so straight for that point Peter scampered. Just before he reached it Bubbling Bob flew up, singing as before. He pretended not to notice Peter. Peter squatted down in the grass and watched him. When Bubbling Bob had finished his song he flew down in the grass again, but this time at a different place. Peter hastily looked about the place where Bubbling

Bob had mounted into the air, and finding no nest, scampered straight over to where Bubbling Bob had disappeared. Again Bubbling Bob took to the air and again Peter hunted in vain. And so Bubbling Bob led Peter hither, thither and yon, farther and farther out on the Green Meadows.

At last Peter grew tired and sat down to rest. Then it was that a little way from him he saw something white just above the grass. Bubbling Bob and his nest were forgotten as Peter hurried over there.

"I knew it! I knew it!" cried Peter happily as he drew near. "It is the first Daisy. How I love the Daisies!"[47]

Peter was right. It was the first White Daisy. No one could mistake it for any other flower. It was a sort of pledge that summer would soon replace gentle Mistress Spring, for it is only as Mistress Spring is preparing to leave that the Daisies begin to bloom.

Peter hopped close to that lone Daisy, for he was seeing it with new eyes. That is, he was seeing it for the first time as a Daisy really is. He admired the round center of pure gold and the pure white of the many petal-like parts surrounding it. Such a cheery blossom as it was. How pure and innocent it looked.

"I know you now," said Peter, talking to the Daisy as if it could understand. "I know you now. Once I would have thought you just a single blossom, but now I know better. You are like the Dandelion, a composite flower. That is, you are not just one flower, but a lot of flowers growing all together so as to look like one."

"My, my, how wise we are," said a voice right behind Peter. Peter turned hastily to find Johnny Chuck grinning at him.

"No," said Peter, "I am not wise, but I am wiser than I was. I am learning every day. Isn't this Daisy beautiful, Johnny?"

"I suppose it is if you say so," replied Johnny Chuck carelessly. "It would look a lot more beautiful to me if it were good eating. Even Farmer Brown's cows don't like it and won't eat it. If things are not good to eat what are they good for?"

"To look at," replied Peter promptly. "I guess the Great World needs beautiful things to look at just as much as it does

47   Look at the picture of the White Daisy on page 108.

COMMON WHITE DAISY
Chrysanthemum Leucanthemum

WILD SPIKENARD
Smilacina racemosa

things to eat."

Just then a little Bee alighted on the Daisy and greedily began to load itself with yellow pollen. A Butterfly took the place of the Bee as the latter left and began to feast on nectar.

"There," said Peter triumphantly, "it may not furnish you or me any food, Johnny Chuck, but it supplies food for others. Here comes another Bee."

It was so. While Peter sat there half a dozen kinds of insects visited the Daisy, and none went away empty. So Peter discovered for himself that the White Daisy is not so useless as Johnny Chuck thought.

It is true that from man's point of view its only use is to please the eye. In fact, the White Daisy has become a pest so that it is often called the Whiteweed. Sometimes it is called the Oxeye Daisy. Strangely enough it is a member of the Thistle family. Were it not so common that it often makes the meadows white in June it would be found in every one's garden. As it is man tries to get rid of it instead of cultivating it. The reason that it increases so fast and spreads everywhere is that it attracts so many insects. They in turn pay for the bounty it furnishes them by carrying the pollen from one blossom to another. This means that each plant will bear many strong, vigorous seeds, and the more seeds of course the more plants.

On his way back to the dear Old Briar-patch Peter had another surprise. This time it was a cousin of the Daisy he had just left. But it was very different. In form it was similar, for of course it, too, was a composite flower. Around a large center grew many so-called petals, but instead of being pure white these were bright orange-yellow. Looking closely at these, Peter discovered that each had a tiny notch in the end of it.

Instead of surrounding a golden center these grew out from around the base of a cone-shaped center of a rich purple-brown color, and the flower heads were much larger than the White Daisy. It was the Black-eyed Susan,[48] which also has several other names, including Coneflower, Yellow Daisy and Oxeye Daisy. This latter name is rather confusing because in many parts of the country the White Daisy is given this name, as you

48   Look at the picture of the Black-eyed Susan on page 133.

already know.

Had Peter had eyes for anything but the flowers he would have seen that there was quite a difference in the appearance of the leaves of the two cousins. The leaves of the White Daisy are much divided and cut into teeth, while those of the Black-eyed Susan are long, narrow, pointed, with the edges slightly cut. Both stems and leaves are hairy.

There were several of the Black-eyed Susans open, and Peter discovered that some had twice as many petal-like parts as others. Had Peter pulled one of these off he would have discovered that it really was a little floret, which means tiny flower. He would not, however, have found any stamens carrying the yellow dust called pollen or any pistil. The pollen is in the tiny flowers or florets packed together to form the yellow center, and these florets are in the shape of little tubes with tops spreading into five points. They also have pistils or seed-bearing parts.

Thus the Daisy blossom is made up not only of a great many very tiny flowers, but of two kinds. The same thing is true of the Black-eyed Susan and other composites. Composite is a big word, but it simply means made up of many parts. I guess you can remember that if Peter Rabbit can. The insects and Butter-flies love the Black-eyed Susan just as they do the White Daisy, but it is not loved by the farmer, for his cattle will not eat it. Here are two flowers which may be picked as freely as desired. In fact, the more are picked the better, for beautiful as they are there are altogether too many, and they are constantly spreading.

XX. Peter Finds Three Old Friends

IT WAS over in the Green Forest where the ground was rich and moist that Peter found Solomon's Seal. It was an old friend whom he had long known. There was no mistaking it. Peter would have known it anywhere. He would have known it by the little pale yellow flower bells hanging in pairs along the stalk below the leaves. The stalk was long and slender and bent gracefully above Peter's head. Growing out from opposite sides were smooth-edged, oval leaves, each broader at the base than at the tip. They were smooth above, but covered with very fine hairs on the under-side. The tiny yellow or greenish flowers were like fairy bells, growing almost always in pairs as they swung below the spreading leaves.

Later in the season there would be a blackish berry hanging in the place of each of these pretty little flower bells. Peter had seen them often, for some of his feathered friends occasionally looked for them and Peter had seen them doing it.

Finding the Solomon's Seal reminded Peter of a near relative which in a way looks much like it, and grows near by in a neighborly fashion. It is the Wild Spikenard[49] or False Solomon's Seal, sometimes called Solomon's Zigzag. It ought to be in bloom now, and Peter promptly went to look for it. He found it almost at once. He would have known it even had it not yet been in bloom. The shape of the plant was much like the True Solomon's Seal, but the leaves were larger and the tips were sharply pointed.

Along this stalk were no little fairy bells. Instead, out from the tip grew a thick, pointed cluster or plume of greenish-

49   Look at the picture of the Wild Spikenard on page 108.

white tiny blossoms. These tiny blossoms were set around stems growing out from the main stalk, one above another, the lower ones being longest and the others growing shorter and shorter towards the tip. Small as they were each little flower contained six stamens and a pistil. So tiny were these flowers that together they made that plume seem feathery. Of course Peter Rabbit had never been up in Farmer Brown's flower bed close to his house where lilies-of-the-valley grow. Had he ever seen these, the leaves of both the True Solomon's Seal and of the Wild Spikenard would at once have reminded him of the Lily-of-the-valley leaves, and he might have guessed, what is a fact, that these two friends of his in the Green Forest are members of the Lily-of-the-valley family.

Like the True Solomon's Seal, its cousin bears berries, but of course these grow in a cluster, and instead of being almost black are pale red and speckled. Many of Peter's feathered friends delight to find them and feast on them before making their long journey to the Sunny South for the winter.

For some time Peter aimlessly wandered about in the Green Forest, finding no new flowers to interest him. At last he decided that he would run over to the Old Pasture to see if more of the beautiful Pasture Rose blossoms were open. You know he never tires of admiring them. But when he reached the Old Pasture he forgot all about the Roses. Yes, sir, he did so. You see as he was hopping across a bare, open place on the hillside where the soil was so sandy and dry that it didn't seem as if any plant could grow there, he came upon some flowers that seemed as if they must have taken their color from the blue, blue sky itself. No wonder that Peter forgot the Roses. I think had you been in his place you would have forgotten them.

With a little sigh of pure happiness Peter sat down close to the low branching little plant whose flowers were the color of the sky. It was a brave little plant, for, as I have said, it was grow-ing in a place so sandy and dry that it didn't seem as if anything could grow there. Where other plants would have withered and died it held itself erect, while its lovely blossoms smiled up at jolly, round, bright Mr. Sun smiling down on them. It could do this because of its roots, which went far down into the ground and there found the moisture which other plants with roots spreading near the surface could not have found.

The leaves were like little wheels without rims. Each spoke of these little wheels was a smooth-edged leaflet, broader at the outer end and coming down to a point at the center. In some of these little wheel-like leaves there were seven of these leaflets to form the spokes. In others there were nine, ten and eleven. They did not form quite perfect wheels because some of the leaflets were a little shorter than the others. Down the middle of each leaflet was a rib clear to the tip.

Had Peter happened along there after jolly, round, bright Mr. Sun had gone to bed behind the Purple Hills, and the Black Shadows had crept out over the Old Pasture, he might have discovered a most interesting thing. He might have discovered that these leaves go to sleep at night. The leaflets fold down around the stem much like a closed umbrella. With the return of jolly, round, bright Mr. Sun in the morning they open out flat again.

But of course it was the flowers that Peter was most interested in. These grew out around a long stem and made Peter think of little blue Butterflies clinging to that stem. If you have ever seen sweet peas, or if you have ever seen the white blossoms of the garden peas, you will know right away what the shape of these little blossoms was like. Each blossom had five petals. The upper one stood almost straight up. It is called the standard. Two others were like little blue wings and the edges of the remaining two grew together so as to form a tiny, fairy boat. It is called the keel.

In this, hidden and protected, were the pistils, stamens and the nectar. A Bee came buzzing along and alighted on one of the wings. Her weight caused the boat-like petals to open so that she could get the nectar and at the same time become covered with pollen. When she flew away these petals closed again, once more protecting the precious contents.

Peter had found the Wild Lupine[50] which is also called the Wild Pea because it is a member of the Pea family. Another name for it is Old Maid's Bonnets, for these quaint little blossoms are not unlike tiny blue bonnets such as fairies might love

50   Look at the picture of the Wild Lupine on page 105.

to wear. Later in the summer there would hang from that stem little broad, flat, very hairy pods within which would be tiny peas. Of course you know that peas are really seeds. The peas we gather in the garden and eat are seeds not yet ripe.

The blossoms of the Wild Lupine are not always the beautiful blue of the ones Peter had found. Sometimes they are pinkish and sometimes almost white. But as a rule they are blue, and when many of them are in bloom at one time they will make a hillside seem to be reflecting the color of the sky. This flower is often found along roadsides and along the gravelly banks beside the railroad. It is as if Old Mother Nature could not bear to have any spot unbeautified by flowers some time during the year.

When Peter had admired the Lupine to his heart's content he decided he would go home. But happening to look up in the blue, blue sky, he saw Redtail the Hawk sailing in great circles high up above the Green Meadows, and he knew that Redtail was out hunting for a dinner. Peter promptly changed his mind. This was no time to cross the Green Meadows, so he decided to stay in the Old Pasture and see if he could find anything more of interest there.

xxi. Beautiful, Mischievous Cousins

PETER FOUND no more new flowers in the Old Pasture the day he found the Lupine, and it was some time before he went back there again. June, the first of the summer months, had come. The Pasture Rose bushes were now a mass of beautiful pink blossoms. Where Peter had found the first Lupine in bloom the ground was now blue with them. Parts of the Green Meadows were yellow with Buttercups and other parts were white with Daisies. It seemed as if everywhere there were flowers, for June is of all months the month of flowers.

Following an old cow path up through the Old Pasture, Peter came to a rocky hillside where grew little and big bushes, sometimes singly and sometimes in masses. The leaves were long, oval, smooth and thick. The older ones were a dark green, the new ones being lighter. All winter those older leaves had remained green. Peter knew all about them. They were leaves that he never tasted, not even when the snow was so deep that he had hard work to find anything to eat. Those leaves were poisonous, and Peter knew enough to let them alone. In this he was wiser than some sheep and cattle, many of which are killed every year by eating these tempting-looking leaves.

But Peter gave no thought to those leaves. You see those bushes were covered with great masses of white and delicate pink blossoms. They grew in great clusters, and it seemed to Peter that never had he seen anything more beautiful. One of these bushes was no higher than Peter's head, and he could look at those blossoms as closely as he pleased.

Each flower was an inch or less across, and was shaped like a tiny bowl with five low points. Around the middle on the outside were ten little projections which on the inside formed ten very tiny pockets. Inside, starting from the center, were ten white stamens, but these stamens, instead of standing straight up as do the stamens in most flowers, were bent over like a spring, and the anther, which you know is the little package of pollen at the end of each, was held fast in one of those little pockets I have mentioned. Standing straight up in the middle was a single pale-green pistil.

Peter was so used to seeing the pollen-covered anthers on the tips of the stamens in other flowers that he missed them in this one. You see, when he first saw those bent-over stamens he didn't recognize them as stamens at all. But presently a Bee came along and entered the flower Peter was looking at. Then surprising things happened. She touched one of those bent-over stamens and instantly it straightened up like a spring, bringing with it the little anther which had been held in one of those tiny pockets and had kept the stamen bent over. The sudden springing up of that stamen caused the little anther on its tip to throw a shower of golden pollen on that Bee. You see it was a regular little spring gun. One after another the other stamens did the same thing as the Bee touched them.

Then Peter understood. Old Mother Nature had given this flower these tiny spring guns to make sure that whoever visited them should carry away pollen to leave in the next flower entered. Peter watched that Bee leave that flower and go to another, where of course the same thing happened. The first time he had exclaimed right out because he was so surprised. Even after he had seen a dozen of those little spring guns go off he had that same feeling of surprise each time.

When the Bee had flown away, Peter sat there for a long time hoping that she or another would come back so that he might see more of those little spring guns go off. Finally he ventured to touch one of those blossoms and found that by so doing he could make those little stamens spring up and throw their tiny showers of golden dust. It was great fun. While doing this he discovered that the stems were sticky.

"I wonder why that is," said Peter to himself, but of course he couldn't answer it himself and there was no one there to tell. Had

Old Mother Nature happened along she might have explained to him that it prevented ants and other crawling insects from getting into those flowers. These insects would not carry the pollen from flower to flower as the Bees do.

Perhaps you have guessed what flower it was Peter had found. It was a flower with several names, its most familiar ones being American Laurel and Mountain Laurel.[51] It is also called Calico Bush, Clamoun, Kalmia and Spoonwood. The wood of the Laurel is very hard, and has been much used for making wooden spoons. Of course this is why it is called Spoonwood in some places.

Just before Peter left to go in search of other flowers he discovered a beautiful Swallow-tail Butterfly laying eggs on one of the Laurel leaves. He knew enough about Butterflies to know that they lay their eggs where the caterpillars hatching from them will find food right at hand. This meant that the caterpillars which would come from these eggs would eat the Laurel leaves, and that therefore they could not be poisonous to them as they are to animals.

Peter had gone but a short way when he came to a little bush which he knew at once to be a little cousin of the Mountain Laurel. "The Lambkill is in bloom!" he cried, and eagerly hurried forward to see if this also had those funny little spring guns.

Just as the plant was very much smaller than its big cousin so were the flowers much smaller. They grew in a big cluster around the stem, while the flowers of the Mountain Laurel were at the end of the stem. Standing straight up above each cluster of flowers was the new growth of the year, its leaves reaching straight up, while the old leaves drooped downward. The new leaves were light green, while the old leaves were dark. In shape they were much like those of the Mountain Laurel, but of course much smaller and also narrower.

But the flowers themselves were formed like little Laurel blossoms, and to Peter's joy he found that they also contained the little spring guns. In color they were a deep pink, and the stamens and pistils also were pink. Peter knew this plant well and not for the world would he have eaten one of those leaves.

51   Look at the picture of the Mountain Laurel on page 118.

MOUNTAIN LAUREL
Kalmia latifolia

He knew it to be even more poisonous than the leaves of the Mountain Laurel. That is why it is often called Lambkill and Calfkill and Sheep Poison. Many foolish sheep and young cattle have died because of eating it. It is also called Sheep Laurel[52] and Wicky.

When Peter left the Sheep Laurel he followed an old cow path that led up to the top of the Old Pasture where it joined the foot of the Great Mountain. There one more surprise greeted him just within the edge of the woods. It was almost big enough to be called a small tree. Had Peter been living farther south he might have found some of these plants so large that they really were trees.

One glance at the leaves was enough for Peter to know that here was another cousin of the Mountain Laurel. They were larger and broader than the Mountain Laurel leaves, and a darker green, but in shape and appearance were much the same.

But Peter had eyes only for the wonderful great clusters of beautiful flowers, some of the flowers being almost two inches across. Some were a wonderful soft pink, while others were almost white and were bell-shaped, and as Peter looked up at them appeared to have five petals. Of course the first thing he looked for was to see if these beautiful blossoms also had those wonderful little spring guns. He was disappointed. They didn't have. There were ten stamens, but they stood upright instead of being bent over like little springs.

Peter had found one of the most beautiful of all our wild flowers, the American or Great Rhododendron,[53] also called Great Laurel, Rose Tree or Bay.

---

52   Look at the picture of the Sheep Laurel on page 120.

53   Look at the picture of the Great Rhododendron on page 140.

FRINGED POLYGALA OR GAY-WINGS
Polygala paucifolia

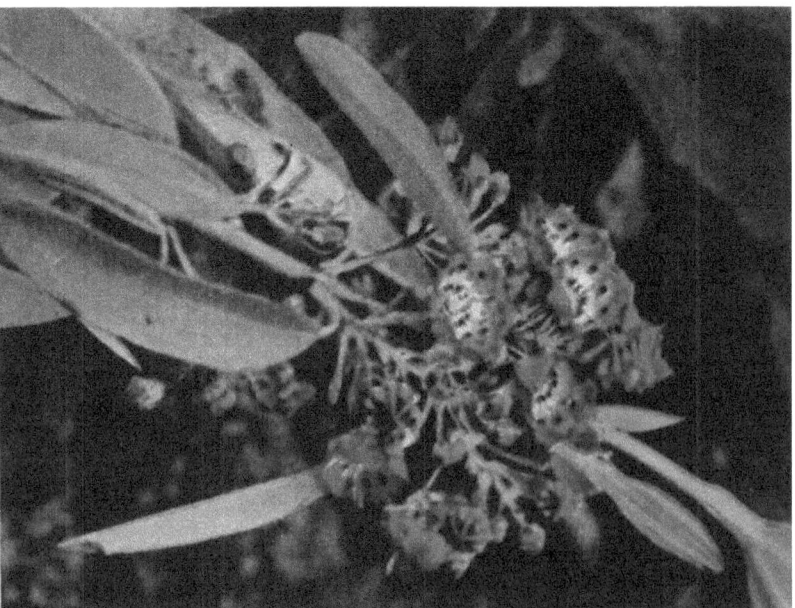

SHEEP LAUREL OR LAMBKILL
Kalmia angustifolia

XXII. Peter Finds Stars in the Grass

"WHEN THE stars are a-twinkle far up in the sky I never can love them because they're too high. So because they are close to the path as I pass I give all my love to the stars in the grass."

"What is that you said, Johnny Chuck?" demanded Peter, hopping out from behind a bunch of tall grass which had hidden him from Johnny.

For an instant Johnny Chuck was startled. He had not supposed that any one was near him. He drew himself up with as much dignity as he could. "I said," replied he, "that I love the stars in the grass. Have you any objections, Peter Rabbit?"

Peter chuckled. "None whatever, Johnny," he replied. "You may love all the stars you please for all I care. But why not talk sense? Whoever heard of stars in the grass?"

"You have now," retorted Johnny Chuck, rather sharply, and turning his back waddled off.

"Don't be cross, Johnny Chuck," begged Peter, hopping after him. "I didn't mean to offend you. You see, I never heard of stars in the grass before. Tell me where they are so that I may see them too."

Go look for them," grunted Johnny Chuck. Your eyes are as good as mine, and if I can find them you can." And not another word could Peter get out of Johnny Chuck.

"Stars in the grass!" repeated Peter to himself, as he sat looking after Johnny Chuck. "I don't know now what he means, but perhaps if I follow that little path he has just come along I'll find out."

So Peter started along the little path through the grass. This time he didn't hurry. He went slowly so as to look on both sides of him. If there were really stars in the grass he didn't want to miss them. He had gone some little distance without seeing anything unusual. Then off at one side he saw several bright yellow star-like flowers, and in a flash he understood what Johnny Chuck had meant. "Johnny Chuck's stars!" cried Peter. "How stupid of me not to think of flowers! Of course these are what he meant."

With two or three quick jumps he was over to them. They were very like six-pointed little stars. They grew in small clusters at the top of a slender, somewhat hairy stalk, but only one flower in each cluster was open, for it is their usual way to open only one at a time. Occasionally there will be two, but rarely if ever more.

The leaves were taller than the flower stalk and were very like blades of grass, each with a rib down the center. Within, the six petal-like parts of the flower were bright yellow, but without they were greenish and hairy. The stamens also were yellow.

Peter at once thought of the Blue-eyed Grass, the small cousin of the Blue Flag which he had found earlier in the season, and he was sure that the two must be cousins. In this, however, he was mistaken, for the Yellow Star Grass,[54] which is the name of the flowers he had just found, belong to quite another family.

"I don't wonder Johnny Chuck loves them," said Peter. "I love them myself."

For some time he sat there admiring them and watching certain small Bees gathering pollen from them to take home for food for their babies. When he had tired of this he started on towards the Smiling Pool. As he drew near he heard Redwing the Blackbird screaming excitedly over in the alders near the head of the Smiling Pool, and at once hurried over to find out what was going on. It was very wet and boggy in there and Peter had to pick his way rather slowly. By the time he got there the excitement was all over. It seems that Redwing had caught sight of Mr. Blacksnake, whom he hates. But Mr. Blacksnake had gone on about his business and disappeared, and Redwing and Mrs. Redwing had resumed the work of hunting for food enough to

54   Look at the picture of the Yellow Star Grass on page 124.

keep the four hungry children in their nest quiet.

Peter had watched hungry young birds being fed too often to be interested, and turned away in disappointment. But within two jumps he saw something that put all thoughts of Redwing and his family out of his head. It was a plant with several beautiful pink flowers more than a foot above the ground at the top of a slender, smooth stalk which bore no leaves. At the first glimpse he thought he had found again the Arethusa or Swamp Pink, which had so delighted him when Longbill the Woodcock had showed it to him earlier in the season. Then he remembered that the Arethusa had but one blossom on a stalk, and as he drew nearer he saw at once that this plant was quite different, though from its appearance he knew it must belong to the same family. It did; it was another member of the beautiful Orchid family.

Looking closely at one of these flowers, Peter found that while it had both sepals and petals they were so much alike that he hardly knew one from the other. As was the case with the other Orchids he had found, this one had one petal very much larger than the others and quite different from them in appearance. Such a petal is, as you already know, called the lip. In the Arethusa this lip is the lower petal, and has three little ridges of hairs. In the Lady's-slipper the lip is in the shape of a bag and is also the lower petal. But in the flower Peter was now looking at the lip was the upper petal and stood nearly erect. It was covered thickly with white, yellow and pinkish hairs which looked almost like stamens.

Peter thought right away that the flower looked very much as if it were upside down. As was the case with the Arethusa the pistil looked to Peter much as if it were made up of three petals. Probably when you see this flower for the first time you will think the same thing.

As Peter sat there admiring the beautiful pink blossoms, along came Lady Bee and alighted on that hairy lip. Then a surprising thing happened. It happened so unexpectedly that it made Peter blink. That lip dropped down as if hinged at the bottom so that Lady Bee was forced down where she would come against the pollen, some of which would stick to her. Of course when she visited another of these flowers the same thing would happen,

YELLOW STAR GRASS
Hypoxis hirsuta

CALOPOGON OR GRASS PINK
Calopogon pulchellus

and some of that pollen from the first flower would be left in the second flower.

When he thought to look for the leaves Peter found but one, and this grew out of the ground close to the bottom of the flower stalk. It was long, narrow and quite like a blade of grass. Peter counted the flowers on the stalk and found seven. A little way off was another stalk, and this had a dozen flowers and buds. As a matter of fact there are sometimes as many as fifteen.

"Well," said Peter, "I don't know what I have found, but it certainly is lovely."

"You've found the Grass Pink," said Redwing the Blackbird, who happened to come along just in time to overhear Peter. "When you said that it is lovely you told the truth for once."

Of course Grass Pink is simply a common name for this plant. Its real name is Calopogon,[55] and while it is one of the loveliest of the Orchids it is not as rare as some of the others. Like its relatives it should not be picked. It is one of those flowers to be hunted for, and when found, admired and then left untouched.

Peter felt that he had found enough for that day, and when he had looked at those flowers to his heart's content he headed back for the dear Old Briar-patch to tell Mrs. Peter about them. He knew she wouldn't be interested, but he just had to tell someone. He knew she would think he had been wasting his time, but he knew better. Adding to knowledge is never a waste of time, and Peter knew that he had learned much that morning.

---

55   Look at the picture of the Calopogon on page 124.

XXIII. Lilies of Meadow and Wood

Peter sat just on the edge of the dear Old Briar-patch trying to make up his mind where to go. Mrs. Peter sat under a bramble bush in the Old Briar-patch and told Peter just what she thought of him for wanting to leave the safety of the dear Old Briar-patch at all.

"One of these days you'll never come back," declared little Mrs. Peter. "Then what will I do? You don't seem to think of me at all. If you really had to go, I wouldn't say a word."

"I do have to go," retorted Peter.

"Why, Peter Rabbit, how can you say such a thing?" demanded little Mrs. Peter. "You know very well that you don't have to do anything of the kind."

"Yes, I do," replied Peter. "I just have to go. Something inside makes me. There are ever and ever so many things in the Great World that I don't know about yet, and I simply must learn. I couldn't be happy otherwise. You wouldn't want me unhappy all the time, would you?"

"No-o-o," replied little Mrs. Peter, hesitatingly. "No, of course I wouldn't want you unhappy. But I don't see why you should be unhappy here with me in the dear Old Briar-patch. It's selfishness on your part, Peter Rabbit. That's all it is, selfishness. You don't want to be unhappy by staying, but you don't think anything about my unhappiness in being left alone."

Peter shifted about uneasily. There was truth in what Mrs. Peter said and he knew it. It made him uncomfortable. He didn't mean to needlessly worry Mrs. Peter. He didn't want to make her unhappy any more than he wanted to be unhappy himself. He just ached to go somewhere, but he didn't want to be selfish.

With a sigh Peter made up his mind that he would stay at home. He had just opened his mouth to say so when far away on the Green Meadows some yellow specks caught his attention. He sat up a little straighter that he might see better. What could they be? He hadn't the least idea. They appeared not to move. Peter forgot his just formed resolution to stay home. He forgot everything but curiosity about those yellow specks. He must find out what they were. He simply must. So without so much as saying good-by to little Mrs. Peter away he went, lipperty-lipperty-lip.

Every few jumps Peter sat up to see if those yellow specks were still there. They were. They hadn't moved a bit. The nearer he got to them, the larger they grew. Now despite his curiosity, Peter wasn't reckless. The nearer he got to those yellow things, the more slowly and carefully he moved. He wanted to see, but be himself unseen. The grass was long, and Peter crept through it with the greatest care. When he thought he was near enough, he very slowly sat up so as to look over the tops of the grasses. Then with a squeal of pleasure he bounded forward. There was nothing to be afraid of. No, sir, there was nothing to be afraid of. Those things which at a distance had appeared as yellow specks were flowers, and big flowers at that! They were quite the biggest flowers he had yet found.

To see them at all closely Peter had to sit up and then tip his head back. Even then they were some distance above his head. They hung like so many yellow bells on long, slender stems from the top of a smooth, quite stout stalk, around which at even distances grew circles of half a dozen or more oval, quite long leaves, each having three ribs.

On this particular stalk Peter counted five wide-open blossoms and two buds. Some stalks growing near had more and some had less. One of the blossoms hung directly over Peter's head. There were six petal-like parts, each pointed and curling backward. On the inner side each of these was deeper yellow than on the outside, and was thickly spotted with dark, reddish-brown. Peter counted the stamens. There were six. They were long and in color were green. On the tip of each was a big brown cap, the pollen package. Instead of being yellow this pollen was brown. Peter discovered this when a little was shaken out in his face by a mischievous Merry Little Breeze.

Peter didn't need to be told that this was a member of the Lily family. "It is the Meadow Lily!"[56] he cried. "Oh, I am so glad I have found the first ones in bloom. Now I know that summer is here."

Peter had called it the Meadow Lily. This is probably its most common name. But it has several other names. In some places it is called the Field Lily; in others the Wild Yellow Lily; in still others the Nodding Lily; and many people know it as the Canada Lily.

A member of the Bee family, one whom Peter had not seen before, came along and promptly entered one of the flowers. When she came out Peter was ready with a question. "Did you find any sweetness in there?"

"Of course I did," she replied rather testily.

"Do you suppose I would have wasted my time in there if there hadn't been sweetness? That was a foolish question."

Peter suspected that she was right, and that it was a foolish question. "They are beautiful flowers, aren't they?" he ventured.

"I suppose they are," replied the Bee, "though I don't know that they are any more beautiful than their red cousins over on the edge of the Green Forest."

My, you should have seen Peter prick up his ears. "Do you mean that there are other Lilies in bloom now?" he asked eagerly.

But already the Bee was out of hearing. She was too busy to waste time gossiping. Peter waited around awhile, hoping she would return. But she didn't. So he decided that he would go look for those other Lilies himself. She had said that they were growing on the edge of the Green Forest.

"If they are as big and showy as these, I ought to be able to find them without much trouble," muttered Peter, as he headed for the Green Forest.

When he reached the edge of it he looked eagerly everywhere, but no sign of a Lily did he find. You see he had not reached the Green Forest at the right place. Of course he was disappointed. But Peter knows that a thing worth finding is worth

56　　　Look at the picture of the Meadow Lily on page 130.

looking for, so he refused to be discouraged. He hopped along through the thickets on the edge of the Green Forest until he at last came to a place where the ground was high and dry. There to his delight he found what he was in search of. Growing on the edge of the thicket were plants with leaves which in shape and arrangement around the stalk were much like those he had just left. The plants were not quite as tall, but still the tops were well above Peter's head.

But of course it was the flowers that Peter was most interested in. Some plants bore only one blossom, while others had three or four, and one had five. Peter knew at once that they were cousins of the Meadow Lily. No one could mistake one of these flowers for a member of any other family. But they were quite different from their nodding bell-like cousins. These flowers did not nod. Each stood erect, and was like a cup with a curving brim. As with the Meadow Lily each flower had six petal-like parts. The color was a bright orange-red, and within, near the base, was more or less yellow spotted with dark purple.

While these petal-like parts were broad in the middle and had somewhat rounded points, at the base they were so narrow that it looked almost as if each grew on a stem. As usual Peter counted the stamens. There were six, and these were long and pink, each with a little brown package of pollen on the tip. The pistil also had a brown tip.

Never having heard the name of this Lily, Peter promptly gave it a name himself. He called it the Wood Lily,[57] and this happens to be the very name by which it is known to very many people. It is also called the Red Lily, the Flame Lily and the Philadelphia Lily.

His curiosity having been satisfied, Peter's conscience suddenly pricked him. He remembered how he really had intended to stay in the dear Old Briar-patch that morning to please little Mrs. Peter. He felt a little ashamed, so he promptly headed back for the dear Old Briar-patch and scampered as only he can scamper when he is in a hurry. And there, to Peter's credit, he remained all the rest of that day.

---

57   Look at the picture of the Wood Lily on page 130.

MEADOW OR FIELD LILY
Lilium canadense

RED, WOOD OR PHILADELPHIA LILY
Lilium philadelphicum

xxiv. Bells of Blue and Others

Peter Rabbit had gone over to the Green Forest for a call on his big cousin, Jumper the Hare. If Peter wants to see Jumper, he has to go to the Green Forest, for that is Jumper's home, and he is such a timid fellow that he rarely even pokes his nose outside of it. Peter didn't find Jumper where he expected to, and so started to look for him. He visited one place after another where Jumper was in the habit of going, but without success. Now Peter had no particular reason for wanting to see Jumper, but when he couldn't find him he grew more and more determined that he would find him. You see, having started to do that thing Peter hated to give up.

So he hopped along farther and farther into the Green Forest until at last he reached a part where he had been only once or twice before in all his life. By this time he had about made up his mind that it would be useless to look farther. He was hesitating whether to keep on or to turn back when who should appear but Jumper himself.

"Hello, Cousin Peter. What are you doing way over here?" exclaimed Jumper.

"I've been looking for you," replied Peter. "And I had just about made up my mind that something had happened to you. What's the news over here in the Green Forest?"

"There is no particular news that I know of," replied Jumper, "unless it is news that the Blue Bells are open."

"Blue Bells!" cried Peter. "What are Blue Bells?"

"If you don't know the Blue Bells, Cousin Peter, it is high time you did," replied Jumper. "If you are not too tired, follow me and I will show them to you."

131

Now Peter was tired, but he promptly forgot it. Curiosity was greater than the mere tired feeling. "Lead the way, Cousin Jumper, and I'll follow," replied Peter, promptly.

So Jumper led the way still farther into the Green Forest until at last they came to a place where the Laughing Brook flowed between high, rocky banks. Jumper led Peter to the edge of the bank. "Look down on that little ledge of rock below us," said Jumper.

Peter looked, and then he drew a long breath of pure delight. That ledge was damp and covered with patches of moss. But what had caused Peter to draw that long breath was a little group of beautiful blue flowers more than half an inch in length swinging in the wind like little bells. So delicate were they and so beautiful was their color that it was no wonder Peter drew that long breath.

The stalks on which they grew were quite long, but so slender that they were almost like fine wires, and the faintest breath of air made them sway back and forth. Some of the stalks were branched and some were single. The leaves scattered along the stalks were long, pointed and so narrow that they hardly seemed like leaves.

As I have said before, each flower was like a little bell. There were no separate petals, but the edge was divided into five rather pointed divisions as if in the long-ago days when the world was young the flowers from which these had descended might have had five separate petals, which for reasons of her own Old Mother Nature had caused to grow together for more than half their length. There were five slender stamens, and a greenish-white pistil. Some of the flowers were almost the color of the blue, blue sky, while others were more purplish.

Jumper had called them Blue Bells. Often they are called Blue Bells of Scotland. Because of their fine stems they are also called Harebells,[58] and occasionally they are called Lady's-thimble. But no name fits them better than the one Jumper had given them. Though the place where Peter had found them was the kind of a place they love best, they are also found on dry, rocky cliffs, sometimes in meadows and in rocky woods. Once in a while

58   Look at the picture of the Harebell on page 133.

BLACK-EYED SUSAN
Rudbeckia hirta

HAREBELL
Campanula rotundifolia

FIREWEED
Epilobium angustifolium

GREAT MULLEIN
Verbascum Thapsus

they will be found in sandy fields.

For a long time Peter and Jumper visited together on the top of that bank where they could admire the Blue Bells while they gossiped. "Do you know of any other flowers I haven't yet seen?" asked Peter, at last.

"Have you seen the Showy Lady's-slipper[59] yet?" Jumper inquired.

Peter scratched his head as if in doubt. "I don't know," said he. "I've seen the Pink Lady's-slipper and the Yellow Lady's-slipper and the White Lady's-slipper. Is there any other?"

"I should say there is!" exclaimed Jumper. "Those are all lovely, but wait until you see the Showy Lady's-slipper. That is the loveliest of all. Come along with me and I'll show it to you."

Jumper led the way down along the bank of the Laughing Brook. By and by they came to a swamp where the ground was very wet and soft, and where ferns and various plants grew high and close together. Into this swamp Jumper hopped with Peter right at his heels. "There!" cried Jumper, at last. "What do you think of that, Peter Rabbit?"

He had stopped before a stout plant about two feet high. The stalk was covered with tiny hairs like fine down, and the leaves which sprang out from it all the way to the top were also downy. In appearance they were very like the leaves of the Yellow Lady's-slipper, and had there been no flowers on the plant, Peter would have known it at once for a member of the Lady's-slipper family.

But there were flowers. There were two at the top of this particular plant. On another plant a little way off was one, and on a third plant there were three. "What did I tell you?" cried Jumper, triumphantly.

"You told me the truth," replied Peter. "It is the loveliest Lady's-slipper of all. I am so glad you brought me over here. Not for anything would I have missed seeing it."

In general shape the flowers were much like those of the Yellow Lady's-slipper. But the two side petals, instead of being long, narrow and twisted, were fairly wide with rounding points,

---

59   Look at the picture of the Showy Lady's-slipper on page 135.

SHOWY LADY'S-SLIPPER
Cypropedium hirsutum

SWAMP MILKWEED
Asclopias incarnata

and were pure white. The sepals were also white, and broad and spreading. But it was the big pouch or lip which caused Peter to exclaim right out. It was white, beautifully marked with pink spots and stripes. Showy this flower certainly is, but at the same time it is delicately beautiful. These flowers also have a delightful fragrance.

Peter parted with Jumper there in the swamp and kept on along the Laughing Brook through the swamp, and finally out to the Smiling Pool on the Green Meadows. He had it in mind to pay his respects to Grandfather Frog, but when he reached the Smiling Pool he forgot all about Grandfather Frog. Seeming to float on the surface of the water were beautiful great white flowers with hearts of gold.

"Pond Lilies!" cried Peter, delightedly. "I didn't know it was time for them yet."

"Chug-arum!" exclaimed a deep, gruff voice. "Of course it is time for them. They have been in bloom for a week. If you visited your old friends a little oftener, you wouldn't be behind the times, Peter Rabbit." It was Grandfather Frog, who was sitting on a big green lily pad a little way out from shore.

"I know it, Grandfather Frog," said Peter. "I know it. But I can't be everywhere at once, and there is so much to see these beautiful June days. How lovely those Lilies are! They look as if they are simply floating on the water, but of course that cannot be."

"Of course not," replied Grandfather Frog. "They have long, hollow, rubbery stems which go clear down to the roots in the mud at the bottom of the Smiling Pool."

Peter looked out at the many-petaled blossoms longingly. Some of them he could see were slightly tinged with pink, but most of them were pure white. "Tell me, Grandfather Frog," said he. "Have they any scent?"

"I should say they have!" replied Grandfather Frog. "They have a lovely scent, and that is why they are often called the Sweet-scented White Water Lily.[60] You can talk all you please about your land flowers, but you can't make me believe that

---

60   Look at the picture of the White Water Lily on page 102.

there are any lovelier than these. Do you know that they close at night, Peter Rabbit?"

"Do they?" asked Peter.

"They certainly do," replied Grandfather Frog. "That is, they do for two nights after first opening. The third night they do not close, but remain open until they fade. You see, they bloom for three days. They love the sunshine. But they open just the same even if the sun isn't shining.

Now tell me truly, Peter, have you seen anything lovelier this summer?"

Peter thought of all the lovely flowers he had seen, but he had to confess that he had seen nothing more lovely than these beautiful white blossoms surrounded by their broad, green leaves which, like themselves, seemed to float on the water. Once a Merry Little Breeze lifted one of these leaves so that Peter saw the under side of it, and to his surprise he discovered that instead of being green it was reddish.

Peter remained long enough to see some of those Lilies begin to close. Then he decided that he had seen enough for one day and that it was high time for him to return to the dear Old Briar-patch.

xxv. The Merry Little Breezes Help Peter

ABUSY month is June in the Green Forest, on the Green Meadows, in the Old Pasture, everywhere. Of all the months of the year it is the busiest. By the middle of June most of the feathered folk have families, either just starting out in the Great World or almost ready to start out. Most of the little people who wear fur are teaching their children those lessons which they must learn before going out in the Great World for themselves. And in no month are there such hosts of flowers to keep the Butterflies, Bees and other insects busy from daylight to dark.

It was now well past the middle of June, yet Peter Rabbit's interest in the flowers was as great as when, in the early spring, he had first started out to get acquainted with them. In fact, it was even greater, for each new find was always in the nature of a surprise. Always it was different from any flower he had seen before and added to his wonder that Old Mother Nature could have created such a variety, each adapted perfectly to the conditions surrounding it. And with the finding of each he wondered what the next one would be.

Not a day passed that Peter did not find one or more flowers he had not seen before. On the day following his visit to Jumper the Hare in the Green Forest he went to a part of the Green Meadows where the ground was low and damp. Farmer Brown had dug a ditch down there to drain off the water. Beside this ditch were growing many plants and small bushes. Peter paid no attention to these for his mind was on something else. It was just chance that caused him to look up just as he was passing a straight little shrub about three feet high and somewhat branched near the top. He stopped abruptly. Above his head standing straight up was a long, pointed cluster of feathery flowers just faintly touched with pink.

"Hello!" exclaimed Peter. "This is a new one and I nearly passed it. I wonder what it can be. My, but it is pretty!"

"You ought to know what it is, Peter Rabbit!" cried a Merry Little Breeze. "You must have seen it here last year and the year before, for it has been growing here ever since this ditch was dug."

I suppose I ought to know," replied Peter, just as there are many other things I ought to know. But, you see, I never was interested in flowers until this year, and so never took any notice of them. What did you say is the name of this one?"

"I didn't say," replied the Merry Little Breeze, rumpling up Peter's fur.

"Well, say it now," begged Peter. "There isn't any use in finding a flower and not being able to name it."

"True enough," replied the good-natured Merry Little Breeze. "True enough, Peter. Most people call this the Meadowsweet.[61] Some call it Quaker Lady, though why I don't know. Others call it Queen-of-the-meadow, which, when you come to think of it, isn't such a bad name. But its most common name is Meadowsweet."

"Is that because it is sweet smelling?" inquired Peter. "Those flowers are so far above my head that I cannot smell of them."

"No," replied the Merry Little Breeze. "There is very little odor to them. I guess whoever chose that name did so because they look as if they ought to be fragrant."

Peter tipped his head back and studied those flowers as best he could. The tall, straight, woody stalk was smooth and of a reddish color. The leaves, which grew rather closely for almost its whole length, were oval in shape and the edges were cut into fine teeth. Above the last leaf the tiny flowers grew in little clusters on short stems springing out from all sides of the stalk, and these little clusters in turn formed a big pointed cluster.

The dainty little flowers, crowded close together, were not more than a fourth of an inch across and had five slightly curved and rounding petals. Each tiny flower had many long, rosy stamens and several pistils. It was the great number and length of

---

61   Look at the picture of the Meadowsweet on page 140.

AMERICAN OR GREAT RHODODENDRON
Rhododendron maximum

MEADOWSWEET OR QUEEN OF THE MEADOW
Spiraea laiifolia

the dainty stamens that gave the big flower cluster a feathery appearance just as was the case with the Foamflower Peter had found some weeks before.

Many flies and insects were busy among these little flowers, for though they were not sweet smelling they contained plenty of sweet nectar for those who could get it.

The Merry Little Breeze, which simply couldn't keep still, had danced away, leaving Peter to find out what he could for himself. Just as Peter had made up his mind that he had learned all he could by just looking and was trying to decide where to go next the Merry Little Breeze came dancing back. "Have you seen the Milkweed yet?" cried the Merry Little Breeze.

Peter shook his head. "No," said he. "I don't believe it is in bloom yet."

"Yes, it is," cried the Merry Little Breeze. "I saw it only a few minutes ago."

"Tell me where that I may see it too," cried Peter, eagerly.

The Merry Little Breeze came close to Peter, and whispered in one of his long ears as if the matter were a secret, which of course it wasn't at all. "Follow your nose, Peter, straight along the side of this ditch, and use your eyes." Once more the Merry Little Breeze rumpled Peter's fur and then danced away across the Green Meadows.

Slowly Peter hopped along beside the ditch. He knew that he would recognize the Milkweed plant as soon as he saw it, even though the blossoms might not yet be open. Ever since he could remember Peter had known the Common Milkweed,[62] for with its tall, rather stout-looking stalk, with long, rather thick, oval leaves, smooth and grayish-green above and downy and silvery beneath, growing out in pairs from opposite sides at regular distances apart, it is unlike any other plant. More than once had he found one of these plants broken, and always the hollow stalk was filled with a milky white, sticky juice. It is this milky looking juice which gives the plant its name.

Peter had gone only a little way when he saw just ahead of him one of these plants. Now of course the first thing he did

---

62   Look at the picture of the Common Milkweed on page 135.

was to look for flowers. He was not disappointed. Springing out from between the upper leaves were two or three large, loose bunches of small purplish-pink flowers. At least, that is the color they appeared to be at first glance. If Peter had looked closely enough he would have found that the base of each of the petal-like parts was greenish, above this white, and finally the purplish-pink which gave the general color to the mass.

Half a dozen Butterflies were fluttering around these clusters of flowers, and Peter knew by that that they contained plenty of nectar. Could he have looked at one of those little flowers very closely, he would have found that Old Mother Nature had formed it very wonderfully to make sure that the visitors to it should be unable to get any of that sweet nectar without paying for it by bringing to it pollen from the last blossom visited. The arrangements for this purpose are almost as wonderful as in the Orchids.

Peter had found the most common of all the Milkweeds, and that is why it is called the Common Milkweed. Later he would find other kinds, for there are very many. But most of them are much alike in general appearance. Late in the summer in place of these bunches of flowers would be big brown pods packed tightly with little seeds, each one attached to a tuft of silky white, fluffy hairs. When the seeds were fully ripe the pods would open, and the first Merry Little Breeze to come along would send those seeds sailing far across the Green Meadows just as the Dandelion seeds sail. It is in this way that the Milkweed spreads so fast.

XXVI. Treasures of the Old Pasture

Sammy Jay had stopped in the dear Old Briar-patch for a bit of gossip and also to see what his sharp eyes might discover there. You know how it is with Sammy Jay. There is no one among the little people who wear feathers or fur who does more spying on his neighbors and is more interested in their affairs than this blue-coated scamp. He arrived silently, as is his way when he is spying. It wasn't until he had looked all through the dear Old Briar-patch with those sharp eyes of his and made sure that there was nothing new there that he made his presence known. He spoke suddenly from just above Peter's head.

"Hello, Peter!" said he.

Peter, who had been sitting half asleep, jumped at the sound of that harsh voice. "What are you doing, Sammy Jay, trying to scare a fellow to death?" he demanded rather crossly.

Sammy chuckled. It always tickles him to scare people. "Not at all, Peter. Not at all," said he.

"You must be nervous this morning. I didn't expect to find you at home. How does it happen you are not out looking for flowers?"

"I've found so many that I don't believe there can be any more," replied Peter, still speaking rather crossly.

Sammy Jay chuckled again. "That shows your ignorance, Peter Rabbit," said he. "I don't suppose there is a day passes during this month that some new flower cannot be found by those who know where and how to look for them. I saw a couple this morning which I hadn't seen before this year, though that is probably because I hadn't been where they are."

Peter pricked up his ears. "Where did you see them?" he demanded.

"Over in the Old Pasture," replied Sammy. "They were pink," he added.

Peter turned up his wobbly little nose. "Pasture Roses," said he. "I found them some time ago."

"Nothing of the kind," retorted Sammy Jay, rather sharply, for he didn't like Peter's tone of voice. "Don't you suppose I know a Rose when I see it? Besides, I said that I saw two, and they were not at all alike and not at all like a Rose."

Once more Peter became interested. "What were they like?" he asked rather eagerly.

"I'm not going to tell you, Mr. Smarty," replied Sammy. "Go find them for yourself, if you want to know what they are like."

"In what part of the Old Pasture did you say you saw them?" inquired Peter.

"I didn't say, and I don't intend to say. They are there for anyone who wants to look at them." And without another word Sammy spread his blue wings and flew away.

He was hardly out of sight before Peter was on his way to the Old Pasture. You see Peter couldn't bear to think that Sammy Jay had found flowers of which he knew nothing. "He might have told me where to look," grumbled Peter, as he hopped along, lipperty-lipperty-lip. "The Old Pasture is a big place, and I may hunt all day without finding them. However, I may as well be over there as at home doing nothing."

But Peter didn't have to hunt all day. In fact, he found the first one on the very edge of the Old Pasture. It was his good fortune to reach the edge of the Old Pasture at the place where an old stone wall divided the Old Pasture from the Green Meadows. Along this old wall bushes grew thickly. Even before he was quite there Peter saw something pink in the bushes, and at once became much excited. Could that be one of the pink flowers that Sammy Jay had seen?

When he was near enough to see clearly he discovered a big, bell-shaped flower which was pink and white. The outer edge had five scallops or points. The small part of the bell was white, while the upper and spreading part was pink with a white strip running down into the heart of it, from each one of the points. The flower was so far above Peter's head that he could not see into it, and so could not see the five stamens which it contained.

"I didn't know there was any bush with a flower at all like this," said Peter, talking aloud to himself.

"There isn't. At least if there is, I don't know it," buzzed Lady Bumblebee, so close to one of Peter's long ears that he ducked his head.

"Well, isn't that flower right up there on a bush?" demanded Peter.

"It is and it isn't," buzzed Lady Bumblebee. "Use your eyes a little. Don't you see that there are two kinds of leaves up there? One kind belongs to that bush. The other kind, those that are shaped like an arrowhead, are on a vine, and that vine is climbing all over the bush. That flower belongs to the vine, not to the bush. Up in Farmer Brown's garden I've seen flowers that look very much like this one. They open just in the morning and are called Morning-glories. I guess this flower here belongs to the same family."

Lady Bumblebee had made a very good guess.

The flower Peter was looking up at was the Wild Morning-glory,[63] or Great Bindweed, also called Hedge Bindweed. In some places it is called Lady's Nightcap. The reason it is called Bindweed is because it grows on a very fast-growing vine that twists around bushes and plants so tightly that often it chokes them. It is very fond of climbing over old stone walls and fences, and often is found trailing over the ground. If you have ever seen the Morning-glory in a garden you cannot mistake the Bindweed when you find it.

"Well," said Peter, "I've found one of Sammy Jay's two pink flowers, so now I'll go hunt for the other. I haven't the least idea where to go, so I suppose one place is as good as another."

So Peter hopped along aimlessly here and there, following old cow paths which twisted and turned through the Old Pasture. He was beginning to be discouraged and was thinking of turning back when he drew near a part of the Old Pasture which the year before had been swept over by the Red Terror, which we call fire. Peter remembered how black and dreadful that place had looked. "It will be of no use to keep on in this direction,"

63   Look at the picture of the Wild Morning-glory on page 146.

GREAT BINDWEED OR WILD MORNING-GLORY
Convolvulus sepium

PICKEREL WEED
Pontederia cordata

thought Peter. Then desire to see if the place still looked as ugly and bare as he remembered it led Peter to keep on.

When he reached this place, he was delighted and surprised to find that it was no longer a black waste. The bushes were still bare and black, for they were dead. But everywhere grass and green plants were springing up so that the ground no longer appeared a blackened waste. But an even greater surprise awaited Peter. Growing all about in the open places, where the Red Terror had burned most fearfully, were tall plants varying from twice as high as was Peter, when he sat up, to three and four times as high. Long, narrow leaves which made Peter think of the leaves of the willow tree grew out from the stalk on very short stems.

But Peter gave the leaves hardly a glance, for above them were pink flowers growing in a long, loose cluster. Only the lower ones were open. Above these many buds drooped, or hung with heads down. Those nearest the open flowers were almost ready to open. Above these were buds but half grown. Above these were still smaller buds and so on to the very tip, where the buds were very tiny. Of course this meant that the plant would bear flowers for a long time. As fast as the lower ones faded there would be new ones just above.

The open blossoms were a beautiful pink. Each flower had four wide-spreading, rounded petals which were broadest above the middle. Each of these flowers was about an inch across. Each contained eight stamens and a single pistil which near the bottom was hairy. The tip of the pistil was divided into four parts. Peter had found the first of these flowers to blossom. Had he been a week later these first blossoms would have dropped, and in place of them he would have found little narrow, purplish pods which later would split open and set free tiny seeds attached to a downy, silky substance, which the Merry Little Breezes would send floating far away.

It was the Great or Spiked Willow-herb which Peter had found, this name being given to it because of its willow-like leaves. A far more common name for it, however, is the Fireweed,[64] for there is no other flower which so quickly follows where the Red Terror has been. It is in such places that it delights to grow, and

[64]   Look at the picture of the Fireweed on page 133.

its bright masses do much to make beautiful the places which fire has blackened and laid waste.

When he had admired the Fireweed to his heart's content Peter decided that he had just about time enough to run over to the Green Forest, so away he went, lipperty-lipperty-lip. He didn't really expect to find any more flowers over there, but of course he kept his eyes open. It is well that he did. Otherwise he might have missed a most charming little flower.

He was hopping along rather aimlessly where the ground was dry, but where decayed leaves had made it fairly rich, when off at one side he saw some white, waxy little flowers on curved stems a few inches above the ground. Hurrying over to them, he discovered that each flower had five petals and that some were pinkish instead of pure white. The pistil was very large and thick and green. Around it were ten stamens. As he drew close to them Peter's wobbly little nose discovered that these flowers had a delicate fragrance. The little blossoms grew in a cluster at the top of a smooth stem which seemed to spring out from the center of an upper circle of leaves at the top of a short reddish stalk. Below this circle of leaves other leaves grew.

It was when he looked at these leaves that Peter squealed right out with pleasure. He knew that plant. He knew it at once, for it was one of the very few plants that remained green all winter. The leaves were rather thick, a dark shining green, with white markings along the veins and were lance-shaped and toothed around the edges. It was the Spotted Pipsissewa, or Spotted Wintergreen.[65]

Had Peter looked more closely, he would have discovered that what seemed to be the stalk of the plant was really a branch, and that the main stalk crept along the ground like a vine, sometimes partly buried in the soil, the branches standing upright like separate little plants. Some bore flowers and some did not. It is a member of the Wintergreen family.

"Well, I have learned something," said Peter, when at last he started for home. "I didn't know until now that this plant has flowers. I'm so glad I came over here."

---

65   Look at the picture of the Spotted Wintergreen on page 149.

SPOTTED WINTERGREEN
Chimaphila maculata

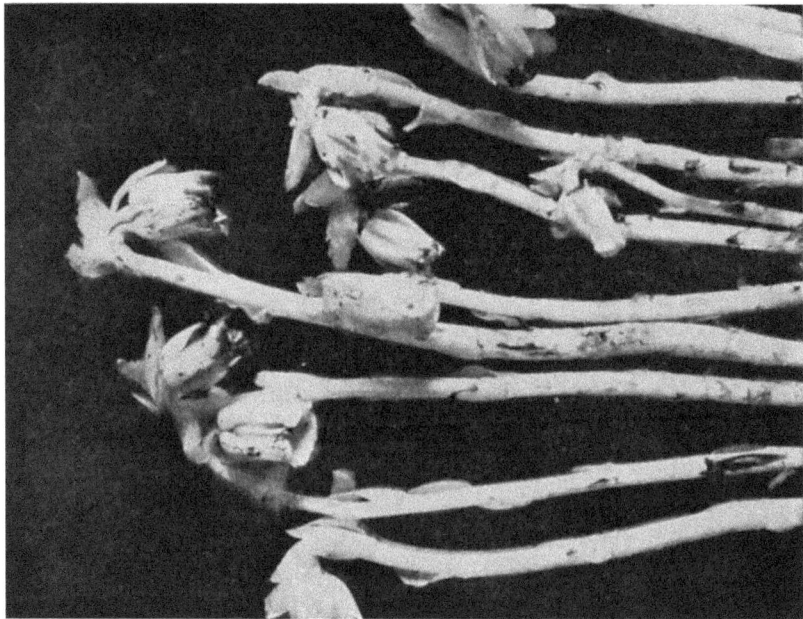

INDIAN PIPE
Monotropa uniflora

XXVII. HONEYBALLS AND LEAFLESS PLANTS

"Down in the swamp where the Buttonbush grows,
   Down in the swamp where the Honeyballs are,
Bees hum their joy, and in gay colored crowds
   Butterflies gather from ever so far."

"WHAT IS that?" demanded Peter Rabbit, pricking up his long ears. "What is that you are saying, Little Friend?"

Little Friend the Song Sparrow cocked his head on one side and his bright little eyes twinkled as he looked down at Peter Rabbit. "I was just talking to myself, Peter," said he. "I have just been over in the swamp and I was thinking of the things I saw there. There are many interesting things in a swamp, Peter; things a great many people miss because they are afraid of getting their feet wet."

"Huh!" said Peter. "I'm not afraid of getting my feet wet! What is a Buttonbush, and what are Honeyballs?"

"Honeyballs grow on the Buttonbush, and the Buttonbush grows in the swamp, and that's all I'm going to tell you," replied Little Friend. "If you want to know more, ask the Bees and the Butterflies."

Little Friend flew away before Peter could ask another question, and a few minutes later Peter heard his tinkling song from over near the Laughing Brook. "Honeyballs," said Peter to himself. "Honeyballs. Now what can they be? The name sounds as if they must be sweet. I suppose if I want to find out about them I'll have to go over to the swamp. I haven't the least idea what to look for, and I don't know how I'm going to know those Honeyballs if I find them. Little Friend said they grow on a bush, and that is all I have to go by. I haven't anything else to do, so I may as well see if I can find them. I would like to know what a Honeyball looks like."

So away went Peter for the swamp. When he got there of course he had no idea in what direction to go. For some time he simply wandered about aimlessly. Every bush he came to he looked at closely. Of course he was looking for Honeyballs, though he hadn't the least idea what Honeyballs were like. He was discouraged and about ready to give up the search when from a point just to one side he heard the humming of Bees. Looking in that direction, he caught a glimpse of a Butterfly. Then he remembered what Little Friend the Song Sparrow had said about the Bees and the Butterflies gathering around the Honeyballs. Perhaps you can guess how eagerly Peter hurried towards the sound of that humming.

He stopped beside a bush three or four feet high. On it were many creamy white balls, and Peter didn't need to sniff the sweet fragrance from them to know that these were flowers. Bees and Butterflies and many other insects were hovering about them or alighting on them. Sure proof that they were filled with nectar. Peter didn't need to be told that he had found the Honeyballs.

Each ball or flower head was about an inch across and was made up of a great number of tiny tubelike flowers packed closely together. From the heart of each tiny tube a long pistil stood out. If Peter had known anything about such things, he might have been reminded of little round cushions stuffed full of pins. Besides being called Buttonbush[66] and Honeyballs it is called Globeflower and Riverbush. It blooms practically all summer. Sometimes this bush grows as high as twelve feet.

When Peter started on he headed for the Green Forest which the swamp joins. He was still thinking of the Honeyballs when he left the swamp to enter the Green Forest. The ground was wet and rich, but it was not muddy nor was there standing water as in the swamp. Almost at once Peter saw a tall, stately plant that put all thought of the Honeyballs out of his head. The leaves of this plant grew in clusters around the stem, three to nine in a cluster. They were long, narrow and tapering, and the edges

66   Look at the picture of the Buttonbush on page 171.

were cut into little teeth.

But Peter hardly gave the leaves a look. It was the top of the plant that interested and delighted him. Growing from the very top were three or four long spikes crowded with tiny white flowers. Peter had to sit up and tip his head as far back as he could in order to see them. These spikes were smaller toward the tips, and some of the tips bent over. The tiny flowers were crowded closely the whole length of these spikes. Each little flower was in the shape of a tiny tube with the outer edge in four rounded scallops. Standing out from each were two stamens and a pistil.

That those little tubes contained nectar Peter knew by the Bees and insects busy about them. Looking about, Peter discovered another plant of the same kind. The flowers on this instead of being white were slightly bluish; otherwise they were the same.

What the name of the plant was he had found Peter didn't know. It was a plant with several names. Some people call it Culver's Root.[67] Some call it Culver's Physic. Some call it Bowman's Root, and by some it is known simply as Blackroot. It is said that the Indians and early settlers used to make use of this plant as a medicine. Later Peter found this plant growing on the edge of the Green Meadows where it was damp, and also along an old road.

Going on into the Green Forest, Peter hopped about this way and that for some time without finding any new flowers. At last he came to that part of the Green Forest where the pine trees grow. Peter always liked to hop about under the pines on the thick carpet of brown needles. He didn't expect to find any flowers there and wasn't looking for them. So his surprise was all the greater when he came upon a little group of the strangest plants he had yet found.

Flower and stalk were of one color, or perhaps I should say that they were colorless, for they were waxy white. The stalk was quite thick and had no leaves. Here and there along it were small white scales. The flower grew from the top of the stalk, which bent sharply so that the flower hung head down as if in shame. It had four or five oblong petals, which seemed more like scales than petals. They overlapped each other so as to make

67   Look at the picture of Culver's Root on page 153.

CULVER'S ROOT
Veronica virginica

WILD CARROT
Daucus Carota

the flower bell-shaped. Within were eight or ten hairy stamens.

They did not seem like real flowers, but more like white ghosts of flowers hiding from the sunshine. Had Peter scraped away the pine needles and a little of the earth from around them, he would have found that each plant was springing from a ball of fine, brittle rootlets which had no real home in the earth. Peter stretched out his wobbly little nose and touched one of the flowers. There was no odor, and he didn't like the feeling of it. It was cold.

He knew what he had found, for often he had seen them before. He had found the Indian Pipe,[68] or Ice Plant, also called Ghost Flower and Corpse Plant.

Had one of those flowers been picked, it would have turned black in a very short time, or had the sun been able to creep in there and shine fully on them, the same thing would have happened. Occasionally this plant is tinted with pink, but this is not often. It is one of the lowest orders of plant life.

Of course Peter didn't know these things, and he rather admired the curious little white plants growing where no other flowers grew. But he couldn't help noticing that there were no Bees or Butterflies about these. They were left quite to themselves. In fact, Peter himself soon lost interest in them and went on his way. Had he returned that way later, he might have found that those little plants had lifted their heads. These are held proudly erect to bear the seeds.

---

68   Look at the picture of the Indian Pipe on page 149.

XXVIII. A Lesson in Beauty

"The rarest beauty often lies
In things so common that the eyes
Of those who pass, unseeing, miss
The very thing they seek, I wis."

"WHAT DO you mean by that?" demanded Peter Rabbit of Carol the Meadowlark, who had alighted on a fence post not far from where Peter happened to be sitting.

"I mean," replied Carol, "that there are some things which are very beautiful, yet so common that few people think of them as being beautiful at all. If they were rare no one would pass them without thinking of their beauty."

"What, for instance?" asked Peter.

"That plant growing just a few feet back of you," replied Carol.

Peter turned quickly. Sure enough, there was a plant with a slender, hairy stalk about two feet high, and leaves cut into such fine leaflets that they seemed to be almost lacy. At the top of a long stem was a broad, flat, circular, white flower head. It was the first Peter had seen, but he knew it instantly. "Pooh!" said he. "That is nothing but a Wild Carrot![69] Pretty soon you'll see them everywhere. There's nothing beautiful about that."

Carol the Meadowlark chuckled happily. "I thought you'd say that," said he. "All your life you have seen the Wild Carrot so often that it has become common to you, and I'll venture to say that you never once have looked at it closely or given it a thought. Yet there are few flowers I know of with more real beauty in them."

69   Look at the picture of the Wild Carrot on page 153.

Peter looked over at that plant with new interest. Then slowly he hopped over for a closer look. He didn't like to admit that Carol was right, but he had to. The longer he looked, the more the beauty of this common weed, for this is what farmers call it, grew on him. It was beautiful. There was no use in denying it. That big, flat flower head was made up of very many tiny, delicate flowers, so dainty that the whole thing was not unlike a piece of fine lace. In fact it is often called Queen Anne's Lace.

Peter sat up close to it that he might see it better. Then he discovered that this big flower head was made up of many small groups, each little group on a separate stem. These little groups were composed of tiny, five-parted flowers with the smallest of yellow-tipped stamens. The flowers on the outer edge of the flower head were larger than those near the center.

Then he discovered something which he never had noticed before because he had never stopped to really look at a Wild Carrot. In the very center was a single, tiny flower wholly different from the others. Instead of being white it was dark purple.

But if until now Peter had known nothing of this plant, which all his life he had unheedingly passed, there were plenty of others who knew all about it and loved it. As he sat looking at it, it seemed to him that he never had seen so many kinds of insects around a flower as he now saw visiting that Wild Carrot. There were many kinds of Flies, small Bees and Wasps, and flying insects coming and going, and he knew by this that each of those tiny flowers contained nectar easy to obtain by even those with the shortest of tongues.

When Peter finally turned away he was honest enough to admit that Carol the Meadowlark had been right, and he wisely resolved that in the future he would not make the mistake of taking no notice of things because they were common and familiar. The Wild Carrot is beautiful, and the more Peter had looked at it, the more beautiful it had seemed. I am afraid, however, that had Farmer Brown come along he would have seen no beauty in it. To him it would have been simply one of the worst pests in his fields, for there is no plant which spreads more rapidly and which is harder to get rid of. It is not a native of America, but has come from Europe to make its home here and take possession of the land. When the flowers fade and the seeds are to be formed, all the little stems that make up the big, flat flower head turn upward to make something very like a nest. From this habit the plant has won the name of the Bird's Nest, though of course no bird uses it for a nest.

Peter was very thoughtful as he left the Wild Carrot. He was wondering how many times he had looked at things without really seeing them, and how often he had passed something interesting without giving it so much as a thought simply because it was common. All the time he kept his eyes open, looking this way and that way that he might not overlook anything.

At last he reached a piece of stony waste ground. "There isn't likely to be anything here worth seeing," muttered Peter, and half turned to go in another direction. As he did so he caught sight of a tall, straight, stout plant growing in the middle of that waste ground. Even at that distance Peter recognized it as an old acquaintance. Turning, he hurried over to see if it bore any flowers yet.

When he reached it he found a thick tuft or rosette of large, pale green leaves, sharply pointed at the tips, fairly broad in the middle and narrow at the base. From the middle of them a thick leafy stalk grew straight up for several feet above Peter's head. There were no stems to the leaves growing out from this stalk, and they were narrower than the leaves close to the ground.

Those leaves were the woolliest leaves of which Peter knew. They were so covered with very fine hairs that they were almost like velvet. The tall, stout stalk also was closely covered with fine hairs. It was as if the whole plant wore a coat of short, fine wool.

Crowded as closely as they could be packed around the upper part of the stalk so as to form a long spike were flower buds. At first Peter thought none was open, but when he hopped around to the other side of the plant he discovered that one was open, and he guessed that this was the very first one. It was light yellow and nearly an inch across. He could count the petals. There were five and they were quite broad and rounded. Looking closely he discovered to his surprise that they were not of equal size. Neither were the five orange-tipped stamens of equal length. Three of these were fuzzy and were shorter than the other two.

The latter were smooth. The pistil was green.

A Bee in search of pollen alighted on the flower. "Buz-z-z-z," said the Bee. "I wish more of these flowers opened at a time. It would save me a lot of work."

"Perhaps more will be open to-morrow," spoke up Peter.

"Certainly. Of course," replied the Bee, rather crossly. "But there won't be more than two or three, or at most half a dozen. Only a few ever open at a time, and if I am not on hand the day they open I miss them altogether. If they remained open two or three days it would help some."

"Don't they?" asked Peter, in surprise.

"No," replied the Bee, shortly. "They are open one day, and that is all. If I hadn't happened along today I would have missed this flower altogether."

"They are so pretty it is a pity they don't last longer," said Peter. "But by the number of buds I guess they make it up in the length of time flowers are to be found. It looks as if there would be flowers on this plant the rest of the summer."

Peter was right. He had found the Great Mullein,[70] also called Velvet or Flannel Plant because of its woolly leaves, and it blooms from June to September. Peter remembered how he had often seen in winter the tall, brown stalks of the Mullein standing above the snow. Later Peter found a near relative, the Moth Mullein, a smaller plant but with flowers as big or bigger. Some were yellow and some were white. They were on separate plants and grew in spike-like clusters. Usually there were no leaves.

---

70   Look at the picture of the Great Mullein on page 133.

xxix. Two Water Lovers

Peter Rabbit sat on the bank of the Smiling Pool, thinking, and, as he thought, he talked to himself, which is a way he has when he thinks he is alone. "It is a queer thing how a fellow can see a thing day after day and not really see it at all," said Peter. "Now every summer since I can remember I have seen the Wild Carrot and the Great Mullein, yet until yesterday I didn't realize that the former is beautiful, and didn't know that the blossoms of the latter open for only one day."

"Chug-arum! There's nothing queer about it, Peter Rabbit. It is always the way with people who do not use their eyes," said a gruff voice.

"Hello, Grandfather Frog!" exclaimed Peter. "I didn't see you at all. I thought I was all alone."

"Chug-arum! That goes to prove what I have just said; you do not use your eyes," retorted Grandfather Frog. "I have been sitting here on this big, green lily pad ever since you arrived. What flower did you say opens for one day only?"

"The Great Mullein," replied Peter. "The flower is yellow and quite large, but it blooms for one day only. Don't you think that is queer?"

"No, I don't," replied Grandfather Frog gruffly. "I am used to flowers that bloom only for a day."

At that Peter's long ears pricked up quickly, you may be sure. "What flowers?" he demanded eagerly. "Tell me, Grandfather Frog, what flowers do you know that open only for a day?"

Grandfather Frog opened his big mouth and laughed. At the same time he rolled his big goggly eyes up at Peter with a funny twinkle in them. "What are those two eyes of yours for, anyway, Peter Rabbit?" he demanded. "You have been looking right at those flowers ever since you sat there, yet you haven't seen them."

Peter rubbed his eyes and rather foolishly stared all about him on the bank of the Smiling Pool. Then he looked down at Grandfather Frog and opened his mouth to demand rather sharply what Grandfather Frog meant. But he closed it without saying a word, for there, just to the right of the big green lily pad on which Grandfather Frog sat, was a spike of bright blue flowers a foot above the water. Of course, they had been there all the time, yet until that instant Peter hadn't seen them at all. You see, he hadn't thought of finding flowers in the Smiling Pool, and he had been so busy thinking of other flowers that he had looked right at these without seeing them at all.

Grandfather Frog laughed again at the foolish look on Peter's face. Peter laughed too. He had to. "Of course you mean those ragged-looking little blue flowers over there," said he. "Is it really true that they bloom only for one day?"

Grandfather Frog nodded. "All those that you see today will be gone to-morrow," said he. "But there will be plenty more to take their places," he added.

Peter hopped a little closer to the water that he might see better. The flowers were very small in the form of little tubes opening out into six petal-like parts not all of the same size, which gave them rather a ragged look. Each little flower was wholly blue, even the stamens and pistil. They grew on a long spike at the end of a large, smooth, stout stem. From halfway up the stem or stalk grew out a single, large, arrow-shaped, rather thick, glossy leaf of dark green. Could Peter have gotten near enough to smell of the flowers, he would have turned up his wobbly little nose, for the scent is not at all pleasant.

"What do you call it?" asked Peter.

"The Pickerel Weed,"[71] replied Grandfather Frog. "At least, that is what I have always heard it called. I believe Pickerel are supposed to lay their eggs under its leaves, but they do that quite as much under the leaves of other water plants, so I guess there isn't any real reason for this name. However, I suppose one name

71   Look at the picture of the Pickerel Weed on page 146.

is as good as another. There is one thing I like about this plant and that is that it keeps blooming all summer. That spike keeps growing longer and longer, and every day new flowers open."

"I'm ever so glad I came over here this morning," said Peter. "I hadn't thought of looking in the Smiling Pool for flowers since the Pond Lilies began to bloom. I don't suppose there are any more here."

"Yes, there are," replied Grandfather Frog. "If you will go up around that little bend you will find a wholly different flower growing in the water close to the shore."

Peter could hardly wait to thank Grandfather Frog properly, he was in such a hurry to see this new flower. He hurried along the bank around the bend, and there, sure enough, in a little cove were flowers wholly different from those he had left. While most of the plants bearing these flowers were growing in the water, a few were not in the water at all, but growing out of the mud at the water's edge. This gave Peter a chance to get as close to them as he pleased.

All the leaves of the plants not in the water were shaped like the head of an arrow. Some were quite narrow and sharply pointed, while others were broader and had more rounded points. But all were of the arrowhead shape. They were rather rubbery and in color a dark green. Looking from those plants on shore to those growing well out in the water, Peter made a surprising discovery. Those in the water had two kinds of leaves! Yes, sir, they had two kinds of leaves! The leaves standing above the water were like those of the plants on shore, but growing beneath the surface of the water were leaves entirely different. These were long and narrow, quite grass-like.

But of course it was the flowers in which Peter was most interested. These were in groups of three along a fairly tall stalk. On some plants the stalks were slender, while on others they were rather stout. The flowers were quite large, being an inch or more across. Each had three sepals and three spreading, rounded, white petals. Each flower grew out from the stalk on a short stem.

Again Peter made a surprising discovery. On some plants the flowers had a cluster of many yellow stamens in the center of each. On other plants the flowers had no pretty yellow centers, for there were no stamens at all. Instead the centers were of green pistils. Those with the stamens had no pistils at all. And then Peter found several plants with both kinds of flowers on the same stalk. Those with yellow centers were the upper flowers, while those lower down on the stalk had the green centers. Of course the yellow-centered flowers, the ones with the stamens, were the prettiest. At least Peter thought so, and I think you would agree with him.

While Peter was still admiring them, who should come stalking along but Longlegs the Great Blue Heron. "What are you doing here, Mr. Curiosity?" Longlegs asked.

"Wondering what flowers these are. Do you know?" replied Peter.

"Of course I know. It would be funny if I didn't. I supposed everybody knew them," declared Longlegs.

"I don't," said Peter honestly. "What are they called?"

"The Arrowhead, the Broad-leaved Arrowhead,"[72] replied Longlegs.

"It is a good name, a very good name," declared Peter, looking at the leaves. "One has only to look at one of these leaves to remember it. My, but it is getting late and I must hurry home! I'm much obliged to you, Longlegs."

"Don't mention it," replied Longlegs, as Peter started off lipperty-lipperty-lip.

---

72   See the picture of the Broad-leaved Arrowhead on page 191.

xxx. Friends by the Wayside

Peter did not go directly home from the Smiling Pool. He went by a roundabout way which took him along an old road. Growing in a dry place beside this road he discovered a tall, rather stout plant, the leaves of which were narrow and pointed, and reminded him of the leaves of the willow tree. Those nearest the ground were longer than those above. They grew thickly all the way up the tall stalk.

Probably Peter would not have given the plant another thought had it not been that he noticed several wilted yellow flowers hanging near the top. They were so wilted that he could get no idea what they had been like.

"Those flowers must have been in bloom yesterday," thought Peter. "It is too bad I didn't come along here then. I wonder if there will be any more in bloom here to-morrow. I wonder if it can be that these are like the Great Mullein and Pickerel Weed, opening only for one day.

Hello, here is another of these plants! And this one is branched. And there is still another without any branches. I wonder what they are. I'll come over here the very first thing to-morrow morning."

Peter had intended to stay at home in the dear Old Briar-patch the rest of that day, but he didn't. No, sir, he didn't. You know Peter is possessed of the wandering foot. Late that afternoon he started out again. It was just as the Black Shadows came creeping out from the Purple Hills. Of course, Peter had no thought of looking for flowers at that hour. He was out on other business altogether. The truth is, he was starting for Farmer Brown's garden to sample some of the tender green things growing there.

His way led him along the same old road he had traveled on his way home that morning. When he reached those tall plants on which he had seen the wilted yellow flowers, he glanced up to see if they still hung there. What he saw put all thought of Farmer Brown's garden out of his head for the time being. At the top of the tall plant he had first discovered was a fully opened blossom. Close to it was another half-opened, and several others which looked as if they were beginning to open. Peter was too astonished to do anything but sit right there and stare at those blossoms. Slowly, very slowly, the half-opened blossom opened wider and wider until it was fully open. Another did the same thing. They opened right before Peter's eyes, for he was so interested and pleased and surprised that he sat there for a long time, long enough for those flowers to get fully open, though they opened so slowly.

Then Peter's wobbly little nose caught a delightfully sweet scent, which he hadn't noticed at all when he was there that morning. He guessed at once that it came from those newly opened flowers. Each flower had four spreading petals of a soft beautiful yellow, and eight long, golden-tipped, spreading stamens. There were also four long, pale yellow sepals, which curved backward.

"There is one thing sure and that is that these flowers cannot have many visitors at this hour," thought Peter. But hardly had the thought entered his head when a night-flying Moth arrived, followed by a second and third. These began at once to suck nectar eagerly from these blossoms. What Peter didn't know was that these Moths have very long tongues, and only such tongues could reach the nectar in these flowers. Perhaps it was for this reason that they opened in the evening instead of during the day. Peter had found the Evening Primrose.[73]

The next day Peter again visited the plants, hoping to find some of those blossoms still open that he might see them better. But he was disappointed. They hung as wilted as the flowers he had seen there the day before. Then he knew that the flowers of this plant bloom only for one evening. Very late in the summer, on a dull day when the light was weak, Peter did find

73   Look at the picture of the Evening Primrose on page 165.

CORN COCKLE OR
RED CAMPION
Agrostemma Githago

YARROW OR MILFOIL
Achillea Millefolium

EVENING PRIMROSE
Oenothera biennis

COMMON BURDOCK
Arctium minus

a few open during the day, but in the early part of the summer he found them only in the evening.

It was near this same old road by which he had found the Evening Primroses that Peter found another old friend the very next morning. "Butter and Eggs!"[74] cried Peter joyfully when he first saw it, and that is the name by which it is most commonly known, though it is also called Eggs-and-bacon, Yellow Toad-flax, Flaxweed and Brideweed. It had been one of Peter's most familiar flower friends every summer since he could remember.

When he stopped to look at it he realized that here was another blossom he had never before really seen because it was so common. Never had he thought of these flowers as being beautiful, and the discovery now that they really were beautiful was a happy surprise.

The light yellow and orange flowers were growing in the form of a spike around the top of a slender stalk a foot or more high. The leaves growing out from that stalk all the way up to where the flowers began were very narrow and pointed at both ends. Indeed, they were much like blades of grass. They, as well as the stalk, were a very pale green.

The flowers were odd in shape. Each was about an inch long. In a way they reminded Peter of the blossoms of the Wild Pea or Lupine, although when he looked at them closely he found they were quite different. Each flower formed at the base a very small, though quite long, tube which is called a spur. This tube opened out into two parts, called lips, the upper one standing up and curving over the lower one and formed of two petal-like parts. The lower lip was spreading and formed of three petal-like parts, the center one being the smallest. On this lower lip was a large orange-colored swelling that nearly closed the throat of the flower and hid the four stamens and pistil. Excepting for this orange-colored part the flower was a clear light yellow.

Lady Bumblebee came along and alighted on the lower lip of one of them. Her weight pressed down the lower lip and caused the throat of the flower to open so that the stamens and pistil could be seen. In she went to suck up the nectar in that spurlike tube, and when she came out she carried away with her some

74   Look at the picture of the Butter and Eggs on page 167.

COMMON MILKWEED OR SILKWEED
Asclepias syriaca

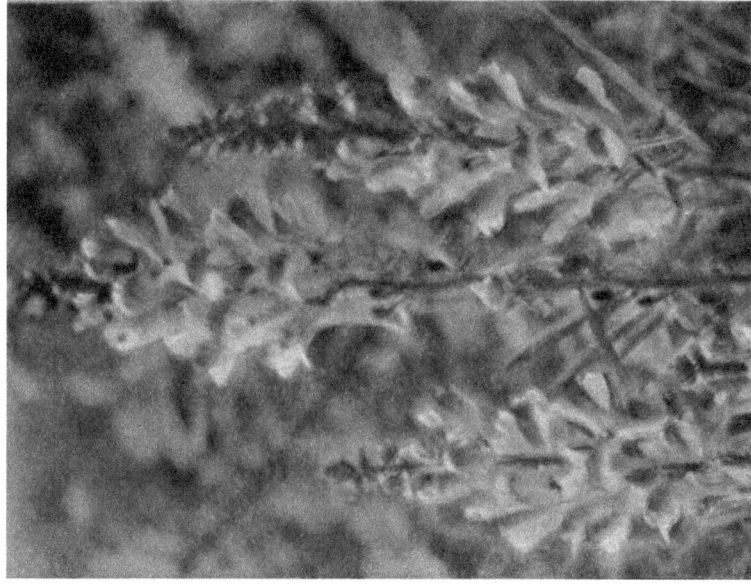

BUTTER AND EGGS
Linaria vulgaris

of the pollen to leave at the next flower she visited.

Watching this performance Peter realized that this common little flower is quite as wonderful as it is beautiful, and when he left to search for other flowers it was with greater respect than ever for common things. A little later in the season he found Butter and Eggs everywhere along the roadsides and in the fields, especially on waste land.

It was quite in order that the next flower Peter found was another very common one known everywhere. It was the Yarrow,[75] also called Milfoil, Nosebleed and Old-man's-pepper. The slender stalk was nearly two feet high, and growing out from it were leaves so finely divided into tiny leaflets that they reminded Peter of ferns. They were curled and feathery and very pleasing to look at.

At the top was a big, grayish-white flat flower head, made up of what seemed like very many small flowers. But when Peter came to look at these closely, he discovered that each of these was in turn made up of tiny flowers, or florets, as they are called, after the manner of the Daisy. The outer ones were white like the so-called Daisy petals, and of these there were four to six around a closely packed head of yellowish or brownish florets, the whole seated in a little green cup. These little flower heads grew on short stems in little groups, and these little groups together made up the big, flat flower head. They gave off a rather pleasant scent which Peter liked.

The Yarrow is found all over America, but is not a native. It was brought here from Europe, where it is also common. In times past it was much used as a medicine and was believed to be helpful in stopping nosebleed. From this it gets one of its names. Some folks confuse it with the Wild Carrot, but if you remember that the latter is like fine lace you will never make that mistake.

---

75   Look at the picture of the Yarrow on page 165.

xxxi. Pests That are Beautiful

J UNE, THE month of flowers, had passed and midsummer
had come. The July heat made Peter lazy. It was much more
comfortable to remain quiet through the day and do his running
about in the cool of the evening and night. But most flowers are
to be found only during the day, and so every once in a while
Peter would slip out of the dear Old Briar-patch early in the
morning and go in search of new flowers. You see, he was so
interested that not even the hot weather could make him give
up altogether. On some of these trips he found no new ones at
all, and this was discouraging. But he knew that some plants do
not bloom until midsummer, and so each time he would start
out with renewed hope that he would find some of these.

He had gone up to the Old Pasture early one morning, and
had hopped this way and that way without finding any flowers
he had not seen before until he had become so discouraged
that he had about made up his mind to go home. In fact, he had
already started in that direction, when in an open place that
was high and dry he came upon a plant a little more than a foot
high which had a slender, stiff and somewhat rough stalk, which
towards the top was much branched. The leaves were rather
long, very narrow and pointed at the tips. They were shiny, and
the upper ones were shorter and smaller than the lower ones.
Each of the branches was in turn branched into many flower
stems, and at the tops of these flower stems were white flowers
that made Peter think at once of little Daisies. Together these
flowers formed a loose cluster.

Of course, being like Daisies, each flower head was made up
of two kinds of flowers, the outer ones snowy white just as in

the Daisy, while the tiny flowers or florets crowded together in the center were a pale yellowish-green. Of the white ones each little flower head had from ten to twenty.

Peter knew it for an Aster right away. It was the Upland White Aster.[76] There are many kinds of Asters, several of them white, but the Upland is the first of the white ones to bloom. The others bloom in August. It reminded Peter that summer was passing rapidly.

It was several days before Peter found another flower which was new to him. This time he happened to be hopping along the edge of Farmer Brown's wheatfield. A spot of bright color in among the wheat plants caught his attention. He guessed right away that it must be a flower and of course he stopped to look.

"This is the last place I would have thought of looking for flowers," muttered Peter, as he made his way in through the wheat. "It is lucky I just happened to glance in here, and it is also lucky that this flower is of such a bright color; otherwise I wouldn't have seen it at all."

By this time he had reached the flower and was where he could have a good look at it. It was about two feet above the ground at the top of a straight, very hairy stalk, and these hairs were whitish. The leaves, which were long, pointed and narrow, were also hairy. The flower stem growing from the top of the stalk was quite long and rather stout.

The flower was large, purplish-red and very pretty. At least, Peter thought so. It was more than an inch across and the large, rounded, broad petals were opened out almost flat. Between the petals were narrow green sepals, almost like leaves, and these were longer than the petals. There were ten stamens and the pistil was divided into five parts. Together these so filled the heart of the flower that only insects with long, slender tongues could reach the nectar at the bottom of the tube.

Looking about, Peter soon found several more of the plants, one or two of which were slightly branched and bore one or two flowers at the end of each branch.

"I don't know what this flower is, but whatever it is, it is pretty. Yes, sir, it is pretty. I like to look at it. I hope I will see it

76   Look at the picture of the Upland White Aster on page 171.

UPLAND WHITE ASTER
Aster ptarmicoides

BUTTONBUSH
Cephalanthus occidentalis

often," said Peter, talking to himself as is his way.

Farmer Brown wouldn't have agreed with Peter at all. You see that flower was the Corn Cockle,[77] sometimes called the Corn Rose, the Red Campion and Crown-of-the-field, a plant which is considered a great pest in grain fields, and one which is poisonous. It is not a native American, but long ago was brought from Europe and has liked this country so well that it has spread all over it. It is a member of the Pink family.

It happened that the very next flower Peter found was also one from Europe, which has liked this country so well that it has spread all over it. He didn't need to be told what this one was. He was acquainted with it. Yes, indeed, he was well acquainted with it. It was a plant for which he had no love at all, for more than once it had caused him no end of trouble. It was the Common Burdock,[78] which is also called Beggar's-buttons. It was the plant which bears what are commonly known as burs, which really are the flower heads gone to seed. Many times had Peter patiently worked pulling them out of his fur.

The plant which Peter found was growing beside a fence. It was a big plant, branching so that it was quite bushy. The stalk was large, round and grooved. The lower leaves were large, broad and somewhat heart-shaped, and the stems of these leaves were hollow. The leaves were woolly on the under side.

At the ends of the branches were the flower heads growing in clusters. The florets were tiny tubes, purplish and white, and rather soft and silky looking as they peeped out from the midst of a thick covering of sharp, spreading bristles with long hooks. Now they were rather innocent looking and pretty green balls, tipped with purple and white. But later they would turn brown and those tiny hooks would cling to whatever touched them, so that it would carry away the whole bur. This is the way in which the plant distributes its seeds.

The burs cling to the tails of cattle and become so entangled that it is hard work to get them out. They cling to the clothing of people who brush against them. Boys and girls love to

---

77   Look at the picture of the Corn Cockle on page 165.

78   Look at the picture of the Common Burdock on page 165.

make balls, baskets, nests and other things of the green burs, for when pressed together they cling closely by means of those little hooks. The roots and fresh leaves are sometimes used for medicine. Peter had once tasted one of those leaves, and once was enough; it was bitter and sour.

xxxii. Peter Finds the Steeplebush

A LITTLE farther along the fence, where he had found the Burdock, Peter came to another tall, stout plant. It was quite four feet high, woolly and had no branches. The leaves were large, broad and pointed. The first thing Peter noticed about them was that some of them had no stems; they grew out from around the stalk and some of them circled the stalk at their bases. It looked almost as if the stalk grew up through these particular leaves. The lower leaves were the largest and these had slender stems.

The second thing Peter noticed was that the leaves were rather thick, rough on the upper sides and woolly on the under sides, and the edges were cut into fine teeth.

But as usual Peter's interest was chiefly in the flowers. These were at the top of the plant, each on a quite long, stout stem. They were yellow, showy and big, some more than three inches across. At the first glance Peter knew that each was really a flower head like the Daisy and the Dandelion. It was one of those flowers which are called composite because made up of a great number of tiny flowers growing together to seem like one.

The round center, as in the Daisy, was composed of ever and ever so many tiny yellowish florets so crowded together as to seem almost like a solid mass. The outer florets, which are commonly called petals, but which properly speaking should be called rays, were quite long and a bright yellow. Instead of standing out straight and evenly, as do the white rays of the Daisy, these long, narrow rays were rather limp and gave the flower head rather a ragged appearance. Just beneath each flower head was a small, pointed leaf.

Peter had found the Elecampane.[79] It has two other names, the Horseheal and the Yellow Starwort. The name of Horseheal was long ago given to it because its roots were formerly much used in making a medicine for horses. But for that matter it might just as well have been called "Manheal," for it is said that for more than two thousand years this plant has been used as a medicine for man.

It was for this reason that it was first brought to this country, for like so many other plants now common it is not a native. At first it grew only in the gardens of the early settlers, but it quickly spread beyond the gardens and in time became what we now call a weed. Although it looks nothing at all like a Thistle it belongs to the Thistle family. So also does the Burdock. Sometimes the Elecampane grows as high as six feet. Sometimes it is only two feet high. Once in a while it is slightly branched, but not as a rule.

"Oh, who has seen the Steeplebush, the Steeplebush, the
        Steeplebush?
Oh, who has seen the Steeplebush that in the pasture grows?
Oh, I have seen the Steeplebush, the Steeplebush, the
        Steeplebush.
Oh, I have seen the Steeplebush that blushes like the Rose."

Peter pricked up his long ears. He knew that voice. Yes, sir, he knew that voice. It was the voice of Brownie the Thrasher. Twice more Brownie sang that little verse before Peter discovered him in the bushes along one side of the old road.

"What is the Steeplebush?" Peter asked eagerly, hurrying over to where Brownie was.

"Run over to the Old Pasture and find out for yourself," replied Brownie teasingly. "You know there is nothing like finding out for yourself."

"All right, I will," declared Peter, when he found that Brownie wouldn't tell him what the Steeplebush was. "But I think you might at least tell me whereabouts in the Old Pasture to look for it."

------

79   Look at the picture of the Elecampane on page 177.

Brownie cocked his brown head on one side and appeared to think the matter over. Finally, when Peter began to get impatient, he seemed to make up his mind. "I will do that much," said he. "Look where the ground is wet."

"But the ground is wet in a number of places," protested Peter.

"So it is. So it is," replied Brownie, nodding his head. "That means that you will have several places to look." And this was all Peter could get from Brownie.

So Peter started for the Old Pasture as fast as his legs could take him. He went straight to a place where he knew that even in midsummer the ground was wet. He looked carefully everywhere, but he found no flower that he had not already seen. Then he hurried to another place where the ground was wet. Once more he was disappointed. He fared no better at the third place.

By this time Peter was discouraged. "I don't believe there is such a thing as a Steeplebush," he grumbled. "I believe Brownie sent me over here just for a joke. If he did, it was a mean trick. Yes, sir, it was a mean trick. I'm not going to waste any more time here."

Having made up his mind to this he started for home. He was hopping along an old cow path on the side of a hill when he came to a muddy place. He hopped out of the path to go around that muddy place. He was halfway around it when right in front of him he saw something which caused him to stop abruptly and catch his breath. He didn't need to be told that he had found the Steeplebush.[80]

A little more than two feet above the ground was a long, pointed, very thick cluster of tiny pink flowers. It was largest at the base and gradually grew smaller and smaller to the pointed top just like a steeple. The flowers reminded Peter at once of the lovely Meadowsweet he had found earlier in the season. They were smaller, but they also had five sepals and five rounded petals, and very many little stamens. No one would need to be told that these two flowers were cousins.

These flowers were a little more closely crowded together than were the flowers of the Meadowsweet, and so did not appear quite so fleecy. But while the flowers of the Meadowsweet

80   Look at the picture of the Steeplebush on page 177.

ELECAMPANE OR
HORSEHEAL
Inula Helenium

HARDHACK OR
STEEPLEBUSH
Spiraea tomeniosa

CARDINAL FLOWER
Lobelia cardinalis

GREAT OR BLUE LOBELIA
Lobelia syphilitica

were white, with just a tinge of pink, these flowers were quite pink, a soft rosy pink. Later in the season Peter found some plants of the Steeplebush with white flowers, but these were comparatively rare.

One thing Peter noticed right away, and this was that the flowers at the tip were the first to open, so of course were the first to fade. The topmost ones were already brown while at the base of the little steeple the buds had not yet opened.

The stalk, at the top of which the flowers grew, was light brown, woolly and rather woody. The leaves were dark green above, but so covered with woolly hairs on the under sides that they appeared whitish. They had short stems that curved upward from the stalk so that the leaves pointed upward. They were oval, pointed at the tips and cut into fine teeth around the edge.

A little later in the season Peter would find the Steeplebush or Hardhack, for that is another of its common names, plentiful in many parts of the Old Pasture, on the edges of the swamp, and along roadside ditches. Like the Meadowsweet and so many other flowers, it is a member of the Rose family, though not looking the least bit like a Rose.

xxxiii. Lady Bumblebee's Friends

THERE WERE some of those July days so hot that nothing could have tempted Peter Rabbit to leave the dear Old Briar-patch until after jolly, round, bright Mr. Sun had gone to bed behind the Purple Hills. Peter had little interest in anything except trying to keep cool. On those days he didn't give flowers a single thought.

But there were other days when the Merry Little Breezes cooled the air, and clouds shut away the rays from Mr. Sun. On such days Peter was often abroad. One of these comfortable days he decided to run over to the Green Forest by way of the swamp where the Laughing Brook enters the Green Meadows.

"When I get over there I'll be comfortable anyway, even if the Merry Little Breezes do stop blowing and the clouds stop hiding the face of bright Mr. Sun," thought Peter.

So he hopped along across the Green Meadows. As he was making his way through the tall grass not far from the edge of the swamp, he came upon some bright, purple flowers which he had not seen before and which caused him to squeal aloud with pleasure. They grew in a group or cluster about a foot and a half above the ground at the top of a light green stalk, which, instead of being round, as are the stalks of most plants, was square. It was somewhat hairy, and growing out from it in pairs were thin, oval leaves, pointed and without stems. Each leaf had three ribs.

Only two or three flowers were open, though there were a number of buds, some of which would open within a day or two. The open flowers were about an inch or a little more across, and at first glance they reminded Peter of something, though just what it was he couldn't think for a few minutes. Then it came to him. They reminded him of the Evening Primrose. Had they been yellow instead of purple, he might at first glance have mistaken them for Primroses. They were on slender, leafy branches which sprang out in pairs, one from each side of the stalk at a point where a pair of leaves grew.

The petals, of which there were four, were rounded and quite broad, joined together for about half their length. There were eight long, purplish stamens, each having on its tip a bright yellow anther, which is, as you know, the name given to the little package of pollen. There was one pistil and this was slender, long and somewhat crooked.

"What a beauty!" exclaimed Peter.

"Of course," said Lady Bumblebee, coming up just in time to overhear him. "That is its name, Meadow Beauty.[81] I'm told that it is often called Deergrass, though why anybody should call such a plant grass is more than I can understand. What are you doing over here, Peter?"

"I am on my way to the Green Forest," replied Peter. "Of course when I found these flowers I just had to stop to admire them. I don't suppose I'll find any new flowers over in the Green Forest, but at least it will be fairly comfortable over there."

"Have you seen the Bee Balm yet?" inquired Lady Bee.

Peter shook his head. "No," said he. "Where is it?" "It has just begun to bloom over in the Green Forest," replied Lady Bee. And then before Peter could ask just where, Lady Bee flew away.

"Bee Balm," said Peter to himself. "I wonder what that is like. I'll hurry right over there and see if I can find it."

So, with a last look at the beautiful Meadow Beauty, Peter started on and entered the swamp. He was hardly beyond the edge of it when he spied what at first he thought to be an old friend, the Common Milkweed. But when he noticed the leaves he knew that it was not. It was a Milkweed beyond a doubt, for there is no mistaking the members of this family, but it was not the Common Milkweed. The leaves were somewhat narrower and came to more of a point. Then, too, the leaves were not so hairy on the under side, and the plant itself was branched.

81   Look at the picture of the Meadow Beauty on page 181.

MEADOW BEAUTY OR DEER GRASS
Rhexia virginica

LARGER OR HYSSOP SKULLCAP
Scuiellaria integrifolia

The flowers were a somewhat deeper purple. It was the Swamp Milkweed,[82] a close relative of the Common Milkweed, but coming into bloom a little later, and a lover of wet, swampy places.

Peter wasted little time there, for his thoughts were of that Bee Balm Lady Bumblebee had mentioned. He hurried on through the swamp into the Green Forest. The Green Forest is a big place, and Peter had no idea in which direction to go. "I may as well go one way as another," thought he. "I think I'll follow up the bank of the Laughing Brook."

He hopped along slowly. It was cooler in there than out on the Green Meadows, but still too warm to hurry. For some distance he found no flowers he had not already seen, and he had just about made up his mind to leave the Laughing Brook when around a little bend he came suddenly upon such a brilliant patch of color that it fairly took his breath away.

Growing in a shady spot near the bank was a clump of tall, rather stout plants, each bearing at the top a big, ragged-looking flower head of bright red. Only the flowers around the outer edge were open, and these were in the shape of slender tubes with very wide mouths, the upper half or lip being sharp-pointed and arched. The lower half or lip was wide-spreading and in three parts, the center one being longer than the others. There were two long stamens and a pistil, and these also were bright red. The flowers were one and a half to two inches long.

At first Peter had eyes only for those odd, brilliant flowers. When at last he looked at the stalks, he discovered that they were square instead of being round. Of course this interested him at once, for you know he already had found a plant with a square stalk that very morning, the Meadow Beauty. Not only were the stalks square, but they were hairy. The leaves were dark green, and were oval with rather long, sharp tips. They grew in pairs from opposite sides of the stalk, and the edges were cut into little saw-like teeth. The stems were hairy. Happening to sniff at these leaves, Peter discovered that they had a pleasant, spicy smell.

Years ago the Indians, so it is said, made tea from these

---

82   Look at the picture of the Swamp Milkweed on page 167.

leaves. And from them the early settlers learned to do the same thing. Perhaps this is why the plant is sometimes called Oswego Tea. Other names for it are Fragrant Balm, Indian's-plume and Mountain Mint. The last name probably comes from the fact that it is a member of the Mint family.

While Peter was still admiring these flowers Lady Bumblebee arrived. "I see you have found it, Peter," said she.

"Found what?" asked Peter.

"The Bee Balm,[83] of course," replied Lady Bumblebee, running her long tongue into one of the flowers.

So that is the name by which Peter knows it, as do very many other people. Perhaps some day you may find it as Peter did beside the Laughing Brook. And if you do, I know you will be as delighted as he was.

---

83   Look at the picture of the Bee Balm on page 184.

AMERICAN BEE BALM OR OSWEGO TEA
Monarda didyma

COMMON, BUR OR SPEAR THISTLE
Cirsium lanceolatum

XXXIV. SURPRISES ALONG THE LAUGHING BROOK

IT HAPPENED that the very next flower Peter found was also a member of the Mint family, though not at all like the showy Bee Balm. He came upon it quite unexpectedly in some tall grass on the edge of a thicket, a place he had never thought to look in before. He at once knew that that plant had been blooming for some time, for already there were some little seed pods on it. It must have begun blooming early in the month before.

The stalk was square like that of the Bee Balm. Moreover it was covered with very fine hairs, as were the rounded, oblong leaves which grew in pairs on opposite sides of the stalk. Those toward the top were smaller than those at the bottom.

The flowers were bright blue and about an inch long. These, like so many other flowers Peter had found, were in the shape of little trumpet-like tubes. Like the flowers of the Bee Balm these had two lips arranged much as in the Bee Balm, excepting that the two lips were of about equal length.

The part which forms the outer covering of the buds and which opens when the flower blooms, and of which the sepals are a part, is called the calyx. The calyx of this flower was also two-lipped, and on the upper lip was a queer-shaped little growth which some people have imagined is like the helmets which the knights of old used to wear. It is from this that the plant gets its name of Skullcap, or Helmet Flower. This particular one was the Larger or Hyssop Skullcap,[84] which is not so common as a very much smaller cousin, but is far more beautiful.

Remembering the delightful surprise the Bee Balm had given

---

84   See picture of the Larger or Hyssop Skullcap on page 181.

him, Peter decided to visit the Laughing Brook once more in the hope that he might be as pleasantly surprised again. He didn't really expect to be, but one of the joys in hunting for flowers is the unexpected. You know unexpected things often give a degree of pleasure which expected things cannot.

Peter hopped along the bank of the Laughing Brook quite a distance without finding any new flowers. Of course he visited the Bee Balm again, for he simply couldn't be near it and not run over for a look at it. This time he went down the Laughing Brook towards where it entered the swamp. One reason he didn't expect to find any new flowers was because he had passed that way only a few days before. But by this time he had learned that a place which had no flowers yesterday may today contain flowers which have just opened for the first time.

It happened just so this time. On the bank of the Laughing Brook, quite close to the water and near the edge of the swamp, he came upon a plant perhaps a little over two feet high. The stalk was straight, smooth and, like several other plants he had recently found, was square. Had he broken it he would have found that it was hollow. The dark green leaves were shaped like lance heads, and grew in pairs on opposite sides of the stalk. The edges were cut into fine teeth.

At the very top of the stalk was a long cluster of flower buds of which only two or three were open, and these were the lowest ones. Though they were white with just a tinge of pink, the instant Peter saw them he was reminded of one of his friends, Spotty the Turtle. Yes, sir, he was so. You see, the shape of each of those open flowers was very much the shape of Spotty's head. It seems queer, but it was so.

These flowers were quite large and, like so many of Peter's recent finds, were tubelike. Like the Bee Balm, each was divided into two lip-like parts forming a wide mouth. But while in the Bee Balm the mouth was wide open, in these flowers it was almost closed, so nearly so that at first glance it seemed to be entirely closed. But it wasn't quite, as Peter saw when he looked closely. It looked that way because the broad upper lip was arched over the lower lip. From between them the five dark stamens, only four of which carried anthers on their tips, barely peeped out.

Peter couldn't really see into the throat of that flower. If he could have he would have found it filled with fine, woolly hairs.

As Peter sat there wondering what he had found this time, Lady Bumblebee came along and alighted on the lower lip of one of those flowers. Her weight caused that lip to drop just like the opening of a mouth, and right inside went Lady Bumblebee. Then that lip closed, and Lady Bumblebee was quite lost from sight. It all happened so quickly that it seemed just as if that flower had opened its mouth and swallowed Lady Bumblebee. It quite startled Peter. Moreover, it looked for all the world as if that flower were chewing Lady Bee. Yes, sir, it looked just like that. If Peter was to believe his eyes alone that was just what was happening. But suddenly that mouth opened again and out came Lady Bumblebee and flew to another blossom where just the same thing happened.

Of course those flowers were not chewing or even trying to chew. When Lady Bumblebee alighted on the lower lip, thus opening the mouth of the flower, she had to force her way in. Now that lower lip was springy, and as she struggled to get in, she made it spring up and down, and this was why it looked as if it were actually trying to eat its visitor.

It was so funny that Peter laughed and laughed. He made up his mind that he would come back there often just to see that funny sight. He knew by the big cluster of buds that that plant would be in bloom for some time to come. Besides the cluster at the top there were some buds just peeping out where some of the leaves joined the stalk.

"I don't know what the name of this plant is," said Peter to himself. "But I know what I'm going to call it. I'm going to call it the Turtlehead.[85] Yes, sir, that is just what I'm going to call it, the Turtlehead."

Other people have had the same thought, and this quaint, pretty flower is quite commonly called the Turtlehead. It is also called the Snakehead. A prettier name for it is the Shell Flower. It is also called Balmony.

---

85   Look at the picture of the Turtlehead on page 188.

TURTLEHEAD OR SNAKEHEAD

Chelone glabra

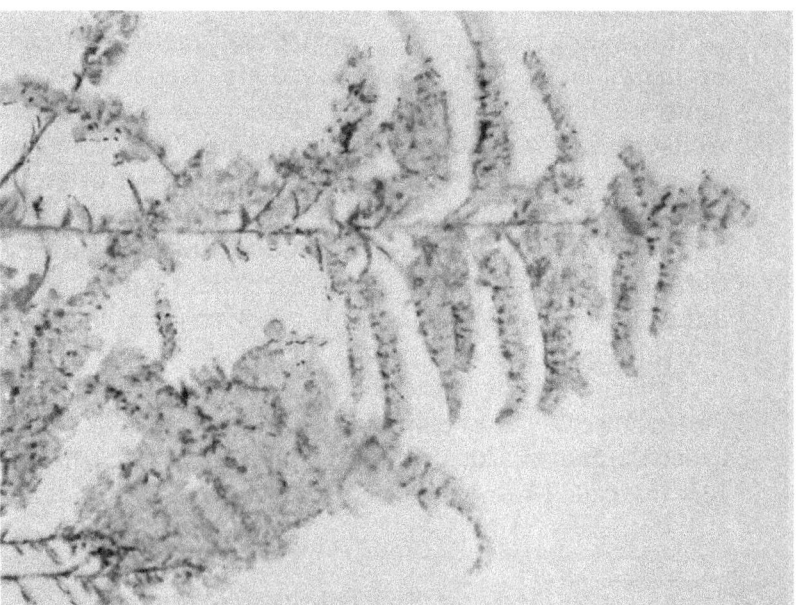

WRINKLED-LEAVED GOLDENROD

Solidago rugosa

xxxv. Wool, Spears and Goldenrod

I<small>T WAS</small> dry. Not for a long time had there been any rain, and everywhere plants were suffering. Wherever Peter went he found them drooping, excepting in the swamp and along the Laughing Brook. It was especially hard on those plants which grew on high and sandy places. Peter felt that it was useless to look for flowers. He felt that if he should find any new ones they would probably be so wilted that he would be sorry he had found them.

But Peter couldn't sit still day after day. He just had to go roaming about some, even though he had nothing special to look for. So it happened that one day he took it into his head to go up in the Old Pasture. He didn't look for flowers. In fact, they never once entered his head. He just wandered about without any purpose at all.

Finally his wanderings brought him to an open place on the side of a hill. It was a place on which jolly, round, bright Mr. Sun shone all day long. It was so dry there that the grass had turned brown and looked as dead as in winter. Right in the middle of it he came upon a plant perhaps a foot and a half high, which seemed not to know that everything about it was drying up.

"Goodness!" exclaimed Peter. "That plant looks as if it has a fur coat!"

It is not to be wondered at that Peter thought so. The stalk seemed to be covered with white wool. It was the same with the under sides of the long, narrow leaves. These were as narrow as blades of grass, those near the bottom being a little broader than those near the top. Above, they were a very pale green, but the undersides were woolly.

Peter didn't know it, but it was this very wool that made it possible for this plant not to mind the dry, hot weather. That wool prevented such moisture as was in the plant from being drawn out as in the case of most other plants.

At the top was a flat head of what appeared to be pearly-white, little flowers with yellow centers. Each was what a White Pond Lily might look like if it were no bigger than one of these. Some of the unopened ones were round and looked like pearls.

Peter touched one of those little flowers, and to his surprise found that what he supposed were petals were not soft and smooth, as had been all petals he had ever touched. Instead, they were dry and stiff. It was as if jolly, round, bright Mr. Sun had dried them instead of wilting them.

The truth is they were not petals at all. They were what are called bracts, which really are tiny leaves changed in form. The true flowers formed the brownish-yellow center. They were tiny florets, each one a little tube, five-parted at the mouth. They do not have both stamens and pistils. The flowers of one plant will have stamens but no pistils, and the flowers of another plant will have pistils, but no stamens.

Peter had found a plant of many names. It is commonly called the Pearly Everlasting.[86] It is also known as the Large-flowered Everlasting, Moonshine, Silverleaf and None-so-pretty. It is a member of the Thistle family, although it does not look in the least like a Thistle. As soon as those flower heads are widely open, the florets in the center turn brownish. Those stiff petal-like bracts remain pearly white, and do not wilt after being picked. That is why the plant is called Everlasting. It may be kept for months looking much the same as when picked.

Not very far from where he found the Everlasting, Peter came upon another plant also in bloom, a plant which he took the greatest care not to touch. Again he was reminded of an acquaintance of his. It wasn't the flower that reminded him this time, but the plant itself. He had come upon one of the Prickly Porkies of the plant world, one which is quite as much respected as is Prickly Porky the Porcupine. It was the Common

---

86   Look at the picture of the Pearly Everlasting on page 191.

BROAD-LEAVED ARROWHEAD
Sagittaria latifolia

PEARLY EVERLASTING
Anaphalis margaritacea

Thistle.[87] It was a big, sturdy plant quite three feet high, and with a number of branches. The stalk was covered with a fine, whitish wool. But to this Peter gave hardly a glance. It was the leaves that interested him most. They were long, dark green, and the edges were cut into all sorts of shapes. Each little projection was armed with a long, stiff spine or point as sharp as a needle.

Here was a plant that was literally covered with little spears, a plant so protected that it had nothing to fear from those who might pass that way. No one who has once carelessly brushed against a Thistle will be so careless again.

On the ends of the branches were big, purple flower heads which looked much like soft, silky plumes quite an inch and a half across. They looked as if bunches of soft, purple silk had been gathered into big, green, egg-shaped cups which were covered with long, very sharp, white little spines.

Later in the season, when the flowers had gone by and the seeds were ripe, those green cups would be filled with a mass of white, fluffy silk, much like that of the Dandelion when it has gone to seed. There are several Thistles and they are all alike in this respect and in having their leaves armed with sharp little needles. The flower heads, however, vary much in size. This one Peter had found is the most common of all and has many names. It is known as the Bur Thistle, Bull Thistle, Spear Thistle, Blue Thistle, Plume Thistle, Button Thistle, Bell Thistle, Bank Thistle and Roadside Thistle. Like all the Thistles, it is a pest to the farmer.

Two members of the same family Peter had found, the Common Thistle and the Everlasting, yet in appearance there was nothing to suggest that there was the least relationship. Before he reached home Peter found a third member of the family, and this was no more like the other two than they were like each other. It was growing near the fence along the edge of the Old Pasture. It was tall, as tall as a tall man. The stalk was very hairy and for its whole length was crowded with lance-shaped, saw-edged leaves slightly wrinkled and very hairy on the under side.

At the top was a broad plume of tiny yellow flowers which

---

87   Look at the picture of the Common Thistle on page 184.

seemed to have caught and held within themselves the gold of the sunshine. Peter knew this flower at first glance, as everybody does. It was the Goldenrod, one of the earliest of the many members of that branch of the Thistle family, for, as I told you before, it is included in that family.

This particular Goldenrod was the Tall or Hairy or Wrinkled-leaved Goldenrod,[88] sometimes called Bitterweed. It cannot be told from its relatives by its height, because it is not by any means always tall. Indeed, sometimes it is not more than a foot high. The fact that it is one of the earliest to bloom, together with the slightly wrinkled form of the leaves, will help you to recognize it. There are so many Goldenrods and some are so much alike that only those who have made a long study of them can tell them apart.

---

88   See picture of the Wrinkled-leaved Goldenrod on page 188.

XXXVI. Along the Edge of the Swamp

PETER WAS tired. In the first place he had wandered a long way from the dear Old Briar-patch. In the second place he had had to do considerable running and dodging, for he had had an unexpected meeting with Reddy Fox. It was so long since he had seen anything of Reddy that he had grown careless, the very worst thing a Rabbit or anyone else can do. The result was that Reddy Fox had surprised him and all but caught him. He had reached a bramble-tangle barely in time. Fortunately, a long time before he had cut some private little paths through that very bramble-tangle, paths just big enough for him and too small for Reddy Fox. There he had found safety.

Though he had rested there for some time, he was still tired when at length he was sure the way was clear and had started on. He had intended to go straight home to the dear Old Briar-patch. But on the edge of the Green Forest, where the ground was somewhat rich and damp, and where there was a thick growth of quite tall bushes, he came to a place just made to rest in. Yes, sir, it was a place made for just that purpose. You see, climbing all over those bushes was a vine, and that vine bore masses of little white flowers with a delicate fragrance that kept Peter's wobbly little nose moving all the time.

It was delightfully shady and cool in there, and Peter decided that he would remain until he was thoroughly rested. Of course he had a splendid chance to look at those flowers to his heart's content. They grew in clusters, each little flower an inch or less across. They varied somewhat, some being almost pure white and others tinged with green.

Peter counted the petals, or what he supposed to be the

petals. There were four. They were not petals, however. They were sepals, so much like petals that only one with thorough knowledge of the parts of flowers would suspect that they were not petals. You remember that the Hepaticas of the early spring are like this, having no true petals, but sepals that look exactly like petals.

One of these clusters of flowers was just above Peter's head so that he could look at them closely. He found that each had many stamens, but though he looked and looked, he couldn't find a pistil in any of them.

"That is queer," said Peter to himself. "There ought to be at least one pistil. I wonder if all the flowers on this vine are just like these."

He found that they were. At least all those near enough for him to see clearly had only stamens. By and by he noticed a cluster growing near the ground farther along on the edge of the thicket. He hopped over for a look at this one. Not one of the flowers in that cluster had a stamen. No, sir, not one had a stamen. But each one had a number of pistils. At once Peter looked to see if these flowers were on the same vine as those he had first seen, and discovered that they were not. It was the same kind of a vine, but from another root altogether. All the blossoms on this vine had pistils, while all the blossoms on the other vine had stamens. Then Peter knew that only this vine bore seeds. He knew that the flowers with the stamens furnished the pollen to be brought by visiting insects and left on the pistils of these other flowers to make seeds.

On both vines the clusters of flowers grew out from the stalk where the leaf stems joined it. The leaves had quite long stems and grew in pairs, each leaf being divided into three or more broad, oval, short-stemmed leaflets, and the edges of these leaflets were cut into rounded teeth. The stalk or vine was round and grooved and appeared to be woody. It was green, stained with purple.

What Peter didn't know then, but what he found out in the fall long after the flowers had disappeared, was that one of those vines, the one whose flowers had pistils but no stamens, is as beautiful in seed time as in flower time. It is covered with masses of curling, silky, feathery plumes, each attached to a ball of seeds.

It was the Virgin's-bower,[89] or wild Clematis which Peter had found. It is also known as the Traveler's-joy and the Old-man's-beard. The latter name has been given it because of those soft silky plumes in the fall. This vine dearly loves to climb over old stone walls and old fences.

The thicket in which Peter had found the Virgin's-bower was close to the edge of the swamp. When Peter was fully rested he went on towards the swamp. Just outside the edge of it, where the Green Meadows were wet, he came upon a bed of plants perhaps a foot and a half high, which he recognized at once as having seen often growing along the Laughing Brook. The stalks were slender and straight, a few slightly branched. Some were more or less hairy and others smooth. The leaves grew in pairs from opposite sides of the stalk and were shaped much like the head of a lance, being quite sharp pointed at the tip and very narrow at the base. The edges were cut into fine teeth.

Perhaps Peter would not have noticed these plants had it not been for that busy, wobbly, little nose of his. It caught a smell which, had Peter been a boy, right away would have made him think of peppermint. He stopped to look at these plants with such a pleasant fragrance, and discovered that growing in close little bunches where the leaves joined the stalk, were tiny white or purplish flowers.

It wasn't necessary to look at those flowers closely to know what he had found. The fragrance, which, by the way, was from the leaves and not from the flowers, told him at once that he had found the American Wild Mint.[90] It belongs to the same family as the Peppermint, Spearmint and Pennyroyal.

On his way home to the dear Old Briar-patch his attention was called to a bushy plant perhaps two feet high, growing where the ground was dry. Very likely he would not have noticed it but for the odd way in which its leaves grew. These leaves were irregular in length, the longest being nearly two inches long,

---

89   Look at the picture of the Virgin's-bower on page 197.

90   Look at the picture of the American Wild Mint on page 197.

WILD MINT
Mentha arvensis, var. canadensis

VIRGIN'S -BOWER
Clematis virginiana

but were so narrow as to hardly seem like leaves at all. They were rounded at the tips, and they grew thickly in little bunches along quite the whole length of the stalk. Towards the top the stalk branched, and at the tip of each little branch was a small cluster of tiny flowers, these small clusters together forming a large flower head. The flowers were white. It was the Hyssop-leaved Thoroughwort,[91] which is a cousin of the Common Thoroughwort or Boneset, which used to be so much used as a medicine. It is easy to recognize by those queer little leaves.

---

91   See picture of the Hyssop-leaved Thoroughwort on page 206.

XXXVII. Cousins in Red and Blue

Summer was just entering its last month, August. Peter didn't need to look at a calendar to know this. Of course, if he had looked at a calendar it would have meant nothing to him, for Rabbits know nothing about the calendar. But Peter knew quite as well as if he had been able to understand the calendar that summer would be over in a few short weeks. He knew because jolly, round, red Mr. Sun went to bed behind the Purple Hills a wee bit earlier each night. He knew because everywhere he went he found berries and seeds on the very plants which had delighted him with their flowers earlier in the season.

So many, many flowers had blossomed and passed that it hardly seemed worth while to look for new ones now. It hardly seemed possible that any plants would wait until so late in the season to put forth their first flowers. But every once in a while Peter would find one just opening its first buds. It was quite as delightful a surprise as the finding of the earlier flowers in the spring, for it was always so unexpected. So, no matter what he was doing or where he was going, Peter always was watching out, not really expecting but always hoping to find a new flower.

It was in this way that one day early in August, as he was going up the Laughing Brook, he came upon one of the most delightful surprises of the whole summer. When he had first caught a glimpse of it ahead of him he had thought it was his old friend, the Bee Balm. But as he drew near it he saw that it was an even brighter red than the Bee Balm, and this made him hurry forward eagerly.

His long ears caught a humming sound as he drew near. "It must be a flower the Bees love, to judge by that humming," thought Peter. And then he gave a little squeal of surprise. He saw no Bees, but there was a visitor there, a quick-moving, flashing small person with wings moving so swiftly that they could not be seen. It was those wings that made the humming sound.

"Hello, Hummer!" cried Peter delightedly. "Hello, yourself!" squeaked Hummer the Ruby-throated Hummingbird, for this is who it was.

"What are you doing way over here?" asked Peter.

"What am I usually doing around flowers?"[92] squeaked Hummer, as he darted his long bill into one flower after another.

Of course Peter knew, and he knew that Hummer knew that he knew, so he didn't think it was necessary to reply. Hummer was getting sweetness from those flowers. "What bright red flowers! I never have seen any like them!" cried Peter.

"And you'll never see any brighter red," replied Hummer. "I know all the red flowers, for red is my favorite color, and there is none like this one."

"Do you mind telling me what it is?" Peter asked.

"Not at all. Not at all," squeaked Hummer, darting like a living jewel from blossom to blossom. "It is the Cardinal Flower or Red Lobelia. I always come over along the Laughing Brook to look for it this time of year."

"I don't wonder," replied Peter. "It certainly is worth looking for and looking at when it is found."

Peter spoke truly. At the top of a hollow, leafy stalk three or more feet above the ground was a long, rather loose, spike-like cluster of brilliant red flowers. These flowers were about an inch long and shaped somewhat like a tube split down one side, and the open part divided into five spreading, petal-like parts. The three middle ones grew together and were separated from the other two, which stood out at right angles and opposite each other. The five stamens were joined together in a tube, and stood out beyond the throat of the flower. From the very shape of these flowers Peter understood why it was that Hummer the Hummingbird had the sweets in them almost to himself. Only such a long tongue as his could get them.

---

92   Look at the picture of the Cardinal Flower on page 177.

The leaves were dark green, just the color needed to set off the brilliant red of the flowers. They were slightly hairy and were lance-shaped. The upper ones had no stems. The edges were cut into irregular little teeth.

None who sees the Cardinal growing beside a stream can fail to admire it. It is a matter for sadness that this admiration almost always results in the picking of these flowers, and so they are rapidly disappearing from the places where once they were abundant. They do not belong in vases, but where they grow, beside the stream. The stream which once had them and then lost them through the thoughtlessness of flower pickers can never again be quite the same.

Peter spent some time admiring the Cardinal Flower, and when he finally did move on along the bank of the Laughing Brook it was rather regretfully. But that regret was soon lost in a new surprise. It was a plant much like the one he had just left, save that the leaves were a lighter green. At the top was a long spike of flowers in shape similar to those of the Cardinal, but a bright blue instead of red, with markings of white.

Peter knew at the first glance that these flowers must be related to the ones he had so recently admired. He had found the Great Lobelia,[93] or Blue Lobelia, sometimes called the Blue Cardinal Flower.

It was a day to be remembered, and Peter didn't even look for any more flowers that day. Though he waited for some time, he saw nothing of Hummer the Hummingbird about the Blue Lobelia. But the long-tongued Bees were there in numbers.

---

93   Look at the picture of the Great Lobelia on page 177.

xxxviii. The Last of the Orchids

Summer was passing swiftly and autumn was drawing near. Peter knew it by signs just as he had known of the approach of spring. Everywhere he went his feathered friends were gathering together in flocks. He knew that this meant that they were getting ready for their long journey to the Sunny South. It hardly seemed worth while to look for new flowers. It was mid-August and it seemed to Peter that no plants wanting to make and ripen seeds would wait until so late to put forth their first blossoms, so he had stopped looking for them.

So his delight was all the greater when one day he discovered in the tall grass of the Green Meadows, near the edge of the swamp where the ground was wet, tall, rounded spikes of wonderful orange and yellow flowers such as he had never before seen. Coming upon them so unexpectedly they quite took his breath away.

"Oh!" he cried softly. "Oh, you lovely things!"

They were lovely. Some were a deep orange and others were a lighter yellow. Some were a little more than a foot above the ground, and some, where the grass was extra tall, were more than two feet high. The stalks were slender, and there were leaves clear to the stem of the flower spike. The lower ones were quite long, pointed and shaped like the head of a lance. They clasped the stalk. That is, they had no stems. The higher they were on the stalk the smaller they became, until near the top they were hardly more than leaflets.

Peter needed but one look at the flowers to know that he had found another member of the Orchid family. No other family could have such flowers as these. They grew rather closely in a long, rounded spike. Those not yet open were like tiny yellow clubs, each with a golden ball on the end. But of course it was by means of the open flowers that Peter was able so quickly to recognize them as Orchids. Each flower had a long, drooping, oblong lip cut into a wonderful fine fringe, and then continued into a very slender tube or spur an inch to an inch and a half long.

Peter had found the Yellow-fringed Orchis,[94] one of the most pleasing of the Orchid family, and one less rare than many of the others. How long Peter would have sat there admiring the lovely flowers, had nothing disturbed him, not even he knows. He had not looked at them half enough when he was startled by approaching footsteps. Like a jack-in-the-box, Peter sat up that he might see better. Then he took to his heels. Coming across the Green Meadows were the boy and girl he had so often seen picking flowers.

"Oh, I do hope they won't find these," muttered Peter as he scampered for a hiding place.

But they did find them. Peter knew it by the cry of delight from the little girl. Peter remained hidden until he saw the boy and girl walking away across the Green Meadows. Each held what at that distance looked like a mass of gold. Anxiously Peter hurried back to the place where he had found those beautiful, wonderful flowers. His worst fears were realized. Not one remained. No, sir, not one remained. Peter didn't remain either. He couldn't. That place, which only so short a time before had been one of beauty and the brightness and gladness which comes from beauty, had become a place of sadness. Peter wanted to get away from there. Something of the brightness and glory of the day was gone. So sadly he headed for the dear Old Briar-patch, and as he hopped along he wondered if another year he would find any of the Yellow-fringed Orchis down there by the edge of the swamp.

"I am afraid I won't find as many, anyway," he thought, "for I am afraid they pulled up some by the roots. Anyway, there will be no new plants, for there there will be no seeds. These human folks are stupid things. They are so. The more rare a flower is the more certain they are to pick it, and so make it

94   Look at the picture of the Yellow-fringed Orchis on page 204.

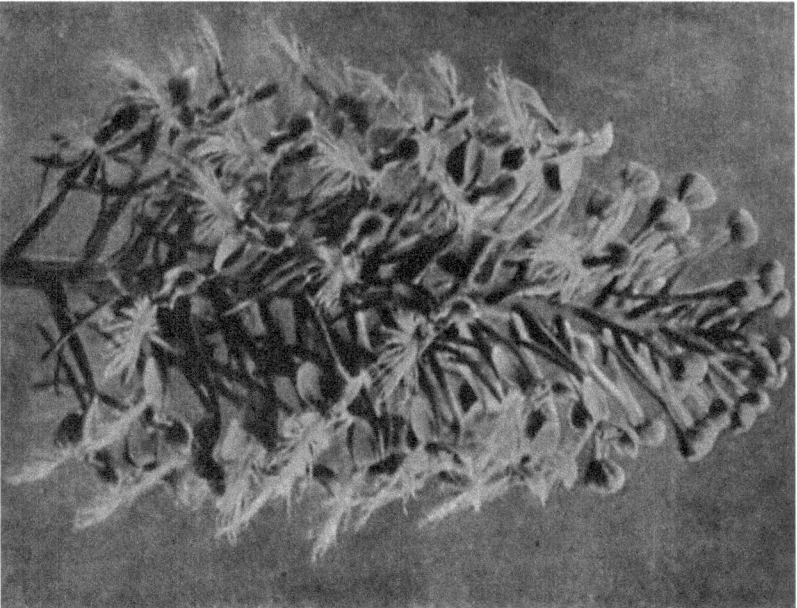

YELLOW-FRINGED ORCHIS
Habenaria ciliaris

JOE-PYE WEED
Eupatorium purpureum

still more rare. I suppose it is thoughtlessness, but it seems to me that it is just lack of good plain, common, everyday sense." Peter was still sputtering to himself about the flower pickers when he reached the dear Old Briar-patch.

It was several days before Peter again visited the home of these beautiful Orchids. He found three or four in bloom, but that was all. The glory of the place was gone, and Peter did not remain there long. He decided he would visit the swamp which was so near at hand. He had almost reached it when in the grass he came upon a group of flowers that caused him to squeal with delight, and for the time being to forget the Yellow-fringed Orchis.

He knew that he had found another member of the same family, the last of all the Orchids to bloom. The long, slim stalks varied in height. Where the grass was short Peter found some not over six inches high, while in the tall grass he found some quite two feet high. The stalks bore no leaves that could really be called leaves. Such as they did have were closely wrapped around them and very small. They are called bracts. Some of the plants had long, very narrow leaves at the base of the stalks, while others had none, for the leaves had disappeared with the blooming of the flowers.

But of course it was the flowers that interested Peter most. They were small, and most of them were white, though a few were slightly yellowish and they were very fragrant. As with other Orchids there was a lip to each little flower. It was broad, rounded and the outer edge was crinkled. There was no spur.

But it is the way in which these little flowers grow that makes it an easy matter to recognize them. They are set on a long spike in threes and grow around the stem in such a way that the whole spike appears to be twisted. Indeed, at a glance it appears much as if it were braided. Perhaps this is why these dainty little flowers are called Ladies'-tresses or Nodding Ladies'-tresses.[95] Peter had often seen them before, for they are more common than most orchids. The Bees know them and love them, for they are generous with their nectar, and it is not so difficult to get as is the case with so many of their relatives.

---

95   Look at the picture of the Ladies'-tresses on page 206.

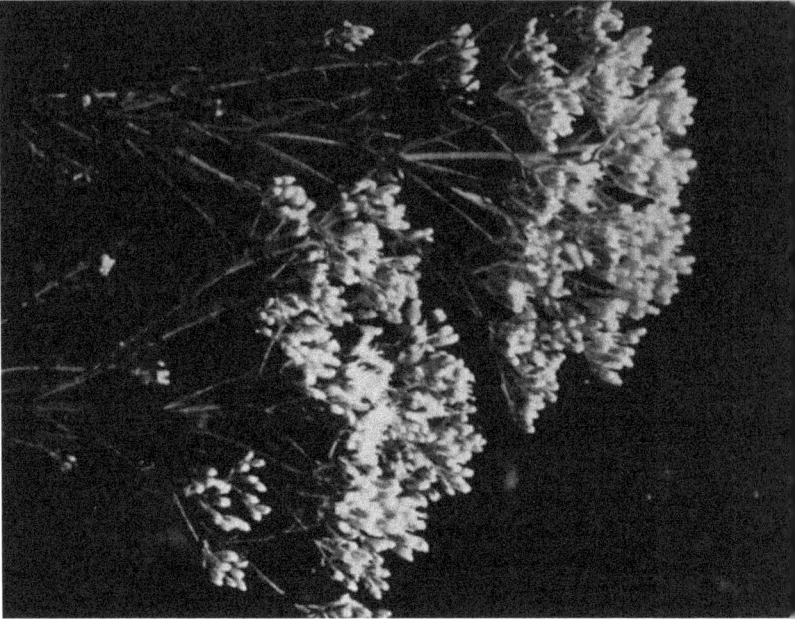

HYSSOP-LEAVED THOROUGHWORT
Eupatorium hyssopifoloim

NODDING LADIES' TRESSES
Spiranthes cerhua

xxxix. Two Who Come in August

A LL SUMMER long Peter's friends and neighbors had laughed at him for spending so much time hunting for flowers. They couldn't see why he was so interested in them. But though they laughed at him and often teased him they didn't forget him when they found flowers they suspected he had not seen. They would tell him about them and where to look for them.

Early one morning late in August Sammy Jay dropped into the dear Old Briar-patch on his way up to the Old Orchard. "Found any new flowers lately, Peter?" he inquired, after they had talked about the weather and such things.

"Not many," replied Peter. "I guess most flowers are through blooming. I don't suppose I can hope to find many more."

"Probably not many," replied Sammy. "But there will be some new ones, just a few even right into the fall. By the way, did you ever see a flower on a fern?"

"No," replied Peter promptly, "and I never expect to see one. Ferns don't have flowers."

"Are you sure of that, Peter? Are you quite sure of that?" inquired Sammy, a twinkle of mischief in his bright eyes.

"Of course I am," replied Peter. "Every one who knows anything about the Green Forest knows that ferns do not have flowers."

"All right, Peter. All right. Have it your own way. I saw some yellow flowers that seemed to be growing on a fern over in a thicket on the edge of the Green Forest this very morning, but of course I may have been mistaken," replied Sammy.

"Where?" demanded Peter, all interest at once. Sammy told him, and then flew away towards the Old Orchard. Peter watched him out of sight. Then, making sure that the way was clear, he started, lipperty-lipperty-lip, for the Green Forest as fast as his legs could take him. "I wonder if he really did see flowers on a fern," he kept saying over and over to himself. "Of course he didn't. He couldn't have. He probably said that to get me over here for nothing. It probably is one of his tricks."

But when Peter reached the thicket Sammy had told him about, a thicket where the ground was high and dry, he at once discovered some dainty, light yellow, bell-like flowers. At first glance they seemed to be growing on a fern. Yes, sir, they did so. For a moment or two Peter was fooled. He actually thought he had found a fern with flowers on it.

But when he looked a little more closely he saw that the plant was not a fern. It looked like a fern because the leaves were fern-like. That is, they were cut into many little leaflets after the manner of a fern. The stalk was very slender and much branched and was perhaps three feet high. Happening to touch it, he found that it was rather sticky. The leaves were light green, soft and downy, and, as I have said before, very fern-like.

The pretty yellow flowers were bell-shaped, more than an inch long, and nearly as broad. The outer edge was in five rounded scallops and these curled back. Peeping into the heart of one of them, Peter could see four stamens. He discovered that the flowers were both hairy and sticky.

"I don't know what I have found, but they are pretty anyway. They ought to have a pretty name," remarked Peter, speaking aloud as is his way sometimes when he thinks he is alone.

"You have found a Fern-leaved False Foxglove,"[96] declared Hummer the Hummingbird, who had come up just in time to overhear Peter.

"Huh!" exclaimed Peter. "I don't like the name. I don't like anything that has anything to do with a Fox."

"But these flowers don't have anything to do with a Fox," squeaked Hummer. "And I never have known a Fox to have anything to do with them."

"Then what are they called Foxgloves for?" demanded Peter indignantly.

96   See picture of the Fern-leaved False Foxglove on page 209.

NEW ENGLAND ASTER
Aster novaeangliae

FERN-LEAVED FALSE
FOXGLOVE
Gerardia pedicularia

TALL OR GIANT SUNFLOWER
Helianthus giganteus

SNEEZEWEED
Helenium autumnale

But this was too much for Hummer, and he darted away without answering.

"I like the first part of the name all right, the Fern-leaved part, but I don't like the rest. I don't like being reminded of Foxes. I have to think enough of them, — too much — as it is. Now I'll never see one of these flowers without thinking of Reddy Fox. People do certainly find queer names for flowers. I would like these ever so much better if they had another name."

Peter stopped talking to himself and turning his back on the pretty yellow flowers, started along the edge of the Green Forest towards the swamp. Of course, it was silly of him to have any such feeling, but you know how constantly Peter has to watch out to keep from furnishing Reddy Fox with a dinner, so perhaps he is not to be blamed for not wanting to be reminded of any such unpleasant thing even by a name.

When he reached the edge of the swamp he came upon a clump of beautiful, purple flowers so high above his head that he had to sit up and tip his head back to look at them. They were Asters. He didn't need to look twice to know this. The daisy-like shape of them enabled him to be sure of this. It seemed to Peter that he had never seen a more beautiful member of the Aster family. Each flower head was nearly two inches across. The petal-like or ray flowers were a rich purple, and there were forty or fifty of these. The tiny center flowers were yellow, stained with purple. A little way from this clump was another clump. The flowers of this were light violet, but they were the same kind of flowers. The stalk was stout, rough and covered with leaves. These were hairy, lance-shaped and pointed at the tips.

It was the New England Aster[97] Peter had found, so pleasing a flower that it frequently is transplanted to gardens. Had Peter been watching it at sunset, he would have seen all those little purple petal-like parts close, to open again the following morning.

---

97   Look at the picture of the New England Aster on page 209.

XL. THE GOLD OF LATE SUMMER

YOU REMEMBER that early in the spring Peter had searched for gold and found it beside the Laughing Brook in the Marsh Marigolds. Later Dandelions and Buttercups made parts of the Green Meadows look as if a cloth of gold had been laid over them. But with the passing of these, yellow gave way to other colors. There were, of course, some yellow flowers all through the season, but not in numbers sufficient to tinge the landscape with their color.

But with the approach of fall yellow again took possession of field and meadow and the edge of the woodlands, as if the flowers were trying to make people forget that the sunshine was daily growing weaker. The gold of the Goldenrod was everywhere, and to add to this glory of rich color now came the Sunflowers.

One of the first of these that Peter found was the Tall or Giant Sunflower.[98] He found it on the edge of the swamp, where of course the ground was damp.

It was so tall that Peter had to tip his head so far back it made his neck ache in order to see the flowers. Some of them were quite ten feet above the ground. Later Peter found some that were not over three feet above the ground, and others that were halfway between the two. In all, the plants and flowers were alike, save that some of the plants were branched and some were not.

The stalk was rough and hairy. It was more or less stained with purple. The leaves were lance-shaped and sharp-pointed, and the edges were cut like the teeth of a saw. They were rough on both sides and on the under side hairy.

98   Look at the picture of the Tall Sunflower on page 209.

The flowers grew on long, rather slender stems with small leaves. Many of the flowers, or flower heads, for that is what they really were, were more than two inches across. As with the Daisies and the Asters, each flower head was really a colony of flowers growing together in a little green, half-round cup. As with the Daisies and the Asters, the outer or ray florets were petal-like. There were ten to twenty of these. They were like little golden banners, and served to attract Bees and insects, for they were so bright that they could be seen a long distance.

The center was, of course, made up of tiny, tubelike, perfect flowers crowded closely together, and these were yellowish. The flower heads made Peter think of giant, all yellow Daisies.

"Pretty, aren't they?" said Little Friend the Song Sparrow, who had stopped to see what Peter was looking at.

"They are lovely!" declared Peter.

"There is a cousin of these in bloom down on the meadows nearer the Laughing Brook. Have you seen it yet?" inquired Little Friend.

Peter was all interest at once. "No," said he, "I haven't. But I'm on my way right now." And off he started, lipperty-lipperty-lip. Sure enough, when he drew near the Laughing Brook he found another Sunflower. He knew it was a Sunflower from its general appearance, although it was much different from the one he had just left. It was only about half as tall and was branched. The leaves were lance-shaped and saw-edged, but not as rough as those of the Giant Sunflower. Peter bit off one and began to chew it. But he didn't chew it long. No, sir, he didn't chew it long. He made a wry face and spat it out. You see it was bitter and not at all to his liking. It left an unpleasant taste in his mouth. There was something familiar about that plant, and presently Peter remembered.

He remembered having found one late in the fall after the leaves had dried, and that he had tramped on some that had fallen to the ground and they had crumpled up into a fine dust, some of which had gotten into his nose and made him sneeze and sneeze until he was afraid he would sneeze his head off. Ever since then he had known this as the Sneezeweed,[99] and that is

99   Look at the picture of the Sneezeweed on page 209.

the name by which a great many people know it. It is also called the Swamp Sunflower and the False Sunflower.

When Peter looked at the flowers he found them quite different from the ones he had been admiring. In the first place the flower heads were not quite so large. They grew in clusters on long, slim stems. The ray florets, which you and I would call petals, were yellow, quite broad, and the tip of each had little cuts or notches in it. Some had three and some had five. These little yellow banners, instead of standing out and up as did those of the Giant Sunflower, drooped downward.

And there was just as great a difference in the centers. Of course these centers were made up of tiny florets, but these were crowded together in little globes or balls, and they were quite brownish. Those globe-like centers and the drooping notched ray florets make it easy to know the Sneezeweed when you find it.

Peter might not like the taste of the leaves, but there was no doubt that the flowers themselves were beloved of the Bees and other insects. Busy Bee the Honey Bee was there, and hardly had she left when Lady Bumblebee arrived. Others of the Bee family paid them a visit, and so did Butterflies and Wasps and Beetles.

What Peter found out about the bitter taste of the leaves many farmers have found out also. You see sometimes cows get some of these leaves in their mouths when they are eating grass, and swallow them. When they do this their milk is almost always sure to be bitter. So farmers do not like the Sneezeweed when it grows where their cows are pastured.

xli. A Day Rich in Beauty

Never will Peter forget the first time he saw the Swamp Rose Mallow,[100] or Mallow Rose. No, sir, Peter never will forget that time. It happened one day at the very end of summer. Peter wasn't thinking of flowers. He had gone over to the Laughing Brook to pay his respects to Grandfather Frog. He is in the habit of doing this every once in a while. He found Grandfather Frog sitting on his favorite big, green, lily pad, looking very much satisfied with the world and things in general.

"You're looking fine, Grandfather Frog," said Peter.

"Chug-arum! Why shouldn't I?" replied Grandfather Frog in his deep bass voice. "Tell me, Peter Rabbit, why shouldn't I look fine?"

"You should and you do," retorted Peter. "It seems to me you are a little stouter than you were in the middle of the summer."

"Perhaps I am," replied Grandfather Frog. "Perhaps I am. If I'm not, it isn't from lack of appetite, or plenty to eat. I like to be a little stout before going to sleep for the winter, and it won't be long now before I shall begin to think about retiring. It is a long time, Peter Rabbit, since you've been over to see me. I thought the Mallows would bring you. In fact, I knew they would. Now be honest, Peter, and tell me if it wasn't to see the Mallows and not to see me that you came over here this morning. "

"Mallows?" said Peter. "Mallows? What are Mallows?"

Grandfather Frog's big goggly eyes opened so wide that they really looked as if trying to pop right out of the top of his head.

"Chug-arum!" said he. "Chug-arum! Do you mean to tell me that you don't know the Rose Mallow?"

---

100   Look at the picture of the Swamp Rose Mallow on page 219.

Peter nodded. "Honest I don't," said he. "Is it an animal or a bird, or what is it?"

Grandfather Frog's eyes popped more than ever. "Gracious!" he exclaimed. "Gracious me, what ignorance! Go over and look among the rushes and cattails and then come back and tell me what you think of what you find there."

Of course Peter's curiosity was aroused at once. Off he started for the upper end of the Laughing Brook. He hadn't the least idea what he would see there, and his curiosity increased with every jump. When he reached the place where the cattails grew he stared eagerly among them. He wondered if he would know the thing he had come to find if he should see it. But he wasn't long in doubt. No, sir, he wasn't long in doubt.

"It's a flower!" he cried. And then he drew a long breath of pure pleasure.

It was a flower, and such a flower as Peter had not dreamed of seeing anywhere outside of Farmer Brown's garden. It was big. In fact it was several inches across, and right away it reminded him of the Hollyhocks he had seen in Farmer Brown's garden. It was shaped much like them. And in color it was pink, — soft, beautiful pink.

Peter looked eagerly for more, and he found that there were a number of them scattered among the rushes. They grew in clusters at the tops of stout, leafy stalks, some of them taller than a tall man. The leaves were pointed at the tip and rounded at the base, and the edges were cut into small, rounded teeth. Above they were smooth and green, but underneath they were covered with a soft, whitish down.

Each of the great, pink blossoms had five rounded petals, and these seemed to have little ribs running the length of them. The pistil in the middle was divided into five tips, each tip like a little button. The stamens were joined together to form a tube around the pistil.

All the flowers that Peter could see were that beautiful rose-pink. Later he was to discover some that were white and others that had a deep, crimson spot in the center. They are lovers of the marshes, and wet places. And there are no more lovely wild flowers in the late summer and early fall.

When Peter had admired the Mallows to his heart's content he went back to tell Grandfather Frog what he thought of them. But Grandfather Frog was nowhere to be seen. Peter waited awhile and then went on to see what more he could find of interest. He hopped along the edge of the swamp, for he remembered that many of the flowers he had found of late grew where the ground was damp. He didn't really expect to find another.

But in this he was happily disappointed. He came to a great clump of tall plants. Some were almost as tall as the Giant Sunflower. The stalks were stout and most of them were stained with purple. The large, lance-shaped leaves with toothed edges grew out around the stalk at regular distances. There were three to six in each group. At the top of each stalk was a great, fuzzy-looking mass of dull pink or purplish flowers. It was a big cluster made up of many smaller clusters, and each small cluster was made up of a number of little tubular flowers from which were thrust out hairy pistils. It was these hairy pistils that gave the mass a fuzzy appearance.

Butterflies were constantly coming and going. There were a few Bees, but it was clear to Peter that the Butterflies were the ones who loved these flowers best. He wondered what the name of this plant was. But there was no one to tell him. It was a plant of many names. The one by which it is best known is Joe-pye Weed,[101] said to have been given it because once, long ago, an Indian Doctor named Joe Pye used it as a medicine. But it is also called the Trumpetweed, the Purple Thoroughwort, the Tall or Purple Boneset, the Gravel-root, the Kidney-root and the Queen-of-the-Meadow. I am quite sure that Peter would have thought the last name the best of all.

When at last he headed for home in the dear Old Briar-patch it was with a feeling that this day had been rich with beauty, and if you have the good fortune to find the Rose Mallow and the Joe-pye Weed I am sure you will agree with Peter.

---

101   Look at the picture of the Joe-pye Weed on page 204.

xlii. The End of Peter's Search

Matching the bluebird in its hue,
Or the autumn skies of cloudless blue;
Shy as a soft-eyed startled fawn
By the Laughing Brook at break of dawn;
A-bloom in a landscape turning sere
In the shortened days of the waning year
The Gentian sways to the wind's caress,
Ethereal in its loveliness.

SEPTEMBER HAD come. Summer was over. Peter no longer
thought of searching for flowers. Many of those which he
had found still were in bloom, but it didn't seem possible that
there could be any that had put off blooming until most plants
had ripened and already scattered their seeds. So Peter's curiosity was concerned with other things, with the doings of his
neighbors who were laying up supplies of food for winter, with
the departure of many feathered friends for the Sunny South,
with the preparations of Johnny Chuck and a few others for that
strange, long sleep through the cold and discomforts of winter.

So it came about that one morning as he was hopping along
the edge of a thicket where the ground was rich and somewhat
damp he stopped abruptly to gaze with round-eyed surprise,
followed by a little gasp of joy, at what he saw before him. It
was a little group of plants about two feet high, bearing clusters
of flowers that seemed to have taken their color from the very
sky itself.

These flowers were an inch to an inch and a half long, and
stood upright in a crowded cluster at the top of the stalk. There

were a few also growing out from the places where the upper leaves joined the stalk. Each flower was a light blue at the base, becoming deeper blue towards the top. Every one of them was closed. They appeared to be buds just ready to open. But they were lovely, very lovely just as they were. Peter went from plant to plant, hoping to find at least one open. But he was disappointed.

"I must come over here again and see them when they are open," said Peter, talking to himself aloud as is his way when he thinks he is alone. "They are lovely just as they are, but they must be lovelier still when they are open."

"Buz-z-z," said a voice almost in his ear. "Buz-z-z. You'll wait a long time if you wait for these flowers to open, Peter Rabbit."

It was the voice of Lady Bumblebee as she alighted on one of those clusters of flowers.

"What do you mean by that?" demanded Peter in surprise.

"I mean that they never will open," replied Lady Bumblebee. "They are in full bloom now."

Then, before Peter could recover from his surprise and this astonishing news sufficiently to find his tongue, Lady Bumblebee thrust her long tongue through a tiny opening in the tip of one of those flowers, and then pushed with all her might until she had forced those petals apart sufficiently to get her head in. Then she kept on until only her hind legs and the tip of her body were outside. She was smart enough not to go wholly inside, knowing that if she did, those petals she had forced open would spring together and make her a prisoner. When she had secured all the nectar she backed out, and Peter could see some little grains of pollen sticking to her head. Then she did the same thing at another flower, and of course she left those little grains in that one. So she went from flower to flower, until she had visited all of them, always carrying some pollen from the one just visited to the next one entered.

Thus it was that Peter became acquainted with the Closed Gentian,[102] sometimes called Blind Gentian and sometimes called Bottle Gentian, and learned that there is at least one flower which does not have to open in order to make perfect seeds. The stalk of this Gentian is smooth and stout, and the leaves

102   Look at the picture of the Closed Gentian on page 219.

CLOSED OR BOTTLE GENTIAN
Gentiana Andrewsii

SWAMP ROSE MALLOW
Hibiscus Moscheutos

grow in pairs on opposite sides and are large, lance-shaped with rather pointed tips, and have smooth edges.

"Well," said Peter, when at last he turned to go on his way, "I guess this is the last flower of the year."

But Peter was mistaken. A little later in the month he had quite as happy a surprise as the closed Gentians had given him. This time it was down on the Green Meadows not far from the Smiling Pool where the ground was damp. There he came upon a little group of one of the loveliest of all our American wild flowers. These also were blue, a lighter blue than the Closed Gentians, a blue that was even nearer to the color of the sky.

The flowers were at the top of a smooth, grooved, rather slender, branching stalk between two and three feet high. Each flower was like a beautiful little vase two inches high, and spreading at the top, where the four petals were wonderfully fringed. It was Peter's good fortune that he found them on a sunny day, for otherwise they would not have been open. On dull and cloudy days they remain closed, and they close at night. When they close, those four fringed petals twist around each other in a most interesting way.

Peter guessed that he had found a cousin of the Closed Gentian, and he was right. He had found the Fringed Gentian,[103] a flower so lovely that it is worth going far to see. It is almost the last flower of the year, and it is fitting that it should be one of the most beautiful.

Peter sat admiring them for a long time. He would have remained even longer had he not been startled by a shout. Instantly he sat up for a look around. There, coming straight towards him, was the boy he had so often seen picking flowers. Peter's first thought was to run. There was time enough for him to get away without being seen. Then he looked at those beautiful Gentians. He knew just what would happen if that boy should find them. He knew that he would pick every one of them. Peter couldn't bear to think of it.

What do you think Peter did? He started off at once, lipperty-lipperty-lip, but not to seek safety by hiding. Instead of running away from that boy he ran straight towards him. You see,

103   Look at the picture of the Fringed Gentian on page 221.

FRINGED GENTIAN
Gentiana crinita

he knew that that boy had no terrible gun, and he wasn't very much afraid of him. He wanted that boy to see him, and so he ran, lipperty-lipperty-lip, to meet him.

Now that boy was like most boys. The instant he saw Peter, he gave a whoop of delight and started after him. Of course he knew he couldn't catch Peter, but he liked to see him run. Peter would run a short distance, then stop. The boy would come on, looking for him. When he was very near, Peter would bound away again, and the boy would whoop. It was like a game, very much like the game of hide-and-seek.

So Peter gradually led the boy across the Green Meadows and into the edge of the Green Forest. When he felt sure that they were so far from where the lovely Gentians were growing that the boy would not go back there, Peter soon got rid of him.

Later, back in the dear Old Briar-patch, Peter thought it all over, and the feeling that he had saved those lovely flowers from being picked made him tingle with gladness. It was a gladness which comes from the doing of a good deed.

How good that deed was not even Peter knew. You see the Fringed Gentian is one of those plants which dies every year. Even the roots die. Therefore it is absolutely necessary that these plants shall ripen their seeds, and these seeds be scattered where they can sprout and grow the next season. If all the flowers are picked there can be no seeds, and of course no more flowers. So Peter had saved not only those flowers that were blooming there on the Green Meadows but the flowers of next year. The Closed Gentian does not have to depend on seeds, for the roots live through the winter, and in the spring new plants spring up from them.

Until the last blossom of the Fringed Gentians faded late in the fall, Peter daily visited the place where he had found them. It was with something of sadness that he turned away from there for the last time. His search for flowers was at an end for that year, and it had been such a happy search. Already he began to look forward to the coming of another spring and the return of the flower friends he had learned to know and love, and of the coming of the many, many whose acquaintance he had not yet made.

"Flowers are wonderful. They are truly wonderful," said Peter to himself, as he hopped along towards the dear Old Briar-patch. "They are as wonderful as they are beautiful, and until this year I had never given them so much as a thought. How queer it is that people with eyes to see often see so little and miss the beauties and the wonders all about them. I have learned a lot about flowers, but I am going to learn more. Yes, sir, I am so."

I am quite certain that Peter will, and I hope that you, too, may do likewise.

THE END

APPENDIX

For the benefit of older boys and girls who are interested in flowers and the adults who may read the book — either to the children or for their own pleasure — this appendix is inserted. It contains in more technical language the facts which should be helpful in identifying and classifying the flowers described.

Adder's-tongue, Yellow: *Erythronium americanum.* Lily family.

FLOWERS. Solitary, bright yellow, bell-shaped, hanging downward, and nodding from long, slender, upright stems. Perianth of six petal-like parts, spreading at tips, and spotted on the inside near the base with rich brown. There are six stamens, and the style is club-shaped.

LEAVES. Two of unequal length, fleshy, long, pointed, oval, pale green, and usually marked with dull reddish or purple irregular spots. The flower stalk rises from between them.

HABITAT AND SEASON. Moist, open woods, thickets and brooksides; March to May; from Nova Scotia to Florida, and westward to the Mississippi.

Anemone, Rue: *Anemonella thalictroides* (*Syndesmon thalictroides*). Crowfoot family.

FLOWERS. White, sometimes tinted with pink; two or more, smaller than Wood Anemone and having five to ten, usually six, petal-like sepals. Stamens numerous, hairlike, short, yellow-tipped, and clustered around several light green pistils.

LEAVES. Involucre compound, growing just beneath an umbel of flowers. The true leaves are compound and grow from the base of the plant after the flowers have gone. The flower stalk is tinged with red.

HABITAT AND SEASON. The same as Wood Anemone. Found throughout Eastern United States and west to Kansas and Minnesota.

Anemone, Wood: *Anemone quinquefolia.* Crowfoot family.

FLOWERS. Solitary, about an inch across, usually white, but sometimes tinted with blue or pink outside. Calyx of four to nine oval, petal-like sepals; no true petals; stamens numerous; many small, green pistils. The stalk is smooth, slender and four to nine inches high.

LEAVES. Involucre of three long-petioled trifoliolate leaves in a whorl about stem midway between blossom and ground. Lobes irregularly notched and center ones larger than others. Basal leaves similar to involucral leaves, but appearing later than flowering stem.

HABITAT AND SEASON. Woodlands, hillsides and in partial shade; April to June; from Canada to Georgia, and west to Rocky Mountains.

Arbutus, Trailing: *Epigcea repens.* Heath family.

FLOWERS. White, pinkish or deep pink, fragrant, in clusters. Calyx of five, dry, overlapping sepals; corolla tubular, spreading into five equal lobes, and hairy; ten stamens; one pistil with a five-lobed stigma.

LEAVES. Alternate, oval, rounded at base, smooth above and more or less hairy below, evergreen with rusty spots on the older ones. Stalk woody and spreading over ground.

HABITAT AND SEASON. Sandy loam in woods and mossy, rocky places; March to May; from Newfoundland to Florida, west to Kentucky and Northwest Territory.

Arethusa: *See* PINK, INDIAN.

Arrowhead, Broad-leaved: *Sagittaria latifolia.* Water-plantain family.

FLOWERS. There are two kinds, sometimes growing on separate plants and sometimes found on the same plant. The staminate flowers have three white, rounded, spreading petals, and a center of many yellow stamens. They are over an inch across and grow in threes on short stems at regular distances along stalk. The pistillate blossoms are green-centered, and unattractive. The stalk is many-angled, milky-juiced, sometimes slender and sometimes stout, and from a few inches to three or four feet high.

LEAVES. Those under water are long and grasslike, while those above water are arrow-shaped, sometimes sharp and narrow, and again blunt and broad. They are thick, rubbery and have long stems.

HABITAT AND SEASON. Shallow water and mud; July to September; throughout the country.

Aster, New England: *Aster novosanglice*. Composite family.

FLOWERS. In numerous heads, one to two inches across, clustered at the ends of branches, and varying in color from rarely white to light violet and rich purple. There are thirty to forty narrow ray-florets, surrounding numerous, five-lobed, tubular, yellow disk-florets, set in a sticky, green cup. The branching stalk is rough, stout and two to eight feet high.

LEAVES. Lance-shaped, toothless, pointed at the tip, heart-shaped at the base and clasp the stalk.

HABITAT AND SEASON. Rich fields and edges of swamps; August to October; from Quebec to South Carolina, west to Northwest Territory, Colorado, Missouri and Kansas.

Aster, Upland White: *Aster ptarmicoides*. Composite family.

FLOWERS. Ten to twenty, white, ray-florets around a flat center of pale yellow-green disk-florets which turn to light brown at maturity. The flower heads are small, barely an inch across, and form a branching cluster. They are the first of the White Asters to bloom.

LEAVES. Grayish-green, shining, grasslike, alternating up the stem, and growing smaller near the top until they become mere bracts among the flowers.

HABITAT AND SEASON. Rocky or dry soil; July to September; northern United States, west to Colorado.

Azalea, Wild; or Pinkster Flower: *Rhododendron nudiflorum (Azalea nudiflora).* Heath family.

FLOWERS. Pink, purplish, or nearly white, one and a half to two inches across, in clusters on a branching shrub two to six feet high. Corolla funnel-shaped with tube narrow and hairy, spreading into five regular lobes; five long, red stamens; one protruding pistil which, like the stamens, is curved.

LEAVES. Oblong, acute at both ends, hairy on midrib, and usually follow the blossoms.

HABITAT AND SEASON. Moist, rocky woods, dry woods and thickets; April to May; from Maine to Florida, west to Illinois.

Baneberry, White: *Aetata alba.* Crowfoot family.

FLOWERS. White, small, in oblong, terminal raceme; three to five petal-like, early falling sepals; four to ten spatulate, clawed petals; numerous, long, white stamens; one pistil with broad stigma. Stalk erect, bushy, one to two feet high.

LEAVES. Dark green, two or three times compounded, with margins sharply notched.

HABITAT AND SEASON. Cool, moist woods; April to June; from Nova Scotia to Georgia, west to Missouri and British Columbia.

Bee Balm, American; or Oswego Tea: *Monarda didyma.* Mint family.

FLOWERS. Deep scarlet, tubular, in circles around a large, round, terminal, dark-red head which is surrounded with a circle of bright reddish, drooping, leafy bracts. Corolla is widest at mouth, two-lipped, and one and a half to two inches long. Two long, anther-bearing stamens protrude. There is one pistil with a two-cleft style. The plant is two to three feet tall, and the stalk is square.

LEAVES. Oval or oblong, lance-shaped, sharply-toothed, thin, dark green, aromatic, with hairy stems; grow in opposite pairs.

HABITAT AND SEASON. Moist soil, especially near streams in hilly country; July to September; from Canada to Georgia, west to Michigan.

Bindweed, Hedge or Great: *See* MORNING-GLORY.

Bitterweed: *See* GOLDENROD.

Black-eyed Susan or Coneflower: *Rudbeckia hirta.* Composite
family.

FLOWERS. Flower head large, of twenty to thirty orange-yellow
ray-florets, notched at the tips, arranged around a purplish-
brown, cone-shaped head of tiny disk-florets at top of hairy,
rough, sometimes branched stalk, one to three feet high.

LEAVES. Long, narrow, oblong to lance-shaped, rough, sparingly notched.

HABITAT AND SEASON. Open, sunny places such as dry fields;
May to September; from Canada to Florida, Colorado and
Texas.

Bloodroot: Sanguinaria *canadensis.* Poppy family.

FLOWERS. Pure white, rarely pinkish, one to one and one half
inches across at top of smooth, naked stem six to fourteen
inches high. There are two sepals and eight to twelve petals tapering at either end. Stamens are numerous aud form
a bright, golden center. The flowers close at night, and are
short-lived.

LEAVES. Usually two, sometimes only one, large, rounded,
deeply lobed at base, and with one to five or more smaller
lobes toward the end, with edges slightly toothed. Upper
surface green and veined; under side silvery white and
coarsely veined. Flower stem and leaves, when broken, exude
orange-red juice, and this is found in quantity in the root.

HABITAT AND SEASON. Rich woods and borders, in colonies;
April to May; from Nova Scotia and Ontario south to Florida,
Missouri and Arkansas.

Blue Bells of Scotland: *See* HAREBELL.

Blue Flag, Larger; or Blue Iris: *Iris versicolor.* Iris family.

FLOWERS. Large, plumy, violet-blue, variegated with white,
green and yellow. Perianth divided into six divisions, the three
outer ones spreading and recurved, one of them bearded; the

three inner divisions shorter and narrower. All are united in a short tube. There are three stamens under three overhanging petal-like parts of the style. These are notched at the tips and violet colored. The flowers are at the top of a stout, straight stalk two to three feet high.

LEAVES. Erect, sword-shaped, one half to one inch wide, growing from the root-stalk.

HABITAT AND SEASON. Marshes and wet meadows; May to July; from Newfoundland and Manitoba to Florida and Arkansas.

Bluets or Innocence: *Houstonia ccerulea.* Madder family.

FLOWERS. Very small, light to purplish-blue or white, with yellow centers, and three to seven inches high. Corolla tubular or funnel-shaped, with four oval, pointed spreading lobes; four stamens inserted on tube of corolla, and two stigmas; calyx four-lobed. The flowers grow in crowded masses.

LEAVES. Tiny, toothless, usually oblong, the lower ones spatulate.

HABITAT and season. Moist, sunny fields, along roadsides and on wet rocks and banks; April to July; from Ontario to Georgia and Alabama, west to Michigan.

Burdock, Common: *Arctium minus.* Composite family.

FLOWERS. Tubular florets of varying shades of purple and white, gathered in small heads, and set in a conical, green bur which is covered with sharp, spreading, long-hooked, sticky bristles. Flower heads are on short stems in terminal clusters on a large, coarse, bushy, leafy stalk which is round and grooved, and is two to four feet high.

LEAVES. Large, the lower ones often a foot long, broadly ovate, toothless, alternating and with hollow stems.

HABITAT AND SEASON. Fields, waste ground and waysides; July to October; throughout the country.

Butter and Eggs or Yellow Toadflax: *Linaria vulgaris* (*Linaria Linaria*). Figwort family.

FLOWERS. Light yellow and orange, two-lipped, tubular, with spur at the base; upper lip two-lobed and curves over lower lip, which has three unequal, out-curving lobes, its base having an orange-colored swelling which nearly closes the tube and hides the four unequal stamens and pistil. The flowers hang on short stems from the axils of leaflets, and grow in a terminal spike, one to three feet high.

LEAVES. Long, narrow, grasslike, tapering at both ends, alternate and clasping the slender, light green stalk, which has a whitish bloom.

HABITAT AND SEASON. Waste land, fields and roadsides; June to October; from Canada to Virginia, west to Nebraska.

Buttercup, Bulbous: *Ranunculus bulbosus.* Crowfoot family.

FLOWERS. Deep glossy yellow, usually with five petals, but sometimes six or seven; sepals bent downward; stamens numerous, yellow, and grouped around numerous green pistils. The stalk is somewhat hairy, and the root is a bulb.

LEAVES. Basal leaves divided into several parts, and each division again cut into lobes. They have long, narrow stems.

HABITAT AND SEASON. Fields, roadsides and waste places; May to July; in many parts of the United States and Canada.

Buttonbush or Honeyballs: *Cephalanthus occidentalism.* Madder family.

FLOWERS. Tiny, white, fragrant, tubular, four-parted, with long, yellow-tipped style protruding. The florets are clustered on a fleshy receptacle forming round heads about an inch across. These are on long peduncles from leaf axils or ends of branches of a shrub three to twelve feet high.

LEAVES. Oval, entire, opposite or in small whorls.

HABITAT AND SEASON. Beside water, swamps, low ground; June to September; from New Brunswick to Florida, west to Arizona and California.

Calico Bush: *See* LAUREL, AMERICAN.

Calopogon: *See* PINK, GRASS.

Cardinal Flower or Red Lobelia: *Lobelia cardinalis.* Lobelia family.

FLOWERS. Intense, vivid red; corolla tubelike, an inch long, split down the upper side, and with five flaring, narrow, pointed lobes bent at right angles, the three middle ones set together and partly separated from the other two, which form the upper lip and are erect. Five stamens are united into a tube around the style. There are two anthers with hairy tufts. The flowers grow in terminal, green-bracted, more or less one-sided racemes on a leafy, hollow stalk two to four feet high.

LEAVES. Oblong to lance-shaped, irregularly toothed, smooth or slightly hairy, dark green, the upper ones clasping stalk.

HABITAT AND SEASON. Wet or low ground, beside streams; July to September; from Nova Scotia to Manitoba, south to Florida, Kansas, Colorado and Mexico.

Carrot, Wild; or Queen Anne's Lace: *Daucus Carota.* Parsley family.

FLOWERS. Tiny, white, usually five-parted, with minute yellow-tipped stamens, and are densely crowded in many, small, flat wheels that in turn are arranged in a flat-topped disk. The central floret of each disk is often dark and once in a while all of the flowers have a delicate, purplish tinge. The outer flowers are largest. The slender stems of the flowers radiate from a common center at top of hairy stalk one to three feet high.

LEAVES. Lower ones much cut and divided, while upper ones are less so.

HABITAT AND SEASON. Fields, roadsides and open waste places; June to September; throughout eastern half of United States and Canada.

Chickweed, Common: *Stellaria media* (Alsine media). Pink family.

FLOWERS. Tiny, white, with five petals so deeply notched as to appear to the careless observer like twice that number; calyx green, five-parted, the sepals being longer and larger than the petals; stamens two to ten; three or four styles.

LEAVES. Small, oval, pointed, smooth, growing in pairs, the lower ones with short stems, while the upper ones clasp the stalk. The latter is branching, slender and spreads over the ground in tufts.

HABITAT AND SEASON. Damp places almost everywhere throughout the year.

Chickweed; Larger Mouse-ear: *Cerastium vulgatum.* Pink family.

FLOWERS. Very small, with five deeply notched white petals, five sepals, and twice as many stamens as petals.

LEAVES. Small and much the shape of ear of a mouse.

HABITAT AND SEASON. Fields and stony places from May to July, and widely distributed. Naturalized from Europe.

Cinquefoil, Common; or Five-finger: *Potentilla canadensis.* Rose family.

FLOWERS. Yellow, quarter to half an inch across, solitary on slender stems from leaf axils. Calyx hairy and green; five petals, broadly oval and notched at the apex; numerous stamens grouped around numerous pistils to form a head.

LEAVES. Divided into five coarsely toothed, strongly veined leaflets arranged like the spread fingers of a hand.

HABITAT AND SEASON. Dry fields, banks, hills and roadsides; April to August; from Quebec to Georgia, west to Minnesota.

Claytonia: *See* SPRING BEAUTY.

Clematis, Wild; or Virgins-bower: *Clematis virginiana.* Crowfoot family.

FLOWERS. Small, white or greenish-white, about one inch across or less, imperfect, growing in loose clusters at the leaf joints of the stalk which is a climbing vine. Four or five rounding, oblong, petal-like sepals take the place of true petals; stamens numerous, and pistils light green in color. Pistillate and staminate flowers grow on separate plants. Flowers are delicately fragrant. In the fall the pistillate flowers are followed by silvery, silky, curled plumes of withered styles.

LEAVES. Large, smooth, dark green, divided into three broad, oval, short-stemmed leaflets with margins cut into coarse notches. The leaves are set on long stems and grow in pairs.

HABITAT AND SEASON. Rich, moist soil, along woodland borders, thickets, fences, walls and roadside shrubbery; July to September; from Nova Scotia to Manitoba, and Georgia to Kansas.

Clover, Common Red: *Trifolium pratense.* Pulse family.

FLOWERS. Tubular corollas set in dense, oval or egg-shaped heads about an inch long, magenta, pink, or rarely whitish. Stalk six inches to two feet high, branching and more or less hairy.

LEAVES. On long petioles, compounded of three or more oval leaflets marked with a white crescent.

HABITAT AND SEASON. Fields, meadows and roadsides; April to November; throughout Canada and the United States.

Clover, White: *Trifolium repens.* Pulse family.

FLOWERS. Round heads of white or pinkish, small, tubular florets set erectly in small, five-parted, light green calyxes.

LEAVES. Divided into three leaflets.

HABITAT AND SEASON. Common in fields and along roadsides; May to December; throughout the country.

Columbine, Wild: *Aquilegia canadensis.* Crowfoot family.

FLOWERS. Red outside, yellow within, one to two inches long; five spreading, red sepals; five funnel-shaped petals narrowing into long, erect, slender, hollow spurs rounded at the tips; numerous stamens; five projecting pistils. Stalk one to two feet high, branching and wiry.

LEAVES. Basal leaves on long, slender stems direct from roots, compound, and each leaflet with three or more lobes; upper leaves small, generally rounded and unite with stalk at the branching joints.

HABITAT AND SEASON. Rocky places, rich woodlands; April to July; from Nova Scotia and Northwest Territory south to Florida and Texas.

Coneflower: *See* BLACK-EYED SUSAN.

Corn Cockle or Corn Rose: *Agrostemma Giihago.* Pink family.

FLOWERS. Large, one to three inches across, magenta or purplish-red, with five broad, rounded petals, ten stamens and five styles, the latter opposite the petals and alternating with the long, narrow lobes of the calyx which extend beyond the petals. The flowers are on long, stout stems from a stalk one to three feet high, which is seldom branched, and is covered with fine, white hairs.

LEAVES. One to four inches long, narrow, pointed, opposite and seated on stem.

HABITAT AND SEASON. Wheat and grain fields and waste places; July to September; throughout United States, but most common in the central and western states. It is a pest.

Cowslip: *See* MARSH MARIGOLD.

Crane's-bill, Spotted: *See* GERANIUM.

Culver's Root or Culver's Physic: *Veronica virginica* (*Leptandra virginica*). Figwort family.

FLOWERS. Small, four-lobed, tubular with two protruding stamens and growing crowded in slender, terminal spikes on straight, erect, usually unbranched stalk, two to seven feet high.

LEAVES. Long, tapering, lance-shaped, sharply-toothed, short-stemmed, in whorls of three to nine.

HABITAT AND SEASON. Rich, moist woods, thickets and meadows; June to September; from Canada to Alabama, west to Nebraska.

Daisy, Common White; or Whiteweed: *Chrysanthemum Leucanthemum.* Composite family.

FLOWERS. Flower head of twenty to thirty, long, spreading ray-florets surrounding yellow center of densely packed tubular florets set in a green disk at top of smooth stem one to three feet high.

LEAVES. Sparingly scattered along stalk, usually lance-shaped and coarsely toothed and divided. Basal leaves have long, slender stems.

HABITAT AND SEASON. Meadows, roadsides and waste land; May to November; throughout Canada and United States.

Daisy, Blue Spring; or Robin's Plantain: *Erigeron yuLchellus.* Composite family.

FLOWERS. Daisy-like head one to one and a half inches across, growing in terminal, flat-topped cluster at top of thick, light green, hairy and juicy stalk, ten to twenty inches high. Ray-florets light bluish-purple to sometimes a faded white; yellow disk-florets set in a green cup.

LEAVES. Stem leaves long, narrow, tapering to the point, hairy and partly clasping stalk. They alternate at infrequent intervals. Basal leaves in a flat tuft about root.

HABITAT AND SEASON. Moist ground, hills, grassy fields; April to June; from Nova Scotia and Ontario to Florida and Louisiana, west to Minnesota.

Dandelion, Common: *Taraxacum officinale (Leontodon Taraxacum).* Composite family.

FLOWERS. A single, yellow head, one to two inches across, composed of a large number of perfect ray-florets in a cup of many narrow, green, leafy bracts at top of smooth, hollow, milky stem.

LEAVES. Long, narrow, irregularly notched, and clustered around base of stem.

HABITAT AND SEASON. Lawns, fields and grassy waste places the year around and the country over.

Dogwood, Flowering: *Cornus florida* (*Cynoxylon floridum*). Dogwood family.

FLOWERS. These appear to be large, with four white or pinkish petals with a notch in the tip of each. These are not petals, but bracts. The true flowers are very small, greenish-yellow, four-parted, and are clustered in the center. They are borne on the twigs of a large shrub or small tree with rough bark and peculiarly hard wood.

LEAVES. Opposite, oval, with unbroken edges.

HABITAT AND SEASON. Woodlands, rocky thickets and wooded roadsides; April to June; from Maine to Florida, west to Ontario and Texas.

Dutchman's-breeches or Whitehearts: *Dicentra CucuUaria* (*Bicuculla CucuUaria*). Fumitory family.

FLOWERS. White, tipped with yellow, nodding in one-sided raceme on smooth stalk five to ten inches high; two scale-like sepals; corolla of four petals in two pairs, one pair forming hollow, flattened, tapered spurs widely separated at tips, and other pair very small, narrow, at right angles to the two longer ones, and extended to form an arch over the six protruding stamens.

LEAVES. Three times compounded and finely cut, making feathery appearance. They spring from base of stalk on slender petioles.

HABITAT AND SEASON. Rich, rocky woods; April to May; from Nova Scotia to North Carolina, west to Nebraska and Missouri.

Elecampane or Horseheal: *Inula Helenium*. Composite family.

FLOWERS. Large, yellow, solitary flower heads of many tubular florets set in a large, flat disk, and surrounded with many, long, narrow, curving, spreading ray-florets. The latter are three-toothed. The plant is usually unbranched, two to six feet high.

LEAVES. Large, broadly oblong, pointed, finely toothed, rough above and downy beneath, and alternate, the lower ones on slender stems, and the upper ones clasping the stalk.

HABITAT AND SEASON. Roadsides, fence rows and fields; July to September; from Nova Scotia to North Carolina, west to Minnesota and Missouri.

Everlasting, Pearly: *Anaphalis margaritacea.* Composite family.

FLOWERS. Small heads formed of many overlapping dry scales of pearly white, inclosing a number of tiny, yellow, tubular florets. These heads form a rather flat-topped cluster at top of a leafy, round, cottony stem one to three feet high. The tubular florets are of two kinds, staminate and pistillate.

LEAVES. Toothless, long and narrow, the lower ones being broadest, somewhat lance-shaped and rolled backward. The leaves are grayish-green above and woolly beneath.

HABITAT AND SEASON. Hillsides, dry fields and open woods; July to September; from Newfoundland to Alaska, and North Carolina to California.

Eyebright: *See* GRASS, BLUE-EYED.

False Solomon's Seal: See *SPIKENARD, WILD.*

Fireweed or Great Willow-herb: *Epilobium angustifolium* (*Chamoenerion angustifolium*). Evening Primrose family.

FLOWERS. Usually magenta or pink, about an inch across, borne in spikelike, terminal raceme on smooth, leafy stalk two to eight feet high. There are four, rounding, spreading petals, eight stamens and one pistil with four-lobed stigma.

LEAVES. Narrow, tapering, willow-like, two to six inches long.

HABITAT AND SEASON. Dry soil, fields and roadsides, especially in burnt-over districts; from June to September; from Atlantic to Pacific, in Canada and United States south to the Carolinas and Arizona.

Five-finger: *See* CINQUEFOIL.

Flannel Plant: *See* MULLEIN.

Foamflower or False Miterwort: *Tiarella cordifolia.* Saxifrage family.

FLOWERS. Small, white, feathery, in a close raceme at top of slender, hairy stalk six to twelve inches high. Calyx white, five-lobed; five-clawed petals, ten long stamens, one pistil with two styles.

LEAVES. Three to seven lobed, the lobes toothed; long-stemmed from root stalk or runners, and broadly heart-shaped at base; downy on veins beneath.

HABITAT AND SEASON. Rich, moist, rocky woods; April to May; from Nova Scotia to Georgia, west to Indiana and Michigan.

Foxglove, Fern-leaved False: *Gerardia pedicularia* (*Dasystoma pedicularia*). Figwort family.

FLOWERS. Light yellow, trumpet-shaped, an inch to an inch and a half long, and almost as wide; hairy and sticky on the outside, and set on short, curving stems in the axils of the leaves. Lobes of the corolla are five in number, rounded and spreading; four stamens. The plant is slender, much branched, one to four feet high.

LEAVES. Light green, soft, downy, deeply cut into many-toothed lobes, much resembling the frond of a fern. They are set in pairs.

HABITAT AND SEASON. Dry woods and thickets; July to September; from Maine and Ontario to Minnesota, Missouri and Florida.

Gentian, Closed; or Bottle Gentian: *Gentiana Andrewsii* (*Dasy Stephana Andrewsii*). Gentian family.

FLOWERS. Intense blue, becoming lighter towards base, in small, crowded, terminal clusters, or set one or two in axils of leaves. The flowers are club-shaped, one to one and one-half inches long, and nearly or quite closed, so that they appear like buds about to unfold. The plant is a leafy stalk, smooth, rather stout and usually unbranched.

LEAVES. Lance-shaped, with long, tapering point, rather large, toothless, often tinged with brown, arranged in opposite pairs clasping the stalk.

HABITAT AND SEASON. Moist, rich soil in meadows and thickets, and along woodland borders; August to October; from Canada to Georgia and Missouri.

Gentian, Fringed: *Gentiana crinita.* Gentian family.

FLOWERS. Bright blue, erect, two inches high, vase-shaped, with the four rounded, spreading lobes finely fringed around the top edge; four stamens inserted on corolla tube, and there is one pistil with two stigmas. The closed flowers have a twisted appearance. They close at night and on dull days. The flowers are borne singly on the tips of branches of a smooth, grooved stalk one to three feet high.

LEAVES. Thin, toothless, heart-shaped at base, tapering to a long point. They clasp the stalk in alternating, opposite pairs.

HABITAT AND SEASON. Moist meadows and woods; September to November; from Quebec to Georgia, west beyond the Mississippi.

Geranium, Wild; or Spotted Crane's-bill: *Geranium macidatum.* Geranium family.

FLOWERS. Pale magenta, lavender or purplish-pink, one to one and one-half inches across, solitary or in pairs, one to two feet high. Five pointed sepals, five petals woolly at base, ten stamens, and one pistil with five styles. Stalk slender, hairy, grooved and sometimes branched.

LEAVES. Large, spreading, divided into five or more parts, each of which is again divided into three more or less notched lobes. Basal leaves long-stemmed, the older ones often spotted with white.

HABITAT AND SEASON. Open woods, thickets and shady places; April to July; from Newfoundland to Georgia, west to Missouri.

Goldenrod, Wrinkled-leaved; or Bitterweed: *Solidago rugosa.* Composite family.

FLOWERS. Tiny, yellow flowers set on one-sided stems which form a spreading, leafy head; ray-florets six to nine, and there are four to seven disk-florets. The stalk is straight, stout, covered with long hairs and crowded with leaves. It may be a foot high or seven feet high.

LEAVES. Broadly oval to lance-shaped, sharply toothed, hairy, especially on the under side, and slightly wrinkled.

HABITAT AND SEASON. Along roadsides, fences and in fields and waste places; July to November; from Newfoundland and Ontario to Florida and Texas.

Grass, Blue-eyed, Eastern; or Eyebright: *Sisyrinchium atlanticum.* Iris family.

FLOWERS. Blue to purple with yellow center; a western variety white. Perianth of six spreading divisions, each pointed with a bristle with a notch; stamens three, the filaments united to above the middle; one pistil with tip divided into three parts. Stalk slender, rigid, two-edged, three to fourteen inches high.

LEAVES. Slender, sharp-pointed, grasslike at base of stalk.

HABITAT AND SEASON. Moist fields and meadows; May to August; from Newfoundland to Virginia, west to British Columbia and eastern slope of Rocky Mountains.

Grass, Deer: *See* MEADOW Beauty.

Grass, Yellow Star: *Hypoxis hirsuta.* Amaryllis family.

FLOWERS. Bright yellow within, greenish and hairy outside, about one-half inch across; perianth six-parted, widely spreading; stamens yellow; buds form a loose cluster at top of rough, hairy scape two to six inches high, only one or two flowers opening at a time.

LEAVES. Slender, grasslike, more or less hairy, grooved, rising from around base of and longer than flower stalk.

HABITAT AND SEASON. Dry, open woods, fields and waste places; May to October; from Maine to Gulf of Mexico and far west.

Hardhack or Steeplebush: *Spiraea tomentosa.* Rose family.

FLOWERS. Tiny, in dense, terminal spikes, on leafy, light brown, woolly stalks two to three feet high. The color is pink or magenta, rarely white, including the stamens, and the corolla has five rounded petals. There are twenty to sixty stamens, and usually five pistils.

LEAVES. One to two inches long, oval, saw-edged, dark green above and covered with whitish, woolly hairs beneath.

HABITAT AND SEASON. Moist ground; July to September; from Nova Scotia to Georgia, west to Manitoba and Kansas.

Harebell or Blue Bells of Scotland: *Campanula rotundifolia.* Bluebell family.

FLOWERS. Bright blue, purplish or violet-blue, bell-shaped, one-half inch long or over, hanging downward on hair-like stems from very slender, simple or branching stalk six inches to three feet high. Five slender stamens alternate with five spreading lobes of the corolla, the greenish-white pistil extending beyond. The calyx is green with five narrow parts.

LEAVES. Basal leaves nearly round, and often wither by the flowering season; the long upper leaves very narrow, smooth and pointed, and seated on stem.

HABITAT AND SEASON. Moist, rocky cliffs, uplands and meadows; June to September; from Labrador to Alaska, south to New Jersey and Pennsylvania, west into the Rocky Mountains and Sierra Nevadas.

Hepatica: *Hepatica triloba (Hepatica Hepatica).* Crowfoot family.

FLOWERS. Six to twelve blue, lavender, pinkish or white petal-like sepals; numerous stamens and pistils; three small, sessile leaves under flower which might be mistaken for a calyx.

LEAVES. Three-lobed, rounded, leathery, evergreen, often mottled with reddish-purple and spreading on the ground.

HABITAT AND SEASON. Woods and hillsides; March to May; from Canada to northern Florida, and Manitoba to Iowa and Missouri.

Honeyballs: *See* BUTTONBUSH.

Honeysuckle, Coral *or Trumpet:* Lonicera sempervirens. Honeysuckle family.

FLOWERS. Corolla tubular, slender, slightly spread below the five-lobed limb; red outside, orange-yellow within, and growing in a whorl around terminal spikes on a high twining vine; five stamens and one pistil.

LEAVES. Opposite, rounded oval, the upper ones united around the stem by their bases to form a cup; evergreen in the South.

HABITAT AND SEASON. Rich, warm soil of hillsides and thickets; April to September; from southern New England to the Gulf States, west to Nebraska.

Horseheal: *See* ELECAMPANE.

Indian Pipe or Ice Plant: *Monotropa uniflora.* Heath family.

FLOWERS. Solitary, white, waxy, oblong, bell-shaped, nodding from top of thick, smooth, fleshy, scaly, white stalk four to ten inches high. There are four or five oblong, scalelike petals, and eight to ten hairy stamens.

LEAVES. There are none, scales taking their place on the flower stalk.

HABITAT AND SEASON. Shaded, moist, rich woods, especially under pine and oak trees; June to August; throughout the country.

Indian Turnip: *See* JACK-IN-THE-PULPIT.

Innocence: *See* BLUETS.

Iris: *See* BLUE FLAG.

Jack-in-the-pulpit or Indian Turnip: *Ariscema triphyllum.* Arum family.

FLOWERS. Tiny, greenish-yellow, around base of a slender, green, club-like spadix within a green, often whitish or purple-striped spathe with broad, pointed flap above it.

LEAVES. One or two, large, spreading, three-parted, overtopping flower hood. The plant is one to three feet high.

HABITAT AND SEASON. Moist woodlands and thickets; April to June; from Nova Scotia to Florida, west to Ontario, Minnesota and Kansas.

Joe-pye Weed or Trumpetweed: *Eupatorium purpureum.* Composite family.

FLOWERS. Dull pink or purple, small, fuzzy appearing, arranged in small groups that form large, terminal clusters on a green or purplish, leafy, often branched stalk, three to ten feet high. The florets are tubular with long, projecting, hairy pistils which give the flower heads a fuzzy appearance.

LEAVES. Large, oval or lance-shaped, saw-edged, thin, rough-surfaced and arranged in whorls of three to six.

HABITAT AND SEASON. Moist meadows, along streams, and in swamps; August to September; from Canada to Gulf of Mexico, west to Manitoba.

Lady's-slipper, Pink; or Moccasin Flower: *Cypripedium acaule* (*Fissipes acaulis*). Orchis family.

FLOWERS. Large, showy, solitary, drooping from end of scape six to twelve inches high. The upper lance-shaped sepal is greenish-purple and the two lower ones are united. Three spreading, curving petals colored like sepals, but narrower and longer; lip an inflated sac, often over two inches long, slit down the middle and folded inward. This is pale magenta, veined with darker pink, the upper part of interior crested with long, white hairs, and open end of pouch nearly closed with curious, broad, sterile anther which shields fertile anthers and stigma beneath.

LEAVES. Two, large, thick, pointed, oval, slightly hairy and many ribbed, clasping scape at base.

HABITAT AND SEASON. Rocky or sandy woods; May to June; from Canada to North Carolina, west to Minnesota and Kentucky.

Lady's-slipper, Showy: *Cypripedium hirsutum* (*Cypripedium regince*). Orchis family.

FLOWERS. One, two or three at top of stout, leafy stalk. The large, pouch-like lip an inch or more long is white, stained with purplish-pink spots and stripes; sepals and petals white, and latter narrower than former.

LEAVES. Three to eight inches long, downy, pointed oval, wavy-edged, ribbed, alternating and clasping the stalk.

HABITAT AND SEASON. Bogs and rich, low, wet woods; June to September; from Nova Scotia to Georgia, west to the Mississippi.

Lady's-slipper, Small Yellow: *Cypripedium parviflwum.* Orchis family.

FLOWERS. Lip or pouch bright yellow, more or less marked with purple stripes or blotches; petals longer and more twisted than those of Large Yellow Lady's-slipper; sepals narrow and curling, sometimes purple or claret-colored.

LEAVES. Oval or lance-shaped, alternate on slender stalk one to two feet high.

HABITAT AND SEASON. Bogs and moist, hilly woodlands; May and June; from Canada south to Missouri and Georgia, west to Washington.

Ladies'-tresses, Nodding: *Spiranthes cernua* (*Ibidium cernuum*). Orchis family.

FLOWERS. Small, waxy, white or yellowish, fragrant, without a spur, the two side sepals spreading, while the upper one forms an arch with the petals. The spreading lip has a crinkled edge. They grow in threes to form a twisted, terminal spike on a stalk six inches to two feet high.

LEAVES. Narrow and grasslike from the base of the stalk, usually disappearing before the flowering season.

HABITAT AND SEASON. Wet meadows and grassy swamps; July to October; from Nova Scotia to Gulf of Mexico, west to Ontario, Minnesota and South Dakota.

Lambkill: *See* LAUREL, SHEEP.

Laurel, American or Mountain; or Calico Bush: *Kalmia latifolia.*
Heath family.

FLOWERS. Pink to white on short, sticky stems, in large, showy,
terminal clusters; corolla an inch or less across, bowl-shaped
with five low points, and ten projections on outside; ten stamens arched over so that each anther is held in a tiny pocket
formed by the outside projections; one pale green pistil.

LEAVES. Oblong to elliptic, pointed at both ends, smooth, shining, evergreen, alternate, or in pairs, or in terminal clusters.
The stiffly branched shrub is two to twenty feet high.

HABITAT AND SEASON. Rocky, hilly woods; May to June; from
New Brunswick and Ontario to Gulf States, west to Ohio.

Laurel, Sheep; or Lambkill: *Kalmia angustifolia.* Heath family.

FLOWERS. Similar to those of the American Laurel, but very
much smaller, usually crimson-pink with purple tips and
pink stamens and pistils. They grow in loose, round clusters
just below or on one side of the new light green, erect leaves.

LEAVES. Oblong or lance-shaped, old ones drooping, evergreen,
frequently marred with rusty spots, and having yellowish
midrib and short stem. The plant is shrubby, six inches to
three feet high.

HABITAT AND SEASON. Moist soil in swamps or hillside pastures;
June to July; from Canada to Georgia.

Lily, Large Yellow Pond; or Spatter-dock: *Nymphcea advena.*
Water Lily family.

FLOWERS. Large, sometimes three and a half inches across,
yellow or greenish outside, yellow within, floating on surface of water or standing above it. The six apparent petals
are really concave sepals, and within this yellow cup are the
true petals which are fleshy, oblong and stamen-like. They
are numerous and comparatively short. The flat top of the
great stigma is composed of many carpels and bears a star-
like design with twelve to twenty-four rays.

LEAVES. Six to twelve inches long, heart-shaped at base, with rounded tip, smooth, shining, leathery, floating on water or standing just above it.

HABITAT AND SEASON. Shallow water; April to September; from New Brunswick to Florida, west to Rocky Mountains.

Lily, Meadow; or Wild Yellow Lily: *Lilium canadense*. Lily family.

FLOWERS. Yellow to orange-red, deeper within and speckled with dark reddish-brown spots, bell-shaped, the six spreading, pointed, petal-like parts two to three inches long with tips curving backward; six stamens with reddish-brown anthers; one pistil having three-lobed stigma. The flowers nod on long, slender stems from top of a leafy stalk two to five feet high.

LEAVES. Lance-shaped to oblong, usually in whorls of from four to ten at regular intervals on stalk; upper leaves sometimes alternate.

HABITAT AND SEASON. Low meadows, moist fields and swamps; June to July; from Nova Scotia to Ontario, south to Georgia, Alabama and Missouri.

Lily, Red, Wood or Philadelphia: *Lilium philadelphicum*. Lily family.

FLOWERS. One to five, large, reddish-orange or flame colored, erect on separate stems from top of stalk. The six petal-like parts of the perianth are broad towards the end and taper to slender, stem-like bases; they are spotted with dark purple and tinged with yellow. The six long, pink stamens and single club-shaped pistil with three-lobed stigma have brown tips.

LEAVES. Lance-shaped, in whorls of three to eight, at regular intervals along stalk.

HABITAT AND SEASON. Dry woods, thickets and borders; June to July; from Maine to Ontario, south to Carolinas and West Virginia.

Lily, Sweet-scented White Water: *Castalia odorata.* Water Lily
family.

FLOWERS. Pure white, or slightly tinged with pink, three to
eight inches across, deliciously fragrant, floating on surface
of water; calyx of four sepals, green outside and lined with
white or pinkish-white; petals numerous, pointed oblong,
arranged alternately in several rows, graduating toward the
center into numerous yellow stamens; pistil compound with
spreading and projecting stigmas.

LEAVES. Large, nearly round, with cleft at base; rich, shining
green above, with underside reddish and more or less hairy.
The leaves, commonly called pads, float on the water at ends
of long, slender, rubbery stems like the stems of the flowers.

HABITAT AND SEASON. Ponds, lakes and slow streams; June
to September; from Nova Scotia to Gulf of Mexico, west to
the Mississippi.

Liver-leaf: *See* HEPATICA.

Lobelia, Great or Blue: *Lobelia syphilitica.* Lobelia family. flowers. Bright blue, fading to pale blue, an inch long, tubular,
split on one side, two-lipped, and irregularly five-lobed. The
lobes are shorter than in the Red Lobelia, and the stamen
tube does not stand out beyond the corolla. They form a
long, dense, terminal spike on a rather stout, leafy, somewhat
hairy stalk, one to three feet high.

LEAVES. Alternate, oblong, irregularly toothed, two to six inches
long, upper ones clasping the stalk.

HABITAT AND SEASON. Moist, wet soil, along streams; July to
October; from Maine and Ontario to Georgia and Louisiana,
west to Kansas.

Lobelia, Red: *See* CARDINAL FLOWER.

Lupine: *See* PEA.

Mallow, Swamp Rose; or Mallow Rose: *Hibiscus Moscheutos.* Mallow family.

FLOWERS. Very large, four to seven inches across, a beautiful rose-pink, or sometimes white, and often with crimson center. Five large petals are rounded, wedge-shaped and strongly veined; stamens united in a tube which incloses a long pistil split into five flat-headed tips. The flowers grow singly or in small clusters on short stems at top of a stout, leafy stalk four to seven feet high.

LEAVES. Oval, tapering to a slender point, three to seven inches long, smooth above, covered with a soft, whitish down beneath, some or all lobed at middle.

HABITAT AND SEASON. Along rivers, lakes and in brackish marshes; August to September; from Massachusetts to Gulf of Mexico, and in the Great Lake region.

Mandrake: *See* MAY APPLE.

Marsh Marigold or Cowslip*: Caltha palustris.* Crowfoot family.

FLOWERS. Shining yellow, one to one and one-half inches across in small groups. Five or more oval, petal-like sepals; no petals; stamens numerous. Stalk stout, smooth, hollow and branching, one to two feet high.

LEAVES. Large, rounded, broad, heart-shaped at base, rich, shining green.

HABITAT AND SEASON. Wet ground, low meadows, swamps, river banks and ditches; April and May; Canada to South Carolina, west to Rocky Mountains.

May Apple or Mandrake: *Podophyllum peltatum.* Barberry family.

FLOWERS. Two inches across, white, with six to nine slightly concave, ovate petals, beautifully marked with fine veins. Stamens as many as petals, or often twice as many, have prominent yellow anthers, and are arranged around a large, thick pistil. The flowers hang from between a pair of terminal leaves at top of stalk from one to one and a half feet high.

LEAVES. Two sets, one on flower stalk and one growing separately, the latter the largest, often measuring a foot in diameter. They are smooth, glossy and divided into seven to nine arrow-shaped lobes. The lobes are two-cleft and toothed at the apex. Ribs and veins are conspicuous. They appear like a closed umbrella when they first come up.

HABITAT AND SEASON. Rich, moist woods; in May; from Quebec to Gulf of Mexico, west to Ontario and Minnesota.

Meadow Beauty or Deer Grass: *Rhexia virginica*. Meadow Beauty family.

FLOWERS. Purplish-pink, one to one and one-half inches across, in small clusters on slender, leafy branches which spring in pairs from the angles of the leaves. The plant is one to one and one-half feet high, and the stalk is square and more or less hairy. There are four rounded, spreading petals joined for half their length; eight equal, prominent stamens; one pistil. They usually open one at a time.

LEAVES. Pointed oval, finely toothed, thin, and arranged in alternating, opposite pairs.

HABITAT AND SEASON. Sandy swamps or near water; July to September; from Maine to Florida, west to Illinois and Missouri.

Meadowsweet: *Spiraea latifolia*. Rose family.

FLOWERS. Small, white, or pink-tinted in fleecy terminal pyramids, two to four feet high; calyx five-lobed; corolla with five slightly curved, rounding petals; many projecting rosy stamens. Stalk simple or bushy, smooth and usually reddish.

LEAVES. Oval or oblong, saw-edged and alternating.

HABITAT AND SEASON. Low meadows, swamps and ditches; June to August; from Newfoundland to Georgia, west to Rocky Mountains.

Milfoil: *See* YARROW.

Milkweed, Common: *Asclepias syriaca.* Milkweed family.

FLOWERS. Large, broad umbels, each flower set on a short, slender stem, the stems springing from the same point on a short, drooping stalk that grows from the axils of the upper leaves; corolla deeply five-clefted, the segments turning backward and varying from green through white to dull purple from base to tip, purple predominating; fragrant.

LEAVES. Opposite, oblong, rather thick, midrib prominent, margin entire, upper surface smooth and grayish-green, while under side is downy and silvery; four to nine inches long.

HABITAT AND SEASON. Roadsides, fields and waste places; June to September; from New Brunswick south to North Carolina, and far westward.

Milkweed, Swamp: *Asclepias incarnata.* Milkweed family.

FLOWERS. Purplish-red or pinkish, arranged in several loose, terminal, flat-topped clusters on a smooth, slender, branched stalk two to four feet high. Lobes of corolla oblong, and hoods shorter than inclosed, incurved horns.

LEAVES. Long, lance-shaped, narrowed toward the base, where they are sometimes heart-shaped.

HABITAT AND SEASON. Swamps and wet places; July to September; from New Brunswick to Louisiana, west to Kansas.

Mint, Wild: *Mentha arvensis,* var. *canadensis.* Mint family.

FLOWERS. White or slightly pinkish, tiny, tubular with four lobes, growing in whorls in the leaf axils. The odor is like pennyroyal. Stalk slender, erect, sometimes branched, more or less hairy, six inches to two feet high.

LEAVES. Opposite, oblong to oblong lanceolate, sharply toothed, one to three inches long.

HABITAT AND SEASON. Marshes, swamps and moist soil; July to October; from New Brunswick to British Columbia, south to Virginia and New Mexico.

Miterwort, False: *See* FOAMFLOWER.

Moccasin Flower: *See* LADY'S-SLIPPER, PINK.

Morning-glory, Wild; or Hedge or Great Bindweed: *Convolvulus septum.* Morning-glory family.

FLOWERS. Large, bell-shaped, about two inches long, light pink with white stripes or all white, on long peduncles from leaf axils; corolla five-lobed, the five stamens inserted on its tube. The main stem or stalk is three to ten feet long, round, leafy, generally smooth, but sometimes minutely hairy, and trails over bushes or along ground.

LEAVES. Triangular or arrow-shaped, two to five inches long, on slender petioles.

HABITAT AND SEASON. Hedges, walls, thickets and fields; June to September; from Nova Scotia to North Carolina, west to Nebraska.

Mullein, Great; or Flannel Plant: *Verbascum Thapsus.* Figwort family.

FLOWERS. Light yellow, wheel-shaped with five unequal, rounded, spreading lobes; five protruding, unequal, orange-tipped stamens, three of which are fuzzy or bearded; one green pistil. The flowers are crowded in long, club-shaped spikes, and open two or three at a time for a day only. The plant is two to seven feet high and very woolly.

LEAVES. Large, thick, velvety, oblong and sharply pointed, the basal ones growing in a rosette around the foot of stalk, and those on stalk alternating and clasping it.

HABITAT AND SEASON. Dry fields and waste land; June to September; from Nova Scotia to Florida, west to Kansas and in California.

New Jersey Tea: *Ceanothus americanus.* Buckthorn family.

FLOWERS. Tiny, white or creamy, in dense, oblong, terminal clusters; five petals, hooded and long-clawed; five stamens with long filaments.

LEAVES. Pointed-oval, set alternately on branches of shrubby stalk two to three feet high.

HABITAT AND SEASON. Dry, open woods and thickets; May to July; from Ontario and Manitoba to Florida and Texas.

Orchis, Yellow-fringed: *Habenaria ciliaris* (*Blephariglottis ciliaris*). Orchis family.

FLOWERS. Orange-yellow, closely set in a large, terminal spike on a slender, leafy stalk a foot to three feet high; sepals oval or almost circular, two spreading, while the upper one forms a sort of hood; petals smaller and generally toothed. A long, drooping, oblong lip is fringed and forms a slender spur an inch to an inch and a half long.

LEAVES. Lance-shaped, long and pointed, becoming bract-like leaflets as they approach the blossoms.

HABITAT AND SEASON. Moist meadows and sandy bogs; July to August; from New England to Ontario, south to the Gulf States.

Oswego Tea: *See* BEE BALM.

Pea, Wild; or Wild Lupine: *Lwpinus perennis.* Pulse family.

FLOWERS. Vivid blue, butterfly-shaped, the corolla having wings, keel and standard, and being about one-half inch long. They are borne in a long, terminal spike on a round, hairy, leafy, erect and branching stalk one to two feet high, and are sweet-scented.

LEAVES. Wheel-shaped, composed of seven to eleven long narrow leaflets, radiating from stem, and are light green and toothless.

HABITAT AND SEASON. Dry, sandy places and hillsides; May to June; throughout eastern half of the United States and Canada.

Pickerel Weed: *Pontederia cordata.* Pickerel Weed family.

FLOWERS. Bright purplish-blue, tubular, slightly curved, unpleasantly scented. The perianth is two-lipped, the upper lip broad and erect with two yellow spots at base of middle lobe; six stamens, three opposite each lip. The flowers are crowded in a dense spike at top of erect, stout, fleshy stalk one to four feet high, but seldom over two feet above water.

LEAVES. One, smooth, thick, leathery, dark green, arrow or heart-shaped, four to eight inches long, midway on flower stalk.

HABITAT AND SEASON. Shallow water; June to October; in eastern half of the United States.

Pink, Grass; or Calopogon: *Calopogon pulchellus* (*Limodorum tuberosum*). Orchis family.

FLOWERS. Three to fifteen, purplish-pink, sweet-scented, in loose, terminal spike from twelve to eighteen inches high; sepals and petals similar, pointed-oval in shape, separated and spreading. A long, upright lip is pale pink with white spots, and is heart or wedge-shaped at summit. It has a dense beard of long, yellow, orange and rose, club-shaped hairs which appear like stamens. The petal-like pistil is long, slender, curving and three-lobed.

LEAVES. Solitary, long, grasslike, direct from bulb.

HABITAT AND SEASON. Swamps, bogs and low meadows; June to July; from Newfoundland to Florida, west to the Mississippi.

Pink, Indian; or Arethusa: *Arethusa bulbosa.* Orchis family.

FLOWERS. Bright purple-pink, one to two inches long, solitary at end of smooth stalk five to ten inches high. Sepals and petals partly united and nearly alike; a conspicuous drooping lip is toothed or fringed, blotched with purple, and with three white, hairy crests.

LEAVES. One, many ribbed and grasslike, appearing after the flower.

HABITAT AND SEASON. Bogs and swamps; May to June; from Canada to North Carolina, west to Indiana.

Pinkster Flower: *See* AZALEA.

Pipsissewa: *See* WINTERGREEN, SPOTTED.

Pitcher Plant: *Sarracenia purpurea.* Pitcher Plant family.

FLOWERS. Single, two inches across at top of scape one to two feet tall, deep reddish-purple, varying sometimes to partly greenish; five sepals and five overlapping petals which inclose a yellowish, umbrella-shaped style with five rays ending in five hooked stigmas; stamens indefinite.

LEAVES. Hollow, pitcher-shaped, their margins being folded together and leaving a broad wing or keel. They curve outward and upward from the root, are yellowish-green lined with purple, and the open end is hooded. They are smooth outside, but covered with fine hairy bristles pointing downward on inside. Usually they are half filled with water.

HABITAT AND SEASON. Peat bogs and mossy swamps; May to June; from Labrador to the Rocky Mountains and south to Florida.

Polygala, Fringed: *See* WINTERGREEN, FLOWERING.

Poppy, California: *Eschscholtzia californica.* Poppy family.

FLOWERS. Large, with four widely flaring petals of golden yellow, turning to orange at the base. Stamens many and long, with long anthers. The flower closes at night and on dull days.

LEAVES. Irregular in shape, finely cut into many divisions, and having long, flattened petiole clasping the stem at its base.

HABITAT AND SEASON. Foothills and desert regions; February to April; in many parts of California. Grown as a garden flower in the East.

Primrose, Evening: *Enothera biennis.* Evening Primrose family.

FLOWERS. Yellow, fragrant, one to two inches across, in leafy-bracted terminal spikes at top of erect stalk one to five feet high. The flowers open at evening, only two or three at a time, and wither the following day. There are four flaring, heart-shaped petals, and eight long, yellow-tipped, spreading stamens.

LEAVES. Lance-shaped, alternating and mostly seated on stem.

HABITAT AND SEASON. Roadsides, thickets and dry fields; June to October; from Labrador to Gulf of Mexico, west to Rocky Mountains.

Queen Anne's Lace: *See* CARROT.

Rhododendron, American or Great: *Rhododendron maximum.* Heath family.

FLOWERS. In large, showy, terminal clusters which nearly cover a tall, branching shrub or tree, as it sometimes grows forty feet high; corolla bell-shaped with five spreading, oval lobes, and sometimes two inches across; color rose, varying to white, greenish in throat, and spotted with yellow or orange; ten spreading stamens and one pistil.

LEAVES. Evergreen, drooping in winter, dark green, leathery, long-oblong, four to ten inches in length, smooth and shining.

HABITAT AND SEASON. Wooded hillsides and mountains near streams; June to July; from Nova Scotia to Georgia, west to Ohio.

Robin's Plantain: *See* DAISY, BLUE SPRING.

Rose, Corn: *See* CORN COCKLE.

Rose, Mallow: *See* MALLOW.

Rose, Pasture: *Rosa humilis* (*Rosa virginiana*). Rose family.

FLOWERS. Fragrant, pink, usually solitary, with five curved, heart-shaped petals around numerous yellow stamens, which in turn surround a cluster of pistils. Calyx has five long, spreading divisions with outer ones lobed.

LEAVES. Usually five thin, oval or sharply pointed, irregularly toothed leaflets make up the compound leaf. Slender, straight thorns, usually in pairs at base of leaf stem. This is the commonest of the wild Roses, and is branching and bushy, six inches to six feet high.

HABITAT AND SEASON. Dry, rocky soil; May to July; from Nova Scotia to Florida, west to Oklahoma.

Rose, Swamp or Wild: *Rosa Carolina.* Rose family.

FLOWERS. Pink, two to three inches broad with five curved, heart-shaped petals and numerous yellow stamens loosely grouped.

LEAVES. Of five to nine finely toothed leaflets, varying from oval to oblong, on bushes one to eight feet high, usually with hooked or curved thorns.

HABITAT AND SEASON. Swamps and low ground; June to August; from Atlantic Coast west to Minnesota and Mississippi.

Saxifrage, Early: *Saxifraga virginiensis* (*Micranthes virginiensis*). Saxifrage family.

FLOWERS. White, small, perfect, in loose panicle at top of sticky, hairy stalk four to twelve inches high. Calyx five-lobed; five petals; ten stamens; one pistil with two styles.

LEAVES. Obovate, toothed, rather thick, narrowed into spatulate-margined petioles, and clustered at base of stalk.

HABITAT AND SEASON. Rocky woodlands and hillsides; March to May; from New Brunswick to Georgia, and west to Minnesota.

Skullcap, Larger or Hyssop: *Scutellaria integrifolia*. Mint family.

FLOWERS. Bright blue, an inch long. Calyx two-lipped, the upper lip having a helmet-like protuberance; corolla two-lipped, the lips of about equal length. The flowers are grouped opposite each other at top of a stalk never more than two feet high. The latter is square and covered with fine down.

LEAVES. Rounded, oblong, with notched edges, and covered with fine down.

HABITAT AND SEASON. In tall grass of roadsides and meadows, and undergrowth of woods and thickets; May to August; from southern New England to Gulf of Mexico, west to Texas.

Skunk Cabbage: *Symplocarpus foetidus* (*Spathyema foetida*). Arum family.

FLOWERS. Tiny, perfect, ill-smelling, greenish-yellow to purplish-brown florets thickly scattered over rounded, fleshy spadix within purplish-brown to greenish-yellow, usually mottled spathe in shape of hood. Appear before leaves.

LEAVES. Large, broadly ovate, often a foot across, with petioles slightly grooved.

HABITAT AND SEASON. Swamps and wet ground; February to April; from Nova Scotia to Florida, west to Minnesota and Iowa.

Snakehead: *See* TURTLEHEAD.

Sneezeweed: *See* SUNFLOWER, SWAMP.

Spatter-dock: *See* LILY, YELLOW POND.

Spikenard, Wild; or False Solomon's Seal: *Smilacina racemosa* (*Vaguer a racemosa*). Lily family.

FLOWERS. In dense terminal raceme, white or greenish, small, with perianth of six spreading segments; six stamens; one pistil. Leafy stalk one to three feet high.

LEAVES. Oblong or lance-shaped, three to six inches long, alternate along stem and finely hairy beneath.

HABITAT AND SEASON. Moist woods and thickets; May to July; from Nova Scotia to Georgia, and British Columbia to Arizona.

Spring Beauty or Claytonia: *Claytonia virginica*. Purslane family.

FLOWERS. Several in terminal, loose raceme. Two ovate sepals; five white petals veined with pink or all pink; five stamens, one inserted in base of each petal; style three cleft.

LEAVES. Linear to lance-shaped. Upper ones shorter than lower ones. The latter are two to three inches long and vary in width.

HABITAT AND SEASON. Moist woods, low meadows; March to May; from Nova Scotia and far westward, south to Georgia and Texas.

Steeplebush: *See* HARD HACK.

Strawberry, Wild or Virginia: *Fragaria virginiana*. Rose family.

FLOWERS. White, loosely clustered at end of erect, hairy scape, usually shorter than leaves. Calyx deeply five cleft, with five bracts between divisions. Five rounded, short-clawed, white petals; stamens numerous, orange-yellow; center green and cone-shaped.

LEAVES. Compound, having three, broad, wedge-shaped, hairy, toothed leaflets.

HABITAT AND SEASON. Dry fields, woodland edges, roadsides; April to June; from New Brunswick to Louisiana, west to South Dakota.

Sunflower, Swamp; or Sneezeweed: *Heleniwn autumnale.* Composite family.

FLOWERS. Large flower heads on long stems in loose, spreading, terminal clusters on a stout, branching stalk two to six feet high; ten to eighteen three-clefted, yellow, spreading, drooping ray-florets surround a yellow, or yellowish-brown disk of tubular florets.

LEAVES. Bright green, pointed, lance-shaped or oblong, toothed, alternating. When dried and powdered they produce violent sneezing; hence, one of the common names.

HABITAT AND SEASON. Banks of streams, swamps and wet ground; August to October; from Quebec to Northwest Territory, south to Florida and Arizona.

Sunflower, Tall or Giant: *Helianthus giganteus.* Composite family.

FLOWERS. Usually several flower heads, one and a half to over two inches broad, on long, rough, terminal stems; ten to twenty pale yellow ray-florets surround numerous, yellowish disk-florets in a green half-round cup. The stalk is purplish stained, rough, hairy, three to twelve feet high, and usually branched near the top.

LEAVES. Lance-shaped, tapering to a point, rough above, and rough-hairy beneath, sometimes entire, but often finely toothed; some have short stems, but most of them clasp the stalk.

HABITAT AND SEASON. Wet meadows, low, damp thickets, swamps; August to October; from Maine and Ontario to Northwest Territory, south to Florida and Louisiana.

Thistle, Common; or Roadside Thistle: *Cirsium lanceolatum.* Composite family.

FLOWERS. Many small, tubular, purple florets in a spreading and rounding head about an inch and a half across, gathered in a green egg-shaped cup covered with long, sharp, white prickles. The flower heads are usually solitary on the ends of the branches of a round, leafy stalk three to five feet high, and covered with fine, whitish wool.

LEAVES. Long, dark green, lance-shaped, with margins deeply and irregularly cut, an exceedingly sharp needle-like point on the tip of each projection, upper surface rough and prickly, while under surface is covered with a thick mat of fine, brownish hairs when young.

HABITAT AND SEASON. Fields, waste places and roadsides; July to November; from Newfoundland to Georgia, west to Minnesota and Missouri.

Thoroughwort, Hyssop-leaved: *Eupatorium hyssopifolium.* Composite family.

FLOWERS. Arranged in heads, about a third of an inch high, and containing about five tubular, white flowers. The flower heads form a flat-topped panicle on a rather bushy stalk one to two feet high.

LEAVES. Narrow, linear or lanceolate, the lower ones sometimes toothed, acute at base.

HABITAT AND SEASON. Dry fields; August and September; from Massachusetts to Florida and Texas.

Toadflax, Yellow: *See* BUTTER AND EGGS.

Trillium, Nodding; or Nodding Wake-robin: *Trillium cernuum.* Lily family.

FLOWERS. Solitary, white or sometimes pinkish, nodding or drooping from peduncle until nearly or quite hidden under the leaves; three petals half an inch long or over, curving backward at maturity; sepals about as long as petals.

LEAVES. Very broad, tapering at points, in whorl of three at top of rather slender stalk eight to twenty inches high.

HABITAT AND SEASON. Damp woods; April to June; from Nova Scotia to Georgia and Missouri, west to Ontario and Minnesota.

Trillium, Painted: *Trillium undulatum.* Lily family.

FLOWERS. Solitary, waxy-white, with stripes of deep pink or wine color at base of petals; three long, pointed, wavy-edged petals widely spreading; three narrow, lance-shaped sepals. The flower has a short stem at top of slender, smooth, green stalk from eight inches to two feet high.

LEAVES. Egg-shaped, with long, tapering points, rounded base and short stem.

HABITAT AND SEASON. Cool, damp, shady woods; May and June; from Nova Scotia to Georgia and Missouri, west to Ontario and Wisconsin.

Trillium, Purple; or Ill-scented Wake-robin: *Trillium erectum.* Lily family.

FLOWERS. Solitary, dull purple or purplish-red; three flaring, pointed, green sepals alternating with three pointed, oval petals; six stamens with anthers longer than filaments; one pistil spreading into three short, recurved stigmas.

LEAVES. Broadly ovate and pointed, arranged in a whorl of three which droop at top of stalk.

HABITAT AND SEASON. Rich, moist woods; April to June; from Nova Scotia to North Carolina, west to Manitoba and Missouri.

Trillium, White; or Large-flowered Wake-robin: *Trillium grandiflorum.* Lily family.

FLOWERS. Solitary, large, waxy-white, with three thin, broad, pointed and veined petals larger and longer than the three spreading, green sepals. The petals curve outward and the flower is borne on a short stem springing from the center of the leaves, which grow in a whorl of three at top of single, smooth, stout stalk.

LEAVES. Large, broad, egg-shaped, tapering to a sharp point, and stemless.

HABITAT AND SEASON. Damp, rich woods; May and June; from Canada to Florida, west to Minnesota and Missouri.

Trumpetweed: *See* JOE-PYE WEED.

Turtlehead or Snakehead: *Chelone glabra.* Fig wort family.

FLOWERS. Pure white or tinged with pink, about an inch long, growing in terminal cluster on smooth, erect, leafy stalk one to three feet high. Corolla broadly tubular and two-lipped, the broad, arched upper lip creased and notched in the middle, the lower lip three-lobed at apex. The throat is filled with woolly hairs, and the five woolly stamens and single pistil are almost hidden by the lips.

LEAVES. Lance-shaped, sharply toothed, tapering to a long point, narrowed at base, and set on stalk in opposite pairs.

HABITAT AND SEASON. Swamps, ditches and beside water; July to September; from Newfoundland to Florida, west to Manitoba and Kansas.

Violet, Bird's-foot: *Viola pedata.* Violet family.

FLOWERS. Largest of the Violets, velvety, somewhat pansy-shaped. Five petals, either all lilac-purple or with the two upper ones dark purple and the lower ones a lighter shade. The lower petal is grooved and has a flat spur; upper petals curve backward. Stamens in center tipped with bright orange.

LEAVES. Cut into five to eleven narrow parts. Divisions of a leaf are so arranged as to suggest the print of a bird's foot.

HABITAT AND SEASON. Dry fields and hillsides from April to June; from southern Ontario to Florida, west to Minnesota.

Violet, Common Blue or Meadow: *Viola papilionacea.* Violet family.

FLOWERS. Vary greatly in color from pale violet to light purple, and occasionally are striped. They also vary greatly in size. There are five petals, the lower one spurred, and the two lateral ones prettily bearded. Orange-tipped stamens form a golden heart.

LEAVES. Large, heart-shaped with prominent rib and scalloped edges. Stem grooved, and the surface is sometimes covered with very fine hairs.

HABITAT AND SEASON. Damp woods and meadows; April to June; from Nova Scotia to Georgia, west to Minnesota.

Violet, Sweet White: *Viola blanda.* Violet family.

FLOWERS. One of the smallest of the Violets; sweet-scented with five white petals, the upper pair often long, narrow and recurved, the lower pair veined with purple; two to five inches high.

LEAVES. Yellow-green, smooth, round, heart-shaped, with finely toothed margins.

HABITAT AND SEASON. Damp places; April to May; from New Brunswick to Louisiana, and many parts of the west, including California.

Virgin's-bower: *See* CLEMATIS.

Wake-robin: *See* TRILLIUM.

Whitehearts: *See* DUTCHMAN'S-BREECHES.

Whiteweed: *See* DAISY, COMMON.

Willow-herb, Great: *See* FIREWEED.

Wintergreen, Flowering; or Fringed Polygala: *Polygala paucifolia.* Milkwort family.

FLOWERS. Purplish-rose, one-half inch long, one to four on short peduncles from among upper leaves and orchid-like in appearance. Five unequal sepals, two of which are wing-like and highly colored like petals; petals form a long, slender tube, the lower ones being extended and beautifully fringed; six stamens and one pistil are inclosed in this tube.

LEAVES. Clustered at top of stalk four to seven inches high. They are pointed oval or oblong, and narrowed into short stems. They become reddish in winter.

HABITAT AND SEASON. Rich, moist woods; May to July; from Canada to Georgia, west to Illinois.

Wintergreen, Spotted; or Spotted Pipsissewa: *Chimaphila maculata.* Heath family.

FLOWERS. White or pinkish, waxy with corolla of five concave, rounded, spreading petals; ten stamens and a short, conical style with round stigma. The stem or stalk creeps along the surface of the ground or just beneath it, sending up branches a few inches high.

LEAVES. Thick, smooth, dark green, mottled with white along the veins, lance-shaped with distant teeth along the margins and arranged in pairs and in whorls on the reddish stalk.

HABITAT AND SEASON. In dry woods; June to August; from Maine and Ontario to Minnesota, Georgia and Mississippi.

Yarrow or Milfoil: *Achillea Millefolium.* Composite family.

FLOWERS. From four to six, grayish-white ray-florets around a tiny head of yellowish or brownish disk-florets seated in a light green cup. These little flower heads are in small, close groups which in turn are gathered into one or more large, flat-topped, terminal clusters, one to two feet high.

LEAVES. Long, narrow, deeply cut, and each part again cut into a fine fringe. Both leaves and flowers are aromatic.

HABITAT AND SEASON. Waste land, roadsides and dry fields; June to November; throughout North America.